Colonial New Mexican Families

Colonial New Mexican Families

COMMUNITY, CHURCH, AND STATE, 1692–1800

Suzanne M. Stamatov

University of New Mexico Press ~ Albuquerque

© 2018 by the University of New Mexico Press
All rights reserved. Published 2018
Printed in the United States of America

First Paperback Edition, 2022
Paperback ISBN: 978-0-8263-6392-3

Library of Congress Cataloging-in-Publication Data
Names: Stamatov, Suzanne M., 1964– author.
Title: Colonial New Mexican families: community, church, and state, 1692–1800 /
Suzanne M. Stamatov.
Other titles: Colonial New Mexican families, community, church, and state, 1692–1800
Description: Albuquerque: University of New Mexico Press, [2018] |
Includes bibliographical references and index. |
Identifiers: LCCN 2017028445 (print) | LCCN 2017029767 (e-book) | ISBN 9780826359216
(e-book) | ISBN 9780826359209 (printed case: alk. paper)
Subjects: LCSH: New Mexico—Social life and customs—18th century. | Families—
New Mexico—History—18th century. | Marriage—New Mexico—History—18th century. |
Marriage—Religious aspects—Catholic Church. | Courtship—New Mexico—History—
18th century. | Hispanic American pioneers—New Mexico—Social life and customs. |
Women—New Mexico—Social conditions—18th century. | Church and state—New Mexico—
History—18th century. | Church and state—Catholic Church—History—18th century. |
Hispanic Americans—New Mexico—History—18th century.
Classification: LCC F799 (e-book) | LCC F799 .S738 2018 (print) |
DDC 306.8509789/09033—dc23
LC record available at https://lccn.loc.gov/2017028445

Designed by Felicia Cedillos
Composed in Minion Pro 10. 25/14

For Jane Stamatov, my beloved mother

CONTENTS

LIST OF ILLUSTRATIONS ix

ACKNOWLEDGMENTS xi

Introduction 1

Chapter 1. The Setting 9

Chapter 2. Civil Authorities, Civil Law, and Family 27

Chapter 3. The Sacrament of Marriage 51

Chapter 4. Sexuality and Courtship 77

Chapter 5. Marriage 107

Chapter 6. Domestic Life and Discord 133

Conclusion 177

Appendix 181

NOTES ON SOURCES 195

NOTES 199

BIBLIOGRAPHY 223

INDEX 237

ILLUSTRATIONS

Figures

1. Tree of Consanguinity 63
2. Genealogy of Mateo and Catalina 66
3. Distribution of Ages for First Marriages among Males, 1694–1800 186
4. Distribution of Ages for Non-First Marriages among Males, 1694–1800 186
5. Distribution of Ages for First Marriages among Females, 1694–1800 187
6. Distribution of Ages for Non-First Marriages among Females, 1694–1800 187
7. Age of First Marriages, 1694–1800 188
8. Surname Clusters for Albuquerque 189
9. Surname Clusters for Santa Fe 190
10. Surname Clusters for Santa Cruz de la Cañada 191

Tables

1. Proportion of Interracial Marriages, 1694–1800 181
2. Pattern of Interracial Marriages, 1694–1800 182
3. Honor Negotiated: A Summary of the Cases 184
4. Proportion of Different Types of Households, 1790 192
5. Distributions of Household Types for Male-Headed Households in Albuquerque, 1790 192
6. Distributions of Household Types for Male-Headed Households in Santa Fe, 1790 193
7. Distributions of Household Types for Male-Headed Households in Santa Cruz, 1790 194

ACKNOWLEDGMENTS

I would like to express my thanks to the many people who have helped me over the years on the journey to publish this book. I am grateful for the help from a number of scholars. Sandra Lauderdale Graham is a thoughtful, incisive historian. She is also generous; she read chapters and took the time to pose piercing questions that always pushed me to think more deeply. I also offer thanks to New Mexico State Historian Rick Hendricks and Deputy State Historian Rob Martinez. Rick shared his incredible knowledge of New Mexico and family history with me, providing me with insightful ideas and comments on my manuscript. Rob offered encouragement throughout the project, helped me to track down the marriage patterns of the Mexico City settlers, and worked with me to uncover the possible marriage rituals that transpired in New Mexico. His encyclopedic grasp of New Mexican genealogy is not only helpful, but provides laughs ("And this is another one of my relatives . . ."). I also gratefully accepted the comments of the anonymous reviewers. Many of their suggestions helped to make the book more accurate and clearer. Laura Calderone, a New Mexico state librarian, always provided willing assistance to find various, obscure texts. Librarians like Laura are invaluable to historians.

I had enormous help from my family members and friends. My husband, George Guthrie, supported me throughout this project and provided technical support. As we raised our own family, George encouraged me to continue my research on the families of the past. My sister, Kristan Winters, edited an early version of the manuscript. More importantly, whenever I felt a bit discouraged, she motivated me to stay on task and to finish.

Some debts of gratitude date back to an earlier incarnation of this project. Linda Hall, Robert Himmerich y Valencia, Durwood Ball, and Sandra Lauderdale Graham gave me advice on adapting my research into a book. I incorporated their ideas and hope that the project meets with their approval.

The New Mexico State Archives continues to be a warm and welcoming place to conduct research. Melissa Salazar, Gail Packard, Sibel Melik, Rob Martinez, Felicia Lujan, and all the other employees provide professional help to the patrons who come in search of their own past or that of others. This atmosphere makes the lonely job of the historian that much brighter.

Finally, I dedicate this book to my mother, Jane Stamatov. Her love and support over the years is forever appreciated.

INTRODUCTION

In 1766, María Luisa de Aragón complained to an ecclesiastical court that her son-in-law had attempted to interfere in her granddaughter's marital plans.[1] Having raised her granddaughter as her own child, she believed his intrusion to be unwarranted and meddlesome. This brief case highlights the many layers of family formation in eighteenth-century New Mexico. As María Luisa's case suggests, family relationships were socially and emotionally complex affairs, involving passion, intergenerational conflict, and community opinion. Moreover, family members often turned to civil and ecclesiastical officials for help in resolving issues that they believed to be of the utmost importance. In this book, I examine how families in colonial New Mexico from 1694 to 1800 formed and functioned, how they interacted with the church and state, and how they were embedded in the community.

In her complaint, María Luisa explained how she had come to rear her granddaughter. Fifteen years earlier, her daughter, María Chávez, had married Pedro Yturrieta against her wishes. After the marriage, the young man had departed on a trip to Mexico City where he stayed for over a year. María Luisa de Aragón explained that during that time her daughter had an affair, succumbing to an "unfortunate fragility, of which all the feminine sex are liable."[2] María Chávez bore a child. When Yturrieta returned, he shunned the child, not allowing his wife to care for her. As a result, María Luisa accepted her grandchild into her house and heart, raising her as her own daughter.

The ecclesiastical judge took the case under advisement. To ascertain the truthfulness of María Luisa's assertions, he interviewed citizens from the community. Three male neighbors came forward and attested to the fact that the grandmother had done an excellent job raising the girl. Don Felipe Silva, resident of Tome, declared that not only he, but the entire neighborhood and the entire jurisdiction, knew that doña María Luisa had taken care of her granddaughter from the time of her birth, supporting, clothing, and educating her. "It is very well-known that she has behaved well and with honor, as a married woman and now as a widow, and with this same behavior and customs, she has looked after and educated her granddaughter." With such exemplary behavior on the part of the widow and her charge, the ecclesiastical judge decided in her favor.[3]

María Luisa de Aragón had appealed to a local church authority in search of a solution to her problem. Her decision was not unusual; New Mexicans frequently invited both civil and religious authorities to mediate tense family situations. In fact, officials of these institutions expected to intervene, seeing their institutions as the underpinnings of family life. These religious and civil institutions formulated policies and implemented rules, intent on creating nuclear families as the foundation of society. Moreover, the state governed the transmission of property from one generation to the next. Church and state depended on community members to provide the necessary information so that they could act on and settle matters.

In her appeal, María Luisa de Aragón mentioned her daughter's sexual affair, referring to women's sexuality as something fragile. The grandmother divulged how her daughter's fragility rent the family apart. She described her son-in-law as incensed upon his return, threatening his wife and ignoring the baby, vowing not to "see her, nor hear about her, nor understand her, nor help her."[4] In fact, the grandmother referred to Pedro Yturrieta's behavior as scandalous. She believed that he should have forgiven his wife and accepted the child. After fifteen years, the tide of public opinion had turned (if it had ever been against María Luisa to begin with). This case shows that people's lives turned on questions of honor and sexuality, but the outcome was not always predictable. A constantly shifting set of factors affected how community members perceived one another.

Most single New Mexicans eventually married, and the marital process proved to be less than uniform as people vied to influence it. The selection of a spouse might have involved parents, children, and other family members.

María Chávez had married in 1751 without her mother's approval. In 1766, María Luisa and her son-in-law struggled for the right to control the granddaughter's marriage. That the grandmother could have an impact on one marriage and not the other mirrors the realities of selecting a spouse during the eighteenth century. At times, parents, perhaps wielding power in the form of property, could finesse a selection. In other instances, young people chose mates on their own, eschewing familial input. Parents and children, however, usually collaborated in the search for the best mates possible. A person who was hardworking, kind, and provided land or animals, for example, was a potential spouse upon which both parents and children could agree. All in all, the process shows variation over the course of the century.

This case also reveals the marital discord that occurred on the husband's return to New Mexico. The husband insisted that the baby be removed from his wife's care. This was a viable course of action because María Luisa de Aragón did not reside with her daughter and son-in-law. Their housing arrangements were typical. During the century under study, most New Mexicans lived in nuclear families. We can only imagine that the removal of the infant lessened the tensions between husband and wife. Little data exist that can help illuminate how husbands and wives interacted after they married. The evidence available deals with marital discord and adultery. In these cases, whether instigated by a family member, a neighbor, or the victim, we can discern their voices, their beliefs about the expected roles of husbands and wives, and how, in these situations, the aggressors had deviated from a societal norm. The civil and ecclesiastical authorities and how they dealt with the accused shed light on how they thought men and women should adhere to religious and civil laws. And in defending themselves and their actions, the men reveal their own ideas about family life in colonial New Mexico.

Though most families were nuclear, many chose to reside near their kin. Usually, this was a practical consideration. Parents divided their land and passed it to their children who then set up their own households. Sisters and brothers were often neighbors. Where people lived influenced their relationships within their homes and with their close relations. In addition to their familial geography within a town or region, the fact that these families lived in New Mexico, the northern frontier of Spain's colonies, also had a direct impact on their lives.

Families on the Frontier

While Governor don Diego de Vargas began actively planning to reconquer the Kingdom of New Mexico in 1691 from the Pueblo Indians, the Spanish colonial government, coupled with the Catholic Church, asserted that the key to a successful conquest involved the settlement of families. It therefore undertook steps to encourage family migration from southern New Mexico and New Spain. Families ventured forth to the far-flung colony, lured north, perhaps, by promises of land or pushed from their homes by threats or extreme poverty. Some colonists had lived in New Mexico since before the Pueblo Revolt in 1680, but they returned to a colony altered by twelve years of their absence. Others encountered a new land and new people for the first time.

Immediately upon arrival, in a cold December of 1693, the Hispanic settlers faced a frontier that was a place of contention as Vargas fought to retake Santa Fe from the Tewa and Tano Pueblo people.[5] On this "contested ground,"[6] the Hispanic families and their offspring had to contend with isolation from the colonial center, a different environment, and the various people who dwelled there or passed through to trade and to raid. Though the government depended on families to multiply and to help establish a productive and secure society, this proved difficult due to poverty, low reproduction, and little imperial support. Initially, families had to labor for their very survival. In the first few years, Hispanics found it difficult to farm productively. Though Governor Vargas offered some supplies, they often proved insufficient. Hispanic families had some allies, however, and turned to nearby Pueblo people for food. In addition to hunger, these settlers had much to fear from Navajos, Comanches, and Utes. Endemic warfare with attacks and counterattacks continued throughout much of the following century. To better survive, the colonial government forged economic and military alliances with the Pueblos.[7]

How did this hard-scrabble life on the frontier affect family formation and family life? Often the conversation turns on the question of honor. Honor, a concept brought to the New World from Iberia, revolved around a person's status, relating to one's legitimate birth and family's class position, and virtue, depending on one's actions. Honor could be won or lost based on other people's perceptions of individuals' actions.[8] It remains difficult, however, to identify all the permutations of honor due to its various interpretations by the historical actors depending on their class, place of origin, and location. According to historian Asunción Lavrin, a precise definition of honor is elusive "since it was a mental construct expressed through a complex set of behavioral codes regulating personal and social conduct."[9] These codes of conduct not only varied based on the class and location of the actors, but changed over time.

Regarding matters of race and class position, scholars of frontier societies find that men's construction of honor differed drastically from that of men in more central regions. Early-modern Iberians judged honor to be based on a family's *limpieza de sangre*, or purity of blood. Society considered those with Jewish, Muslim, or New Christian ancestors as less honorable, as having a stained reputation. Colonial elites expanded this concept in the New World by adding Indians, Africans, and mixed-race peoples as unworthy forebears. Over time, this discriminatory bias lost its sting due to the rise of miscegenation.[10] Race in colonial New Mexico, for example, lost its significance as a marker of honor and became sublimated to men's ability to fight enemy Indians.[11] *Genízaros*, descendants of ransomed Plains Indian captives, gained prestige as they played crucial roles in the defense of the Hispanic villas and pueblos, acting as military scouts and in auxiliary units.[12]

Many men might have expanded their roles as protectors of the colony to be arbiters of justice within their communities. Some historians and anthropologists believe that frontier inhabitants, hardened by their violent experiences, refused to abide by state laws, substituting them with their own rules. The nature of the frontier strengthened these rules based on ideals of honor. Historian Ramón Gutiérrez writes: "An exaggerated moral code for personal public behavior based on honor developed among New Mexico's Spanish colonists because the social and legal institutions that would have provided society an orderly tenor were absent on this remote frontier where might was right."[13]

Men's honor was also tied intricately to the honor of women. Women's honor centered on their sexuality: women who remained chaste before marriage and sexually faithful to their husbands fulfilled the honor code. The anthropologist Ana María Alonso contends that frontiersmen and women lived by a draconian code of honor. Alonso defines women's honor as linked to a public denial of the "natural facts" of sexuality and conception that were so shameful that they needed to be culturally controlled and publicly denied.[14] Some scholars argue that in the military culture of New Spain's northern frontier, men and society often blamed women for sexual transgressions regardless of the circumstances. In this gender-relational concept of frontier honor, women were in a bind—held responsible for their own actions as well as for men's.[15] If a man sullied a woman's chastity, her brothers or father had to avenge her honor in order to recover their own.[16]

In addition to a link between men's honor and women's sexual purity, historians also find that fathers protected their daughters' chastity in order to contrive favorable marriages. In more central regions where stark class divisions existed, elites controlled their daughters' sexuality to maintain a hierarchical, class society.[17] Some believe that even in frontier regions, families developed strategies to contract marriages that increased their social and economic status.[18]

Do these definitions of honor and plans to perpetuate class status illuminate eighteenth-century New Mexico? Regarding women's virtue, the evidence suggests that the situation was more complex than previous studies on the frontier allow since many women did not deny their sexuality and often openly engaged in sexual relationships with men. Historian Ann Twinam finds that elite Spanish American women who had sexual relations maintained their honor if they married afterward or if they hid any subsequent pregnancies.[19] Like elite women, New Mexican women often married after initiating sexual relationships. They did not, however, have the luxury of giving birth privately. Nevertheless, unmarried women whose pregnancies revealed their sexual activity did not necessarily become shunned as fallen women.

Did New Mexican Hispanic parents employ strategies to control their daughters' sexuality to further their class positions and enhance their families' honor? Some of the strategies available to parents were the giving of patrimonies and the selection of cousins as marital partners. Patrimonies involved parents favoring one son with the family inheritance at the time of his marriage to the selected wife.[20] New Mexican parents, however, avoided this method. In fact, documents show that parents tried to implement inheritance laws fairly and endow their male and female children equally. Perhaps because the economy of New Mexico remained stagnant during much of the century and did not support an established economic elite class, few families accumulated enough wealth to use patrimony effectively. Even if a handful of families achieved wealth and status, constant Indian raids and inheritance laws rendered their positions tenuous and limited the perpetuation of their rank and affluence. Although parents might have tried to use available property to influence their children's selection of a spouse, they did not have the means of using a patrimony.

Another strategy elites employed was to select close cousins as mates in order to maintain their honor, social status, blood purity, and familial wealth.[21] Although cousins did marry in New Mexico, it was not necessarily a tactic parents undertook to control marriages. To begin with, very few close cousins, those who shared grandparents, married over the course of the century. Under ecclesiastical law, a couple sharing blood ties (consanguinity) or spiritual ties (affinity) in the fourth degree could not marry unless the bishop or friar granted them a dispensation, a relaxation of the above impediment to marriage. The dispensation cases of New Mexicans show that marriage for cousins was an intricate affair. Even though some mentioned that they married for quality, how they defined quality varied from person to person and over time, and the quality that they sought rarely encompassed both social status and blood purity, as well as wealth.

Although some parents undoubtedly tried to control their daughters' conduct when relating to men, young New Mexicans, their peers, and community members also played an important role, making marriage a many-layered process. In their study of female honor in Piedmont, Italy (1600–1800), historians Sandra Cavallo and Simona Cerutti show that in rural Piedmont, peer groups, in lieu of parents, actually acted as mediators in courtships and that community members followed young people's relationships, offering rebukes if the couples acted inappropriately. The authors find that a rigid code of behavior did not exist; rather, "public judgment had an elasticity that was capable of adapting to individual circumstances."[22] In these cases, then, groups, rather than family members, monitored women's sexuality and helped them select men who would not take advantage of them.

Cavallo and Cerutti's font of evidence (six hundred cases) outweighs the available data for New Mexico. Nevertheless, their findings help historians who study rural areas in colonial Latin America by suggesting that community involvement was a vital part of courtships and marriages and that parental participation might have had less impact. New Mexicans also monitored young people's relationships, observing the behavior of the couples as the relationships blossomed. Their interest enabled them to offer protection to women and to warn others about unruly men and women. As friends and neighbors, moreover, they did not necessarily judge young people harshly. They would continue to live with these young neighbors and their families long after scandals ended.

In these ways then, New Mexicans built their lives and communities around marriage. The church taught that marriage was a sacrament of which all could partake. On the frontier, a Christian marriage distinguished Hispanics from the enemies they named infidels. Marriage also gave a sense of order to society. Married people, for the most part, followed certain rules, such as fidelity, that prevented them from disrupting others. They also raised, educated, and passed property on to their children. Tensions in the system existed, such as out-of-wedlock births, broken promises, adultery, domestic violence, and sexual abuse of servants. The community's responses varied depending on the situations. Some people welcomed an unmarried mother and her children into their homes. Others tried to force couples to marry. In cases of extreme abuse, people appealed to the church and state for intervention. Overall, people recognized that their community's strength lay in living together peacefully. Instead of instituting their own strict codes of conduct, they used the church and state laws as guidelines, inviting governors to intervene in family matters of importance.[23] Also, they interpreted the laws flexibly to avoid alienating the neighbors whom they needed in order to survive in the remote Kingdom of New Mexico. Indeed, the evidence about family life exists because colonists believed that these frontier institutions should decide which party was correct, rejecting outright the idea that might was right.

Chapter 1
The Setting

Geography and Population

THE KINGDOM OF New Mexico, again under Spanish hegemony by 1692, consisted of the settlements along the upper Río Grande and its tributaries, extending a little into the headwaters of the Pecos. To the west, Franciscans served Acoma and Zuni with few Spanish settlers. To the south, another group of riverine colonies centered around El Paso del Norte. This book concentrates on the northern settlements near the Río Grande and its tributaries, namely Albuquerque, Santa Fe, Santa Cruz de la Cañada, and their surrounding communities. The Río Grande flows into these areas through a deep canyon near Taos, and for several hundred kilometers below the range, a narrow alluvial plain has formed along its banks. The valleys are surrounded by the Sangre de Cristo mountain range on the east and the Jemez range to the west.[1] The Sandia Mountains overlook Albuquerque. The climate is dry, with hot summers and cold winter nights. Droughts and blizzards ravage the land periodically.

When Spaniards and their allies initially conquered the region in 1598, they encountered sedentary town dwellers whom they came to call Pueblo Indians. The Pueblos lived in multitiered stone and adobe houses built around a central plaza.[2] They had continually cultivated land along the Río Grande Valley since the fourteenth century. At the beginning of the seventeenth century, the Pueblo population might have numbered close to sixty thousand. By the eighteenth century, their population had dropped to seventeen thousand people, a result of European diseases, famine, and warfare.³ In addition to these complex societies, Spaniards also encountered nonsedentary Indian groups, such as the Apaches, Comanches, Navajos, and Utes, who entered the colony to trade and to raid.⁴

The subjects of this study are the Hispanics who came north in Spain's recolonization of New Mexico and their descendants who were born to this place. The settlers hailed from El Paso del Norte (near present Ciudad Juárez), Zacatecas, Sombrerete, Puebla, and Mexico City. Some Mexican Indians of various backgrounds also resettled the area. The 1695 muster roll of Zacatecan recruits illustrates the various ethnicities of the settlers: of the 141 persons enrolled 30 percent were classified *español* (Spaniards), 39 percent were *mestizo* (Indian/español), 11 percent were *coyote* (mestizo/Indian), 11 percent were *mulatto* (español/black), 2 percent were *lobos* (black/Indian), and 1.5 percent were *castizo* (español/mestizo).⁵ In general, all of these settlers shared Catholic beliefs and rituals, the Spanish language, and the rules and possibilities of an imposed Spanish legal culture.

After the first twenty years of recolonization, fewer and fewer immigrants came to northern New Mexico from New Spain and Spain. In fact, by 1790, census enumerators recorded only eight immigrants in Albuquerque, eight in Santa Fe, and none in Santa Cruz. The sixteen transplants all came from New Spain.⁶ Nevertheless, a constant infusion of people entered the Spanish towns, enriching the culture. During the period 1700–1800, close to 1,360 Plains Indians came to the colony as captives.⁷ Known as genízaros, *criados*, or *huérfanos*, they became an integral part of the Hispanic communities.

Plains Indian groups, including Kiowas, Comanches, and Navajos, sold captives, mostly women and children, to Hispanic settlers at trade fairs. Ostensibly, the Hispanics ransomed the captives, rescuing them from their captors. The colonists baptized them as Catholics and brought them into their homes to acculturate them as Catholics and Hispanics.⁸ In exchange, the genízaros were made to work for ten to twenty years. Their experiences varied, ranging from familial incorporation to outright bondage. Most captives remained in their new society, forming families and building their own communities. They often passed their genízaro status on to their children. Over the course of the century, they came to play an important role in protecting the colony from Indian attacks.⁹ In addition to the genízaros, other Indians also became part of the Hispanic communities. Known as *indios vecinos*, they came from nomadic tribes or nearby pueblos, inserting themselves into Hispanic society.[10] By 1790, they made up at least 4.2 percent of New Mexico's population.[11]

These groups interacted and intermarried from the first years of recolonization. Although friars attempted to keep the Pueblo communities separate to insulate them from the worst aspects of Hispanic culture,[12] some marriage between Hispanics and Pueblo peoples occurred. Although an exact number of interethnic marriages remains difficult to determine due to incomplete records left by the friars, the extant data reveal that all racial groups intermarried to some extent (see tables 1 and 2).

Nevertheless, a racial hierarchy imposed by Spanish civil and ecclesiastical authorities existed. These officials made various attempts to identify the racial composition of the population. Their efforts reveal their own racial and class prejudices and their frustrations in devising and applying the appropriate racial terms to the populace. Friar Francisco Atanasio Domínguez refrained from describing the different classes of people in Santa Fe to avoid long-windedness and confusion. He wrote: "Suffice it to say that most of them pass for Spaniards."[13] The parish priest of Albuquerque in 1801 summed up the citizenry of Albuquerque: "most are Genízaros (which is a mixture of various nations), and the rest are mulattoes, coyotes, and few Spaniards, although most are considered Spaniards without it being so."[14] Civil officials also instituted pernicious laws designed to denigrate one race over another. Governor Pedro Fermín de Mendinueta (1767–1778) issued a decree in which he stated:

> If a man or woman, boy or girl is found with stolen produce or in the act of stealing produce from someone's garden and if that person is of broken color, he or she shall receive twenty-five lashes at the pillory. If the person is white he or she shall be tied to the same pillory with the shameful stolen produce hung around the neck.[15]

The official belief in a stratified society in which the *español* was the worthier and more honorable member of society filtered down to the population at large to some extent. Various remarks found in the documents reveal that racial prejudice existed, yet the degree of that bias remains difficult to determine. Many mixed-race people identified themselves to the authorities as *español*. Nevertheless, they willingly offered information about their ancestors who included Indians and mulattoes. They acknowledged themselves as culturally Hispanic, but did not deny their racially diverse heritages.[16]

The population of New Mexico, never large, grew slowly, showing all the characteristics common to frontier populations. Historian Alicia V. Tjarks writes that for the first eighty years of the eighteenth century, several factors depressed demographic development: geographic isolation, menace from enemy Indian attacks, and a subsistence economy. Moreover, fertility and reproduction rates lagged due to high mortality rates. The Pueblo towns felt these depressive factors more keenly than did the Spanish villas.[17] In a census compiled by Fray Andrés Varo in the mid-eighteenth century (1749), the population of Spanish and *castas* (people of mixed race) in the district of Río Abajo numbered 670 people in Albuquerque. In the more populous region of the district of Río Arriba, the Spanish and castas numbered 1,800 in Santa Fe and 1,560 in Santa Cruz de la Cañada and its environs. By 1790, the Spanish and casta population in the respective villas numbered 5,244, 2,997, and 7,081.[18]

Perhaps the greatest deterrent to robust population growth was the constant raiding by Comanche and Apache Indians. The non-Pueblo population grew approximately 6.3 percent per year between 1750 and 1760. But at the height of the warfare, the rate of growth slowed to only 0.04 percent per year from 1760 to 1765, and about 1.4 percent between 1765 and 1779. After the defeat of the Comanche leader Cuerno Verde, in 1779, and the success of various peace treaties with other Indian nations, population growth soared to more than 16.2 percent annually between 1779 and 1784. From then on the population rate grew steadily into the next century.[19]

Disease also limited population growth in New Mexico. A catastrophic smallpox outbreak struck in the spring of 1780 and reached its climax in January and February 1781. Historian Ross Frank, relying on baptismal books, burial records, and partial censuses, estimates that on average 20 to 25 percent of the populace died during the year.[20] Sporadic outbreaks of smallpox recurred until New Mexicans received inoculations in 1805. Many of the factors that contributed to the slow growth in population also affected the economy.

The Economy

The majority of Hispanic New Mexicans were subsistence farmers. Small, irrigated family farms that supplied local markets characterized land tenure in eighteenth-century New Mexico.[21] Initially, Hispanics depended on viceregal support for supplies of seeds, tools, and livestock.[22] Even with this help, colonists found it difficult to be self-sufficient; unable to feed themselves, they turned to the Pueblo peoples for aid. Nevertheless, they persevered and survived, farming near water, building irrigation ditches, and acquiring skills and knowledge. At the time of the 1790 census, most family heads were farmers.[23]

At the turn of the century, various friars throughout New Mexico, in response to queries from the Merchant Guild of Guadalajara, provided detailed reports regarding the state of the local economy.[24] In his report of 1801, Fray Ambrosio Guerra, parish priest of Albuquerque, stated that his parishioners commonly planted wheat, maize, pinto beans, chile, cotton, anise, peas, and garbanzos. They also planted an herb called *punche* that they used for tobacco. He wrote: "The principal activity of these citizens is planting, each one the little they can for their annual support. They are so poor that there is always a scarcity."[25]

In Santa Cruz de la Cañada, Fray José Mariano Rosete reported that the residents there planted wheat, maize, barley, lentils, peas, anise, cilantro, mustard greens, and pinto, garbanzo, and broad beans. He said: "The harvest of wheat and maize is the most abundant, but only for some individuals. Others barely have enough to eat, and still others are always seeking sustenance." Rosete opined that the scarcity resulted from people's laziness. Hungry, they begged from the more diligent farmers and the Pueblo Indians, "who live with greater care to plant than *gente de razón*."[26]

Father José Bibián de Ortega, a diocesan priest, relayed that a successful harvest in Santa Fe depended on the amount of rain they received. During a wet year, they reaped enough maize and wheat to support themselves. In a dry year, they fared poorly since the river "is so limited that if it snows much in winter, there is some water. If not, it is almost dry because its origin is a shallow lake, and it only fills up a little when the snow melts."[27]

In addition to drought, the friars mentioned other natural conditions that affected the harvest. In Santa Cruz, people had fruit trees, such as pear, apricot, peach, plum, and apple, but Father Rosete wrote that these trees produced little or nothing due to "heavy frosts."[28] Father Guerra summarized the various pests that attacked the crops in Albuquerque. Hares destroyed the garbanzo beans. In some years the *pulguilla* (flea beetle) ate the chile, the *palomilla* (grain moth) the wheat, the *cojoyo* worm (bean beetle) and coyotes the maize.[29] As in most farming communities, natural calamities impacted crop yields from one year to the next.

Another pastoral employment was stock raising. During the initial recolonization, Governor Vargas divided hardy sheep, called *churros*, among the settlers.[30] New Mexicans slowly increased their flocks, though the process proved difficult as a result of droughts, blizzards, and enemy attacks.[31] Father Guerra wrote that farmers raised cattle, horses, mules, sheep, goats, and pigs. He assessed the situation in Albuquerque thusly: "Principally, what do the most damage to all kinds of stock raising above all to equine stock are attacks by the enemy Apaches. For that reason they do not expand as they could. Even though there are pastures in abundance, it is necessary not to let the stock roam free because they will be stolen or killed. For this reason the cold of winter catches them skinny and they die or miscarry."[32]

Over time livestock became more highly valued than land and was often used for dowries.[33] As herds increased, New Mexicans instituted the *partido* system, a pastoral institution in which an owner turned over a certain number of animals to the *partidario*. The partidario accepted responsibility for the ewes and agreed to make annual payments of lambs and wool to the lender (approximately 20 percent of the initial head count).[34] Father Ortega, in evaluating the stock-raising situation in Santa Fe at the beginning of the nineteenth century, stated that some from Santa Fe owned "wool-bearing" stock, but not in the curacy due to distant pasturage and enemy attacks. He noted that they distributed the sheep on the partido system in other parts of the province.[35] Over the course of the century, the partido system led to augmented livestock numbers, making sheep ranching one of the region's most important industries.[36]

The New Mexicans used the wool for weaving, creating blankets, shawls, and clothing. At the end of the eighteenth century in Santa Cruz de la Cañada where they purchased wool from the nearby stockmen, Fray José Mariano Rosete wrote:

> From the wool they purchase, they weave large and small blankets, flannel, very coarse woolen cloth to clothe themselves and to sell. The women embroider bedspreads, rebozos, carpets, sheets, and tablecloths. With the little cotton they acquire, the men weave a few poor quality mantas. The women make fine and ordinary stockings from wool and

cotton, as well as stockings, gaiters, gloves, sashes, belts, and other things. I can assure you that in this country the women work more than many men.[37]

Others engaged in carpentry, tailoring, and barber-surgery. The presidio, in need of weapons and tools, employed armorers and blacksmiths. The state employed officials, such as *alcaldes mayores* (district administrators), while the church paid friars to christianize Native Americans and to care for its flock.

Economic life also revolved around a trade economy that existed between nomadic native groups, such as the Comanches, and the sedentary Pueblo Indians and Hispanic settlers. In 1749, Fray Andrés Varo described the trade fairs:

These Infidel Indians are accustomed to come in peace to the pueblos, and bring buffalo and elk skins, and some young Indians from those that they have imprisoned in the wars that they have among themselves. These they trade to the vecinos, *gente de razón* [non-Indians], Spanish, and Pueblo Indians for horses, mules, knives, awls, clothes, beads, and other things.[38]

In addition to the trade fairs, informal trade centers existed in the numerous mountain settlements, allowing for a steady flow of goods.[39] In turn, this internal trade with the Plains Indians stimulated trade between New Mexico and Mexico, namely Chihuahua and Sonora. In Chihuahua in 1762, the New Mexican merchant José Reaño sold livestock, Plains Indian captives, hides procured from nomadic groups, and woven goods.[40] By 1801, goods traded to Chihuahua included buckskins, *mantas*, piñon, medicinal plants, various resins, stockings, and sheep.[41]

Even so, over the course of the century, raiding deeply affected the livelihoods of New Mexican settlers. Governor Mendinueta mentioned 195 separate raids between 1767 and 1777. The raids resulted in 382 dead, 136 Pueblo Indians and vecinos wounded, and 94 captured.[42] Moreover, Comanches often stole entire herds of livestock and horses.[43] The constant pillaging negatively influenced trade between the northern frontier and its southern neighbors, as trade convoys were frequent targets.[44] Overall, however, the raiding for captives and animals created an economic system that, while destructive at times, led to a redistribution of resources that allowed for survival of both New Mexicans and Plains Indians. Those who had the least resources attacked those with the most wealth, stealing both slaves and livestock. Historian James Brooks writes: "Hence there existed a redistributive transfer of wealth from the higher order (caste, rank, age) in Indian and Euramerican societies to men of lower status."[45]

Due to the strategic importance of New Mexico as a buffer between enemies and valuable mines, crown administrators turned their attention to the frontier and its vulnerabilities. King Carlos III of Spain (1759–1788) and crown administrators, intent on shoring up the weak economy in its colonies and thus increasing royal revenues, enacted a number of fiscal and structural modifications known as the Bourbon reforms. In 1778, Commandant General Teodoro de Croix saw the Comanches as a threat to the rich mining centers of Sonora. He depended on the governors of New Mexico to pacify these enemies.[46] The strategy they devised combined military campaigns and alliances, along with gifts for Indians who complied with treaties, and fiscal reforms to promote trade.[47]

In general, these defensive policies had a salubrious impact on the region's economy. The state, in maintaining peace by supplying gifts to its Indian allies, relied on local artisans to make them.[48] The 1790 census reveals a plethora of New Mexican artisans who benefited from the policy: spinners, carders, weavers, silversmiths, tailors, shoemakers, and blacksmiths.[49] Funds from the royal treasury flowed into the region in the form of troop salaries and military projects.[50] Perhaps the biggest boon to the economy was the lasting peace. Trade between New Mexico and the mining centers to the south flourished, with Sonora demanding livestock and woven goods.[51]

By the second half of the century, a small group of ranchers began to dominate the livestock market.[52] In part, this concentration of power was a result of the smallpox epidemic that left fewer owners to control the herds.[53] By the end of the century, as trade increased, a new commercial hierarchy arose, creating a new social order. Ross Frank writes: "The new commercial order served to divide economic functions between the relatively privileged merchants, agents, and traders who created the export market and the common vecino, Genízaro, Casta, and Pueblo producers."[54]

On the other hand, during the period under study, the continual struggle to overcome adversities led to economic stagnation and resulted in a more fluid class structure. A settler's entire herd, house, and community was often obliterated in a day; the constant raids profoundly affected the rate of material accumulation. Although historian Oakah L. Jones Jr. concludes that class differences came to mean very little in New Mexico,[55] some men and women did amass large flocks of animals and became influential citizens.[56] In many of these instances, however, inheritance laws forced parents to divide their property among their children, preventing great accumulation from generation to generation. At the time he wrote his will in 1739, Cristóbal Baca owned nine hundred ewes. These he bestowed on his nine legitimate children.[57] Although his children benefited from the gift of one hundred ewes each, this type of partition of property led to a society with fewer class divisions than in regions where families entailed properties, passing the bulk of their wealth to their eldest sons.[58]

The Hispanic Communities

After the reconquest, the colonists quickly resettled in Santa Fe and soon populated other towns. On April 19, 1695, Governor Vargas established the town of Santa Cruz de la Cañada with sixty-six families, mostly colonists from Mexico City. Close to a decade later, in the summer of 1706, Viceroy Francisco Fernández de la Cueva, Duke of Alburquerque, ordered a *villa* (town) to be founded near the pueblo of Sandia. Governor Francisco Cuervo y Valdés followed the viceregal dictates and named the town after the duke. Thirty families moved south to inhabit the new villa of Alburquerque, known today as Albuquerque.

Although the crown had promulgated regulations in 1573 that required colonial officials to establish municipalities ordered on a grid system with a rectangular central plaza at its center with straight parallel streets with rectangular blocks and lots for houses and gardens, the New Mexican villas rarely adhered to these plans.[59] Although each town possessed a plaza adjacent to the main church, citizens chose to build their residences away from the town center and close to their fields for the sake of convenience. These small farmsteads were known as *ranchos*. In 1776, Fray Francisco Atanasio Domínguez observed that the villa of Santa Fe "consists of many small ranchos at various distances from one another, with no plan as to their location, for each owner built as he was able, wished to, or found convenient, now for the little farms they have there, now for the small herds of cattle which they keep in corrals of stakes, or else for other reasons."[60] Similar to Santa Feans, residents of Albuquerque and Santa Cruz de la Cañada lived dispersed throughout the regions of their respective villas.[61]

New communities continued to appear throughout the century. Hispanics applied to the governors for small *mercedes* (royal grants of land) on which they lived and farmed.[62] At times groups of people applied for mercedes and the cluster of these land grants became the locus of small villages.[63] In 1768, Governor Pedro Fermín de Mendinueta granted six families a merced to found Vallecitos on the condition that the settlement be constructed in the form of an enclosed plaza. Ignoring the proviso, families followed the usual pattern and established ranchos instead of building a town center.[64]

Royal officials complained about the settlers' insistence on residing in these dispersed settlements. The authorities preferred the plaza-centered towns that were more readily defensible. In 1776, Antonio de Bonilla, secretary to Commandment General don Teodoro de Croix, observed that in New Mexico

> the settlements of the Spaniards are scattered and badly defended . . . and quite exposed to entire ruin. Because the greater number of them are scattered ranches, among which the force of the settlers is divided, they can neither protect themselves nor contribute to the general defense of the country. This, in consequence, results in the abandonment of their weak homes and the terror of seeing themselves incessantly beset by the enemy.[65]

In some of the smaller towns, families took defensive measures placing their homes closely together and constructing towers (*torreones*).[66] In these fortified communities, known as plazas, the houses enclosed a large central square with a large gate standing at one end. During attacks, the families corralled their livestock and barred the gate.[67] Yet these steps often proved deficient, and many people abandoned their towns and ranchos in the face of repeated Indian attacks. In 1772, the settlers of Las Nutrias, located south of Albuquerque, and Carnué, located to the east, abandoned their rich farmlands, irrigated by water from the Río Grande, due to attacks by Apaches.[68]

In 1778, Fray Juan Agustín de Morfi commented that the Spaniards, living in their scattered communities, were not only exposed to enemy attack but allowed to wallow in idleness. With no one to observe them, they ran around naked. "Out of this, other moral disorders proceed which shock even the barbarous Indians.... As a result lewdness holds destructive sway here, more so than among animals. And even robbery is looked upon as a tolerable expedient that does not diminish one's reputation, so that blatant violence is the rule."[69] Morfi's assessment of the Hispanic communities raises the specter of disorganization and isolation. Nevertheless, in spite of their dispersed living arrangements, Hispanics depended on their neighbors for survival and for social interaction. Indeed, their communities proved essential to them, and they willingly defended them.

When Juan Bautista de Anza, governor of New Mexico from 1778 to 1788, attempted to reorder and to concentrate villages as part of his military reorganization, he met with stiff resistance from the settlers.[70] Four different communities sent representatives to travel approximately five hundred miles to Arizpe in northern Sonora, seat of the commandment general, to plead for repeal of Anza's plans. Their grievances reveal what being part of a particular community entailed. The citizens of Santa Fe expressed dismay at the idea of abandoning their town. They had toiled to build the irrigation dams and *acequias* (irrigation ditches), to cultivate their fields, and to maintain the chapel. They complained that Anza's ban on the sale and purchase of Indian servants stripped them of labor and profits and rendered moving more difficult.[71] Genízaros, from the community Analco, feared that relocation would expose their children and women to capture by Comanche raiders.[72] Communal work, Catholicism, economic interests, defense against enemies, and political action in defying Anza's plans all served to bind these settlers together.

Possessions

A material culture also bound Hispanic New Mexicans together, helping to define their communities. They owned or coveted similar objects and shared concepts about which objects had value. In general, settlers brought with them from Mexico and Europe ideas about what constituted decent shelter, which furniture should be used, how farming and animal husbandry should be conducted, which clothes should be worn, and what they should eat. They took these views and adapted them to their new environment, simultaneously borrowing ideas from their Native American neighbors. In this hybrid material culture, New Mexicans imbued things and animals with status and judged their worth. Using objects for work, trade, and religious purposes, they established a familiar world that distinguished them from native communities and helped them establish a pecking order in their own communities.

Over the course of the century, domestic architecture varied slightly. The environment and its offerings limited the type of housing that colonists could build. Due to the lack of timber under 7,500 feet elevation, Hispanic settlers, imitating their Indian neighbors, chose to build with adobe. While Native Americans had used puddle adobe for the construction of walls, the Hispanics introduced adobe bricks. They mixed clay, sand, water, and straw or other plant fiber and shaped them into bricks that they then placed in the sun to dry.[73] Before laying the sun-baked bricks, the builders formed a rough stone foundation on leveled ground. These crude foundations helped to prevent some erosion at ground level. They then arranged the bricks into walls that were eighteen inches to two feet thick.[74]

Most settlers initially constructed one to three rooms that were fifteen feet wide. Builders usually used less cumbersome, moderately sized logs that dictated this width. The length of the room varied and most likely depended on the settlers' resources at the point in time of construction. As the size of their families increased and they acquired more possessions, many added rooms in single file or at times forming an L or U shape. Each room had an outside door and possibly a small window, but usually not both due to the lack of squared timber for woodwork. These rooms might or might not have been interconnected.[75] In his will written in 1729, Diego Márquez of Santa Cruz de la Cañada described his house as having seven rooms with six doors and one window.[76]

Settlers fashioned doors out of thick planks joined by mortises and tenons. Iron, imported from Mexico, proved too costly, so that local builders created a pintle-hinging device out of wood that allowed the door to rotate open and close.[77] It is likely that most did not use wooden doors between openings in the interior, but instead covered them with animal skins or cloth.[78]

When constructing the roofs, builders placed horizontal beams (*vigas*) across the interior space then covered these beams with smaller pieces of wood. Depending on what was locally available, homeowners might have used aspen poles, cottonwood, or split cedar. Afterward, they piled on another layer of brush, cedar bark, or straw and then loaded on adobe earth. The thick layer of dirt kept out the rain and provided insulation, and the layer of straw or brush kept the dirt from sifting into the house. The builders graded the roof and slightly pitched the vigas so that water flowed off the roof into the opening parapets, splashing water away from the adobe walls.[79]

For defensive purposes, New Mexicans opted for very few openings in the walls. If they did make windows, they were very small, facing the east or south elevations. In the earlier years, most homes did not have window glass. The homeowners stuffed the openings with cloth or placed selenite in them. With few or no windows, residents depended on doors for light and ventilation.[80] Some houses did have *portales*, meaning that the roofs extended out past the front door providing shade and shelter from precipitation. One can imagine that people took tasks that required light outside of the home and sat under the *portal*.

Inside the floors were packed earth. To make the floors hard and water resistant, New Mexicans added animal blood and ashes to the earth. A fireplace, or *fogón*, occupied a corner of the room. The hearth usually stood six to eight inches off the ground. The width of the parabola-shaped opening was approximately twenty inches. Due to the shallow firebox, the settlers had to place the logs upright. They also built adobe beehive ovens, called *hornos*, outside their houses.[81]

In addition to houses, the inhabitants also constructed barns, shelters, corrals, storage sheds, and mills. With mills, they mostly used timber because splashing from the mill wheel and seepage from the ditch would have led to the disintegration of adobe walls. They employed *jacal* construction, borrowed from Native Americans, for corrals and chicken pens. The builders placed small timbers vertically and supported these with horizontal grooved rails at the top and bottom or, alternatively, they held the timbers together by weaving them with willow branches. They then covered the surface with mud.[82] Outbuildings, apparently, did not include outhouses. People of the pueblos used chamber pots at night that they emptied in nearby fields the next day, but there is apparently no evidence to illuminate the habits of the Hispanics. Only the friars built latrines.[83]

Unlike outbuildings that had specific uses, the house served many functions, especially if it only contained one room. Those who dwelled there might cook, eat, and sleep in the one room. In larger homes, there was more specialization with a *sala*, or parlor, a kitchen, and storerooms. Some wills reveal that people lived in many-roomed houses with two stories and that the rooms on second floors probably served as sleeping chambers.[84] Juan Manuel Gabaldón, in his will of 1745, declared that his house had fifteen rooms, two portales, a corral, a patio, and the lands that pertained to the house.[85]

Families invited guests into their salas where they displayed their most luxurious possessions. These included furnishings like the *trastero*, or great cupboard. Some trasteros stood seven feet tall with two pairs of doors. One pair had an open grille with hand-carved spindles; the other pair had solid wood panels. The trastero contained small drawers and shelves inside. By the end of the eighteenth century, the carpenters made the cupboards less ornately, with fewer carved details, but continued to paint them with gesso and religious decorations.[86]

Those in search of furniture did not have to go far. They bought furniture from the Indian carpenters of Pecos, who had maintained a fine reputation for furniture making for over a century, or turned to *carpinteros* in the Hispanic towns. By 1790, there were eight carpinteros in Albuquerque and eighteen in Santa Fe.[87]

Carpenters sold a wide variety of furniture to New Mexicans, including beds, tables with drawers, chests, and kneading troughs. Many testators mentioned beds and bed linens in their wills. In 1729, Diego Márquez, who was sick in bed at the time he wrote his will, indicated that he owned a bed with mattress, sheets, blankets, and two pillows.[88] Juana Anaya Almazán left her bed to her husband Lucas Montaño.[89] Although many lay sick in bed while writing their wills, many poorer New Mexicans, who did not leave wills, did without beds. Instead they slept on sheepskins strewn upon the floor.[90]

At times, New Mexicans also chose to purchase imported furniture. One of the most popular items was the *caja de Michoacán*, or chest from Michoacán, Mexico (during the colonial period, Mexico was known as New Spain). Over a third of the testators of colonial wills mentioned these chests; some described them as being used for clothing.[91] They also used the cajas de Michoacán and other chests to store a variety of objects. Tomása Benavides, who died on April 29, 1762, kept one woolen underskirt, one serge petticoat, one linen shirt, and a pair of pearl earrings in her chest, as well as one bottle and two flasks of aguardiente.[92]

Even though colonists possessed a wide variety of furniture, few owned chairs. As in Spain, most people chose to sit on the floor using woolsacks or pelts. Those who did have chairs reserved them for government officials and priests. Accordingly, tables were low, like modern coffee tables. New Mexicans also sat on low stools, or *tarimas*.[93] In addition to the houses and furniture, people owned various tools that facilitated their farming, cooking, and professional tasks. Farmers who grew wheat and corn used farming implements such as the plow pulled by oxen, the ubiquitous digging stick, known as a *coa*, and hoes. In her study of the distribution of goods amongst Santa Cruz settlers in 1712, Angelina Veyna finds that only women received the steel plow points, known as *rejas*.[94] In addition to the steel points, New Mexicans also fashioned wooden plow points.

Men who were soldiers, or who engaged in services for the governor and crown, usually owned the necessary equipment for carrying out their duties. When writing their wills, these men often gave their equipage to their sons, grandsons, or nephews. In 1723, Juan Ruiz Cordero left his saddle, bit, harquebus, leather shield, spurs, cape, long coat, breeches, and his service papers to his son, Francisco Cordero. Luis López, in his will of 1728, indicated that his saddle, harquebus, bit, spurs, and shield were to be given to his grandson, Juan Mascareñas, so that he could enjoy them.[95] In his will of 1767, Manuel Holguín divided his equipage between his two sons. Pedro Antonio was to receive his saddle, stirrups, bridle, spurs, boots, and lariat; whereas his other son, Ventura, was to inherit his gun and case, pouches, a pound and a half of powder, fifty bullets, a leather jacket, and sword and sheath, so that he could serve the king.[96]

Wills also reveal the tools of people's trades such as weaving, carpentry, and barber-surgery. Miguel Lucero, at the time of his death in 1766, owned a loom, two pairs of wool cards, two spinning wheels, and a comb.[97] Woodworkers possessed tools such as planes and chisels.[98] Dimas Jirón de Tejeda's will of 1733 reveals that he was the barber-surgeon of Santa Fe. He owned three books of medicine and had two boxes containing his instruments. In one box, he stored five razors and a rock to sharpen them. In the other, Jirón de Tejeda kept six little lances and a dentist's forceps. He also owned a blood letter, scissors, and cupping glasses—two large and one small.[99]

Upon returning home from their various tasks, New Mexicans needed to prepare the crops or game for their meals. Their kitchens contained a variety of tools, such as ladles, copper kettles, griddles, cauldrons, iron spits, tin plates, spoons, and *manos* and *metates*, the stones for grinding. Also, they required containers to store the food, like flour bins, gourd canteens, and jugs specifically for chocolate or water. The *harinero* or *granero* chest held grain. It had legs at least twenty inches long in order to keep the grain safe from vermin. Imported products like cones of sugar, saffron, chocolate, and cinnamon lined the shelves of some kitchens.[100]

The two main institutions of New Mexico, church and state, also required certain objects to function, so they imported them or purchased them locally. To conduct masses, the priests required the proper vestments, altar cloths, chalices, and thuribles. A baptismal font found in Tome, New Mexico, suggests that settlers worked and formed copper into useful objects.[101] Religious paintings and statues graced the walls of the churches. Many of these objects found their ways into the homes of New Mexicans as well. Local craftsmen, known as *santeros*, painted *santos* (saints) on boards, known as *retablos*, and on animal hides. The santeros also carved *bultos* (sculptures) out of pine or cottonwood that they then painted with gesso and tempera colors.[102] The presidio hired local blacksmiths and armorers to provide a variety of tools, including axes and knives. Both church and state officials also required paper for documentation that needed to be imported. Although state and ecclesiastical officials, at times, needed specialized tools, many of their requirements, like beeswax and ink, for example, were also needs shared by the average citizen. The demand for these objects stimulated both imports and local production.

As settlers' wealth increased, they purchased more and more items of clothing and jewelry, as well as land and houses. With little money circulating in the region, the acquisition of material items proved a wise investment, a practice that occurred in other colonies as well. Historian John Demos finds that colonists in Plymouth invested their wealth in land, household goods, and clothing.[103] New Mexicans apparently did the same; they bought material objects to use and display on their persons, to horde, or to trade at appropriate times or use to buy services.

First and foremost, people liked to display their wealth by wearing expensive clothing, like a red cloth shawl with lace and wide yellow and red ribbons or a cape of Chinese silk with narrow silver thread and jewelry.[104] When Governor Vargas died, he possessed emerald and pearl earrings and a rose diamond ring. Richard Ahlborn writes that "even a poor frontier region boasted high quality goods which served as status symbols and, perhaps, as goals for lesser officials and merchants."[105]

Hispanics owned numerous clothes made from imported lace, linen, silk, serge, and damask. Although some clothes came ready-made, colonists also purchased bolts of imported cloth to be made into clothes by local tailors.[106] On April 19, 1714, doña Francisca de Mizquía, sick in bed, began to enumerate and divide her possessions, choosing to give almost all of her clothing and jewelry to her daughter Lucía. For example, Lucía received, among other items, two gowns known as *tapapiés*, one of green satin and one of red satin, coral bracelets, a blue shirt of Ruan cloth, and a scarlet petticoat. Doña Francisca also indicated that a new gown of green serge and some blue fabric with white and red flowers with yellow-ribbon fringe should be used to pay for her burial and masses.[107] Men also purchased elaborate clothes. Manuel Holguín, in his will of 1767, related that his wardrobe consisted of red breeches with silver buttons and jet buttons surrounded by silver. He also had a short jacket of blue Castilian cloth. Apparently, he changed the look of the coat by changing the lapels, one of which was scarlet in color. In addition, he wore a blue cape made of Mexican cloth lined with red Castilian cloth.[108]

The colonists' fascination with foreign goods and willingness to trade and to buy them meant that the traders braved long distances, bad roads, and Indian attacks to meet the demand and to profit. The goods for sale in New Mexico differed little from what the traders sold in New Spain. Historian Eric Van Young's review of an inventory of a murdered merchant of New Spain included ready-made clothing, such as stockings for both men and women, blouses, *rebozos*, petticoats, jackets, waistcoats, and even a wig. The merchant also had sewing material, such as large quantities of French lace, Chinese ribbon, Portuguese thread, raw silk and silken thread, and cotton cloth from Mexico. Additionally, he carried household items, such as folding knives, brooms, hoes, and raw indigo dye. Rounding out his stock, he had jewelry, religious items, and ornaments made of coral and enamel, beads, earrings, copper rings, silver reliquaries, rosaries, and combs.[109]

In 1752, Governor Tomás Vélez Cachupín captured two French traders and seized their merchandise. The wares they aimed to sell to Hispanics matched the diversity of the Spaniard's stock. The French carried flowered silk, muslin, and lace, in addition to the more common fabrics made of wool, cotton, and linen. They also had shoes, gloves, silk and cotton handkerchiefs, woolen and cotton caps, and beaver hats. The governor also confiscated thread, buttons, sealing wax, copper candlesticks, puzzles, ivory and horn combs, mirrors, and a cape for a bullfighter.[110]

Although New Mexicans purchased imported clothes, they most likely wore more practical clothes on a daily basis while working. Clothes made of local materials included leather jackets, buckskins, and woolen socks. Juan Manuel de Herrera took little interest in the finer, imported clothing of his neighbors. He wore an old cloth cape, a pair of buckskin trousers, and an old hat.[111] Father Guerra of Albuquerque noted that his parishioners made "quite coarse cloth that is used in the clothing of the inhabitants and some ordinary and fine stockings that usually have some worth in Chihuahua."[112]

In addition to wearing these clothes, the colonists traded them with one another and Native Americans. At the time of Juan de Archibeque's death, his son was on a mission, trading wares that included 36 buckskins, 11 painted elk skins, 28 buffalo hides, 12 thick elk skins, 4 leather jackets, and 309 pairs of different colored stockings.[113]

Often times, it was these local goods that people used as bartering chips. When New Mexicans enumerated debts they owed and those due to them, they often listed stockings and/or animal skins. In 1717, Juana Domínguez said that she owed various people, including her comadre, Juana Griego, pairs of stockings and, in addition, four individuals each owed her a pair of stockings.[114] Juan José Moreno, in 1756, stated that Miguel el Chago, a resident of Taos, owed him ten hides at two pesos each, the balance due for an Indian woman.[115]

A discussion of the material culture would not be complete without including the objects that brought pure pleasure to the New Mexicans such as games and toys. Testators did not often include children's toys when listing their goods. Yet it is known that people enjoyed card games since traders from Chihuahua brought cards (originally purchased from the crown which held a monopoly on the printing and sale of playing cards) to sell on the frontier.[116] The French traders carried a puzzle. New Mexicans also played musical instruments like the guitar and harp.[117] And while playing cards or listening to music, they might have smoked punche and relished a glass of wine.

Chapter 2

Civil Authorities, Civil Law, and Family

THE IDEAL HISPANIC society was composed of hierarchically arranged groups and individuals, all finally owing allegiance to the crown. The three traditional estates included the nobility, the clergy, and the commoners, each with its specific duties and privileges, and together they made up the body politic of the monarchy.[1] The inequalities inherent in this society rested on the acquiescence of each person to his or her station with its respective obligations.[2] An 1806 opinion by the Council of the Indies summarized the importance of the corporatist system: "It is undeniable that the existence of various hierarchies and classes is of the greatest importance to the existence and stability of a monarchical state, since a graduated system of dependence and subordination sustains and insures the obedience and respect of the last vassal to the authority of the sovereign."[3]

The Spanish Crown believed that families acted as the foundation of a well-ordered, functional civilization. The family was a metaphor for the king's society in which the man ruled over his family as the king ruled over his kingdom. Within the family, hierarchies also existed, with the members owing obedience to the head of the household, who was husband and father. The historian Silvia Arrom writes, "Because conflict within the vertically segmented groups was unacceptable to this order, effective control from the top down required the inequality of husbands and wives."[4] The father, receiving obedience and respect, provided for his family members and treated them with affection. The realities of family life often clashed with the ideals as people failed to conform to their ascribed roles. At times, conflict ensued and New Mexicans sought state intervention to help mediate.

From the initial settlement and throughout the colonial period, the New Mexican governors, as representatives of the Spanish Crown, and the men they appointed to help them govern, intervened in personal, family matters at the behest of family members. The state supported the church's bid to control and to monitor family life. The laws that affected families most consistently over time were those pertaining to property, namely the dowry and inheritance. In general, the governors took their role as father of the people seriously. When citizens appealed for their help, governors dutifully involved themselves, especially when citizens transgressed inheritance laws or broke vows commonly held to be valued.

The citizens expected civil authorities to intercede in their lives and often appealed to the governors to help mediate contentious familial situations. Women, for example, filed suit against men who had broken promises of marriage. Arrom, when discussing the legislation to protect women, argues that because family matters were private, the courts in Mexico City did not actively intervene on a woman's behalf when a man abused his authority. A woman or her family had to initiate a suit demanding her rights.[5] On occasion, however, community members in New Mexico intervened in the "private matters" of neighbors, becoming involved when they perceived injustices or transgressions of community standards.

Settlement Policies

Hard on the heels of conquest, the Spanish Crown recognized the need to develop policies to cultivate stable settlements. The state, in its effort to establish prosperous communities, looked to the Iberian family as the building blocks, the raw material, for instilling Spanish society in the New World. Concomitantly, authorities viewed unattached men as uncontrollable and causes of social disorder.[6] The crown believed that a colony based on the institution of marriage, family, and Christianity led to social order, the transmission of Spanish culture and moral values, and loyalty to itself.

The idea of imbuing conquest with family policies was by no means a New World phenomenon. Spain, in its long history of conquest and counterconquest with Muslims, saw marriage with new Christians (those who converted to Catholicism) as a means for promoting social stability. Alfonso X, architect of the *Siete Partidas* in 1265, viewed marriage as the preferred state so as "to avoid quarrels, homicides, insolence, violence, and many other wrongful acts which would take place on account of women if marriage did not exist."[7] As soldiers reconquered Iberian land, the crown considered colonization the key objective. The settlement policy stressed the need for matrimony and, subsequently, the conjugal residence of man and wife. The hope was that a married man would settle down and forgo the quest for adventure.[8] The Spanish settlement policies contrast sharply with those of Portugal. Portugal did not aim to control and settle immense expanses of land, but instead founded its colonies on commercial ports and trade routes. Even Brazil, until well into the sixteenth century, functioned largely as a series of trading posts.[9]

In some of the earliest laws emanating from Spain in the sixteenth century, the crown showed a keen concern for the marital status of *encomenderos*, grantees of Indian tribute and labor, and settlers alike.[10] The crown issued numerous decrees encouraging men to marry or to send for wives they had left behind in Spain. In a royal decree in 1539, the crown stated that if an encomendero failed to marry within three years, it would take the *encomienda* and give it to a deserving married man.[11] The crown's belief that women provided a stabilizing force proved true in sixteenth-century Peru where encomenderos' wives offered social and economic continuity, offsetting the instability created by their husbands' civil wars.[12]

At the turn of the eighteenth century, the central regions of the vast colony of New Spain were settled, yet Spanish subjects continued to explore, conquer, and colonize the northern frontiers. Government officials, therefore, confronted the issue of conquest and settlement throughout much of the colonial period. In fact, in the early 1690s, New Mexico remained unconquered. In 1680, the Pueblos had united and revolted against the Spanish colonists, driving them downriver to the vicinity of El Paso.[13] Governor Vargas believed that to reconquer New Mexico and maintain it for the crown, he would need a Hispanicized, Christian citizenry to occupy the region. Vargas initially hoped to recruit five hundred families and one hundred presidial soldiers.[14]

To realize his plan, Vargas appealed to the settlers of the El Paso region, some of whom were survivors of the Pueblo Revolt. After the Indian uprising, close to two thousand settlers had fled to El Paso.[15] The governor conducted a house-by-house census of over one hundred households, informing the people that he wanted them to resettle New Mexico and that the viceroy would provide them with aid. When Vargas visited the home of Mateo Trujillo, he found a willing participant. Trujillo told Vargas that "he is ready to enter with his family to settle this Kingdom of New Mexico and, as his majesty's loyal vassal, for everything that I, the governor and captain general, shall order and command, as he has always done what he has been ordered and what has presented itself to him."[16]

Some of those who responded to Vargas's urgings agreed to go if they received the necessary assistance. Sergeant Major Sebastián González stated that he had served his majesty for thirty years at his own expense without an encomienda. "His majesty's will is his own, and he will need aid in order to move, since he does not even own a shirt."[17] Captain Juan de Valencia stated that, as his majesty's loyal vassal, he was ready to settle this Kingdom of New Mexico, "if he is given the means to be able to move his family, because it is very large and he is too poor to be able to do it."[18] Indeed, poverty among the refugees and settlers in the region was great. Without the promised help, few would have been able to make the trip north.

Other men agreed to go with the governor but stipulated that they wanted to go before their families so that they could make homes. Diego Varela, for example, said that "unencumbered, he will enter to build his house and after it is done, he will come for all his family and enter to settle this kingdom."[19] Antonio Montaño was quite ready to go whenever he was ordered, "but that at present, he will enter alone to reestablish a household and afterward come for his family."[20] These men's responses reveal that they perceived themselves as the protectors of their families. Wisely, they believed that their families should remain where they were and should not go elsewhere until shelter was guaranteed.

Apparently, these men had little choice in the matter. When the time came to leave El Paso on October 4, 1693, whole families left together. The royal supplies did not last the entire trip; provisions ran out and settlers were forced to trade their possessions for food. The lack of shelter also proved disastrous, with many babies dying of exposure. Although men tried to negotiate the terms of their return to New Mexico, they had little power to do so.

These families also insisted that their Indian servants be allowed to migrate north with them. Vargas wrote that the citizens of San Lorenzo (two leagues from El Paso) requested that "those Indians born in Mexico City, who were living together with them in this real and pueblo of San Lorenzo and have accompanied and followed them since the uprising of the apostate Indians of the villa and principal town of Santa Fe and the Kingdom of New Mexico, loyal and obedient to the Divine and human majesty, living and persevering with the hope of returning when this kingdom was recovered and to the royal crown restored, be allowed to live and settle, accompanying them wherever they may settle."[21] The evidence suggests that strong bonds existed between the Hispanic population and its servants. While in exile and living in poverty, they perhaps formed bonds of kinship with each other. They probably also considered that with more hands to work the land and more men to protect the community, their chances of survival and success increased. In the end, these earnest citizens convinced Vargas; he allowed their Indian servants to join the recolonization effort.

Due to the paucity of settlers, Vargas called for more people to help colonize the area. The viceroy heeded his call and began recruiting families in Mexico City. While Governor Vargas worked to enlist settlers in El Paso, Viceroy don Gaspar de Sandoval Cerda Silva y Mendoza, the Conde de Galve, appealed to the citizens of Mexico City, enticing them to relocate to New Mexico. On March 13, 1693, a town crier proclaimed that the reconquered province of New Mexico needed to be repopulated with families and that any persons wishing to go would receive assistance for the trip and be transported in wagons paid for by the king. All those who enlisted would be given privileges and favors and would receive land, water, and all that they required to maintain themselves.[22] The viceregal junta general closely supervised the recruitment and insisted that couples be married and show legal proof.[23] One expedition leader, Fray Francisco Farfán, prohibited unmarried men from enlisting. In September 1693, he wrote to the viceroy, "Also, in attention to the fact that these families are composed precisely of married couples and are taking along some unmarried daughters, it should neither be permitted nor agreed that any unmarried man, even under pretext of being a kinsman, be allowed to go, live, or mix with these families."[24]

Willing recruits signed on to leave Mexico City and venture north. Perhaps they decided to leave because of the floods, famine, and riots that plagued the city. Whatever their reasons, many of the people who agreed to depart did so with foresight, employing a strategy that would make their endeavors less arduous and less lonely. Nine distinct kinship groups agreed to make the journey together. Close to half of the colonists were related to one another by either blood or marriage.[25]

Still in need of additional families, the viceroy directed Vargas to appoint a qualified person to recruit colonists in the Zacatecas region and to accompany them to New Mexico.[26] Governor Vargas entrusted his lieutenant, Juan Páez Hurtado, to enlist families composed of persons of good character and social standing. Páez Hurtado enrolled forty-six families composed of 145 people. They arrived in Santa Fe on May 9, 1695.[27]

These three recruitments for settlers varied markedly and speak to the ideals of settlement policies and the realities therein. When Vargas wrote to the Conde de Galve about the resettlement of the area and his need for money, he congratulated the viceroy: "Thus, I hope in everything you will take the measures you see fit that are so necessary for the stability and safety of that kingdom. The new propagation of our holy faith in it will result from your excellency's zeal. I have certain hopes that, with such a prince and protector as the instrument, not only what has been acquired by evangelical law with painstaking efforts will be held most securely and exalted, but also the increases in the growth of heathen conversions to that law."[28] The viceroy most likely appreciated the importance of evangelism but also recognized the threat of French infiltration and possible invasion of the silver-producing areas of northern Mexico.[29]

As previously mentioned, the viceroy, as supervisor of the enrollment process, insisted on including only legally married couples and their families. His insistence on wedded couples harkens back to the earlier royal policies. In a discussion about whether larger families should receive bigger allowances, the viceroy and the general junta stated that larger families should be compensated in order "to recognize the greater service to his majesty."[30] The viceroy wanted Hispanic families so that the region would be a Spanish stronghold. The church, in the voice of Father Farfán, also played a part. His apprehensive tone connotes an interest in the morality of the settlers. He was probably most concerned, however, with the example the Hispanic families would set for the Indians.

When Vargas arrived with the settlers from the El Paso region, he encountered Pueblo people who resented the return of the Spaniards. The Indian residents of Santa Fe refused to vacate the city and war ensued. Hostilities did not end there, and the recruits from Mexico City, upon being forced to help in military expeditions, complained that they had been promised that they would not be forced to perform military service. The viceroy had assured them a land free of enemies.[31] Instead, the male colonists spent much of their time away on campaigns or simply protecting their families.[32] Due to the dire need for able-bodied men, it comes as a surprise that settlement policies stressed that only families be recruited and not single men.

When Juan Páez Hurtado set out to recruit families, he did so with the same requirements that the viceroy had insisted upon in Mexico City: enroll settler families, not bachelors. Páez Hurtado, however, had few qualms about breaking these rules and enlisted whomever was willing to go. Historian John B. Colligan relates that Páez Hurtado's motives might have been monetary: Páez Hurtado absconded with close to 7,000 pesos owed to the settlers. Colligan also points out that Páez Hurtado's actions were not out of the ordinary; many officials defrauded citizens and the state to pad their own pockets.[33]

Regardless of this fraud, Páez Hurtado willingly recruited single men and women. Instead of the forty-six families on the official list, the group was made up of twenty-one families and twenty-one individuals. Of those twenty-one individuals, sixteen were men.[34] Perhaps Páez Hurtado believed that the colony needed young men who would be able and willing to protect the fledgling community. Páez Hurtado, unlike the viceroy, planned to settle in the region and to remain there. He had a vested interest in the success of the community.

How did settlement policies affect these people? To begin with, the people who ventured north ultimately made the decision to go. They could have stayed home. Of course, they had limited choices. The citizens of El Paso, for example, suffered from extreme poverty. Those who thought they might be better off farther south petitioned to leave, but Vargas denied them the necessary licenses.[35] Vargas knew that he would need every available person to repopulate New Mexico. With some encouragement, people did opt to go to New Mexico. Enticed by promises of land, and hidalgo status, they believed that they would find more opportunities than they had in their home cities.

In summary, before the colonists resolved to leave, they insisted on certain terms that they hoped would facilitate settlement. They considered with whom they would migrate, recognizing the need for a long-term strategy. Those from San Lorenzo petitioned Vargas to allow their servants to make the journey, and the recruits from Mexico City migrated in kinship groups. They also insisted on support for their endeavors. The refugees in El Paso made certain that there would be royal assistance. The recruits from Mexico City wrangled over the money promised to them. Men with large families demanded more, and those families composed of only husband and wife expected the promised 300 pesos.[36] Finally, some men hoped to shield their families from the worst of the colonization process by requesting that they be allowed to go first and establish a home.

Even though the colonists tried to exert influence over their expedition to the north, they were often victims of circumstance and pawns of those who held more power. Instead of finding prosperity, they found war, drought, sickness and famine. In search of food, Vargas led various campaigns against Indians, causing bitter antagonisms that eventually led to an armed uprising against the Hispanics in June 1696.[37] In this dire situation, many Hispanics probably regretted their decisions. During the political conflict between Vargas and his successor, don Pedro Rodríguez Cubero, the citizens had the opportunity to complain about their leaders who had mismanaged supplies, created a hostile environment, and stolen from their meager rations.[38] Little came of their anger, however, for Vargas received his coveted reappointment in 1703 and retained his lieutenant, Juan Páez Hurtado.

The New Mexican State in the Eighteenth Century

The king governed from Spain and depended on his representatives in the New World to uphold his laws and enact his policies. Appointed by the crown, the governor, who held military and administrative authority over his jurisdiction, also dispensed justice in the king's name.[39] The New Mexican *cabildo*, the municipal council, operated only until 1710, leaving the governor with uncontested authority to govern thereafter.[40] According to the *Recopilación de Leyes de los Reynos de las Indias* (5.2.7), the governor's duties were as follows: "You will do justice to all, with no exceptions; and you will adhere to and comply with all the matters of good governance and laws of the kingdom, the *cédulas* and provisions of His Majesty, and those that are made and given, and might be made and given, for the proper order of the Indies."[41] Although governors were not educated in law and jurisprudence, evidence suggests that governors from the early eighteenth century had access to the relevant legal works. Governors also received royal dispatches and pertinent legislation from New Spain.[42]

The governor, as the top judicial representative of the crown at the provincial level, was supposed to foster impartiality and neutrality. The crown forbade marriage between its representatives and locals, and banned nepotism. The governors of New Mexico respected these laws to some degree and agreed not to marry into local families. Many governors already married at the time of their appointments declined to bring their families with them, though some did. And although governors brought their own networks of men, most governors did not appoint their relatives.[43]

Even though most governors dedicated their time and energy to their military responsibilities, governors were also the top judicial representatives of the crown at the provincial level. If a civil or criminal disturbance occurred or someone had a complaint, citizens turned to the governor to seek redress or to arbitrate. In carrying out justice, the governors turned to the alcaldes mayores—local officials appointed by the governors—to investigate the civil and criminal cases. Alcaldes mayores also participated in the execution of wills and settlements of estates (*derecho privado*). Their interaction with the community was more immediate. Historian Charles Cutter argues that although these men had no legal training whatsoever, "their notions of justice and appreciation for the basic precepts of Spanish law allowed them to carry out something of the crown's vision for judicial administration and the maintenance of social harmony."[44]

Though governors were intent on making a profit from their appointments while in New Mexico, they did manage to fulfill their duties with some impartiality due to the fact that they aspired to move onto more lucrative and prestigious posts. Since most governors' terms lasted only six to eight years, they remained somewhat removed from the local affairs, giving the settlers recourse to relatively disinterested judges. If citizens found the current governor unapproachable, they could wait for the next one.[45] In the year 1750 Julián Rael de Aguilar and his siblings filed a civil suit against Antonio de Ulibarrí, the executor of their father's will. They contended that Ulibarrí had failed to deliver their fair inheritance and had beaten Julián and threatened his siblings. Before making his complaint, Rael de Aguilar waited until a new governor took his post, saying, "When another governor came, like the one that is now present, the witnesses would tell everything they know or part of it."[46] The fact that they delayed filing their suits points out that citizens recognized that each governor had his own biases and that those biases might adversely affect their petitions. The act of waiting, however, afforded no guarantees. How could citizens know that the next governor might prove more sympathetic?

Although some citizens chose to await a change in leadership, others had more pressing matters and had to appeal to the current governor. In petition after petition, citizens invoked the aid of the governors, expecting them to fulfill their duties by heeding their calls. In 1736, Manuela de Chávez, fearing for her siblings' well-being, asked the governor to appoint a guardian. She beseeched: "I pray and beg of Your Majesty as judge and father of minors, and who acts in place of our king, whom God preserve, to remove from them our brother [who, she believed, was not protecting her siblings' interests] and that you appoint a person, tutor or guardian ad litem, for them; so that he may govern, teach and educate them, and to take charge of their inheritance."[47] The governor immediately responded by appointing a guardian to watch over the minors' possessions.

Yet there were times when the relationship between the governor and the community was strained. The conflict between Vargas and Cubero was in some ways an aberration in the eighteenth century—the only case in which an outgoing governor wished to retain his post and tried to prevent the incoming governor from succeeding him. At that time, the incipient colony was reeling from an Indian revolt and staggering hunger. When the political conflict between the two governors afforded the colonists the opportunity to choose sides and vent their frustrations, they took it. This exceptional case demonstrates how some people interpreted the social order, what they expected of their leaders, and how they reacted when they perceived this social order to be awry.

On January 2, 1697, the members of the Santa Fe cabildo sent a petition to the viceroy, Conde de Moctezuma, listing their grievances against Governor Vargas. Although they mentioned the governor's failure to heed the warning of the 1696 revolt, his mismanagement of the presidio that led to the endangerment of the settlers, and his financial misdeeds, they began their petition with and emphasized a list of the governor's sexual improprieties. "First, when the governor and captain general entered El Paso to govern in 1691, he brought a woman with him as his mistress." They also said that in New Mexico he later began living with a married woman and permitted his retainers to engage in this immoral behavior as well. Following the lead of the governor and his cohorts, soldiers also cohabitated illegally without reprimand or punishment. Citizens concluded, "As a result, the contagion has infected this Kingdom worse than Sodom ever was."[48]

The righteous indignation of the cabildo members evident in the petition illustrates the complex relationship between the governor and his subjects and the cabildo's perception of a tear in the social fabric. One of the key components of maintaining the order was for the governor to uphold family values and sexual propriety. In this case, the cabildo members saw themselves as the guardians of morality. They wanted citizens to abide by the laws of the church and state and recognized when people behaved immorally and illegally. In the citizens' view, the mandate of the king's representatives was to uphold these laws and obey them as well. They attempted to alter the offensive behavior by filing lawsuits, but the governor stymied these attempts. Instead they turned to the viceroy, hoping he would bring Vargas to heel.

The viceroy, however, disregarded the cabildo's imputation respecting Vargas's alleged moral lapses, and in the end, the Audiencia of Mexico City declared all of the cabildo's accusations, including those of financial malfeasance, as inadmissible.[49] In addition to the fact that the cabildo's legal position was based on flawed premises, the chance of success had also been slim due to the class division between the settlers and Vargas.[50] The hierarchy in colonial New Spain was predicated on distinct social cohorts: a socially superior elite ruled an inferior populace. When one of the rulers came under attack, those of the elite closed ranks and supported one another. Cabildo members and settlers appealed to a viceroy who had much more in common with Vargas than with the mostly illiterate, common-born masses. Historians John Kessell and Rick Hendricks write: "A peninsular outlook, whether acquired by birth or by training and career; a privileged class position; the shared concerns of those accustomed to rule; and, sometimes, simple friendship were the commonalities that linked Vargas to his counterparts in Mexico City."[51] Indeed the viceregal authorities blamed the settlers for the hard times besetting the fledgling colony. Instead of productively using the supplies provided them, the settlers had squandered them through their "inherent laziness."[52]

The social distance between governors and settlers is evident throughout the century. Although governors carried out their duties, and settlers used paternalistic metaphors to address them, governors often disparaged their subjects. At the end of the eighteenth century, Governor don Fernando de la Concha cautioned the incoming governor about the character of many New Mexicans: "Under a simulated appearance of ignorance or rusticity they conceal the most refined malice. He is a rare one in whom the vices of lying and robbing do not occur together."[53] Class divisions often led to misunderstandings; the governors expected their subjects to respect them and follow their orders, and the citizens expected their leaders to understand the realities of New Mexico and to uphold the laws and to abide by them as well. Hailing from the social elite in New Spain, the governors often believed that a great divide separated them from the New Mexicans. Yet, while serving their terms on the remote frontier, the governors recognized that within New Mexico social stratifications existed, and they felt more affinity toward the more powerful and affluent families.

Family Laws

Although differences existed between the governors and the citizens, authorities strove to fulfill their duties in most cases. The governors and the alcaldes mayores endeavored to uphold the laws known as the *derecho indiano*, laws that both emanated from Spain and those that derived from the American experiences, such as the *Recopilación de Leyes de los Reynos de las Indias*. When called upon to deliver justice, colonial magistrates turned to a number of sources to make their decisions. First, they analyzed written law and *doctrina*, which encompassed the written opinions of both national and international jurists. The local customs of a particular place also played a role in the decision-making process. Under Hispanic law, deep-rooted practices carried the weight of authority. Lastly, magistrates also considered *equidad*, or how their decisions would affect the community at large.[54] Due to the lack of legal training of both the governors and the alcaldes mayores, the crown permitted local magistrates to employ simplified criminal and civil procedure. Simplified procedure, however, did not mean that magistrates disregarded the laws. Indeed, magistrates on the frontier had access to both written laws and doctrina.[55]

Derecho indiano offered little in the way of contracts, marriage, and inheritance.[56] Instead, the laws that the magistrates turned to when deciding cases about conflicts among family members, broken marriage promises, or dowry cases were set out in the *Leyes de Toro* (promulgated in 1505) or in the thirteenth-century *Siete Partidas*. Alfonso X "El Sabio" (1221–1284), king of Castile, oversaw the compilation of the *Siete Partidas*, a uniform code of law to be utilized throughout his diverse kingdoms.[57] Touching on all aspects of medieval life, the code became the cornerstone for the legal system in Spain and its colonies.

The fourth *partida* pertained to betrothal and matrimony. Alfonso X deemed matrimony his most important topic, given that it was considered the noblest and most honorable of the seven sacraments. This partida was the architectural centerpiece for the entire law code, with three partidas on either side of the fourth, "just as the heart is placed in the middle of the body where is situated the spirit of man, from whence life proceeds to all his members."[58] For Alfonso X, family began with the union of husband and wife. God showed man "great distinction by creating a woman whom He gave as a companion." United in holy matrimony and becoming one in love, the couple preserved faithfulness to one another, "and, besides, that from this affection offspring might be born, by which the world might be peopled, and He Himself praised and served."[59] When a man and a woman united in holy matrimony, the man became "the lord and the head of his wife."[60] Legally bound, the husband supported, protected, and guided his wife and she, in exchange, owed him obedience.

Although the state's role in marriage was not as central as the role played by the Catholic Church (see chapter 3), the New Mexican state proved an important influence in upholding the laws and values promulgated in the *Siete Partidas*. Betrothals marked the beginning of the marital process. A promise made in the present tense, with both the man and woman repeating a promise such as "I take you as my wife," and "I take you for my husband," rendered the marriage valid.[61] By the eighteenth century, the betrothal promise no longer signified a valid marriage, but the idea that a promise was binding remained a part of societal values.[62] In New Mexico, the state (governors, lieutenant governors, and other appointed men) recognized the importance of the marriage promise. Over the course of the century, in five out of thirteen cases dealing with broken marriage promises, parents and one young woman appealed to the governor to help resolve their conflicts (see table 3). In four out of the five cases, the state imprisoned the men accused of breaking their promises. In 1750 Lieutenant Governor don Bernardo Antonio Bustamante y Tagle even jailed a married man who had broken off his engagement to another woman. Upon releasing him, the lieutenant governor admonished the man to keep his word in the future.[63] In the remaining cases, in which citizens appealed to the ecclesiastical authorities, the state lent the church its support. When the church wanted to imprison a man for breaking a promise, the state supplied the church with the soldiers to arrest the offender and provided access to the jail.[64]

Once the marriage occurred, custom dictated that the couple set up a household separate from their respective parents' homes. In 1714, Governor Juan Ignacio Flores Mogollón issued one of the few gubernatorial decrees concerning family, insisting that married Pueblo Indian couples reside together in separate households. He had received notice of the "bad custom" among these people of having the women stay with their parents or relatives while the husbands resided in another house without "taking care of them or supporting them."[65] He said that they had failed to fulfill the orders of the church regarding the sacrament of marriage and that these customs would lead to horrible consequences. He interpreted this sacrament as meaning: "that the couple lives together in one house with the husband taking care to sustain and to maintain his wife, assisting her in all that is necessary, his work permitting; and the wife looking after her husband and the house, alleviating his work when possible."[66] The governor believed so strongly in his commandment that he threatened the disobedient with corporal punishment and imprisonment.

In 1704, Ana Bernal sought the help of a *procurador*, a self-styled legal representative who petitioned the ecclesiastical court to help her reunite with her estranged husband, Luis López.[67] The husband agreed to live with his wife and resume their marriage. Seeking assurances that the couple would maintain its vows, the ecclesiastical judge appealed to the state for assistance. The judge reasoned that the state would be able to threaten the couple with temporal punishments.[68] Juan Páez Hurtado, the lieutenant governor, ordered the couple to reunite, to resume married life, to love one another as

Christ loves the church, and not to fight. If they failed to abide by these rulings, Luis López would be sent to the Philippines for ten years and Ana Bernal would be placed in prison.[69] Páez Hurtado's strong threats attest to the fact that the state upheld the church's view of marriage as an important sacrament, in which couples lived together and supported one another.

In the latter part of the century on April 7, 1776, Charles III issued the *Pragmática sanción de matrimonios*. In general, the *Pragmática*, similar to other Bourbon reforms, aimed to modernize the imperial state by increasing its efficiency and its power and influence over society and by limiting the authority of the Catholic Church. More particularly, the architects of the *Pragmática* hoped to bolster paternal authority and filial obedience within families that, in turn, would reflect and enhance the kingdom's hierarchical order.[70] With the *Pragmática*, the crown broke with the tenets of the Council of Trent which had affirmed the church's jurisdiction over marriage and the necessity of the bride and groom to consent freely to the marriage.[71]

The *Pragmática*, extended to the Americas in 1778, stated that those under age twenty-five needed parental consent to marry. Parents could oppose the marriages of their children if they deemed the matches as unequal. If the children persisted, parents could disinherit their errant children. Couples, if they thought the opposition unjust, could challenge the parents before a civil judge. Believing that most Americans of African ancestry did not know their fathers, the minister of the Council of Indies tailored the Pragmática for Spanish America and exempted these individuals.[72]

The implementation of the new law did not run smoothly in the Americas. Initially, some circumvented the law by marrying without consent and forgoing the parental inheritance (in many cases too small to make much of a difference). Churchmen asked for clarification about whether couples could relinquish the inheritance and marry as they chose. Some couples complained that they had had premarital sex because they had promised to marry one another. Ensuing pregnancies and uneasy consciences led to lawsuits. All of these nuanced arguments presented by suitors and requests of clarification by both civil and ecclesiastical officials led to continual reviews of the Pragmática by the Council of Indies until the *Real Cédula* of 1803. The cédula stated that all males under age twenty-five and females under age twenty-three needed their fathers' consent to marry. Those who were older did not need permission. The intent was to avoid confusion and discourage lawsuits.[73] News of the Pragmática had arrived in New Mexico by April 24, 1784.[74] Parental interference in marriages existed, but the state's role remained small and did not increase between 1784 and 1800.

King Alfonso X believed in the holiness of marriage, but he also recognized it as an alliance between two people and their families that united properties as well as blood. Much of the fourth partida is dedicated to the dowry and marriage gifts. The dowry was the property a wife brought to her husband at the marriage. The husband took control of the property and was entitled to collect the incomes in order to support himself, his wife, and their children, and to preserve, defend and protect the marriage.[75] The husband had no right to sell, dispose of, or waste the dowry since it remained the property of the wife.[76] Upon the death of the husband, the dowry, free and unencumbered, returned to the wife, to dispose of at her pleasure. Upon the wife's death, the property descended intact to her heirs or, if she had none, to her family.[77]

The law compelled a father to "bestow her in marriage and give a dowry with her." Also, a woman could present her husband with a dowry from her own property or patrons could give a dowry in her name.[78] The law did not require mothers to give dowries, although, if they desired, they could do so. Guardians in charge of young women and their property took a percentage of the property and presented it as a dowry. The laws regarding property persisted with some changes made when the *Leyes de Toro* were promulgated in 1505.[79]

The giving of dowries is evident in eighteenth-century New Mexico, but the role of the state in these transactions was minor. Dowry letters, abundant in the notarial records in New Spain, do not exist in New Mexico. Instead of the involvement of a notary and the archiving of the dotal letters, families apparently conducted dowry transactions informally. In the existing records, the state became involved only when a dispute arose. For example, in 1733, Francisco de Silva, resident of San Felipe de Albuquerque, filed a civil suit against his father-in-law, Nicolás Durán y Chávez, in which he complained that Durán y Chávez had failed to deliver the agreed-upon dowry owed to his wife.[80] Throughout the proceedings, the alcalde mayor of Albuquerque interviewed a number of witnesses who had knowledge of the dowry (what was promised and whether it was delivered). Neither man presented formal documents to prove his points. In the end, however, the two men came to an agreement without any input from the state except in its role as arbiter. In two other cases, disputes over dowries occurred after the deaths of the husbands. The state played an active role since these cases dealt with the wills and inventories. The governors and the alcaldes mayores stood ready to arbitrate and to decide to whom the property belonged, and at times, this meant finding out whether women came to marriages with dowries.

In general, the purpose of the laws of inheritance that the governors and the alcaldes mayores enforced was to safeguard the rights of legally married persons and their legitimate children. Upon the death of a spouse, the living spouse inherited half of the wealth accumulated during the marriage, known as community property (*bienes gananciales*), and whatever property he or she owned separately. Women's dowries returned to them at the death of their husbands. Law required that parents divide their property among the legitimate heirs, with no preference made to boys or girls. Testators could reward a fifth of their estate to someone of their choosing, such as a spouse or a particular child.

State officials were involved in almost every step of the inheritance process. Alcaldes mayores acted as witnesses when people made their wills and helped with the distribution of the property. When people failed to leave wills, the alcaldes mayores recorded the inventories and settled the estates. Settlement proceedings were laborious, especially if the estates were large. In 1744, Carlos Fernández petitioned Governor don Joaquín Codallos y Rabal to assign the alcalde mayor of Santa Cruz to divide his mother-in-law's estate among her heirs. The governor dispatched Francisco Ortiz to Margarita Martín's house where he inventoried all of her goods and furniture. He was then to divide the estate according to her will and, if she had not left one, to apportion the amount to her debts, funeral, masses, burial, and her heirs.[81]

Francisco Ortiz, acting as judge receiver, undertook his duties to divide the property and assiduously began the process by listing all of the deceased woman's goods. Depending on her husband to show him all of her property, he began by listing her house, which had a living area, kitchen, pantry, and two bedrooms. He placed the value at 320 pesos. He then went on to list over fifty-six items that included cows, oxen, sheep, clothing, cooking utensils, gardening tools, and land. He estimated the worth of her estate at 5,298 pesos.

Not only did Margarita Martín leave a large estate, she also left a complicated web of familial relations. To begin with, Martín was a widow when she married don Bernardo Roybal. With her first husband, don Juan Padilla, she had had four children. The eldest, Juana Padilla, was married to Carlos Fernández, the initial petitioner. During her second marriage, she had three children. Except for Juana Padilla, who had become emancipated upon marrying, all the children of both marriages were minors.[82]

Owing to the fact that the heirs had different fathers, Ortiz's task was to ensure that the heirs of the first marriage received their paternal inheritance from Juan Padilla, as well as their maternal inheritance from Margarita Martín.[83] Since the children were minors, Margarita Martín, as the guardian, had undoubtedly been in charge of the paternal inheritances of her children. For example, Ortiz wrote that some land Padilla and Martín acquired from a royal land grant was considered community property of the first marriage. This land, then, was to be divided in half, with the children of the first marriage entitled to receive half as the paternal inheritance from Juan Padilla. The children from both marriages were to receive the other half as their maternal inheritance.[84]

Furthermore, Ortiz needed to identify the community property that had accumulated during the second marriage and then divide this property among her children and don Bernardo Roybal. Roybal was to receive half of the community property. During the proceedings, Roybal informed Ortiz that Martín had come to their marriage with a dowry that included five cows and calves, a bull, a mule, a jack, two yoke of oxen and a plowshare, property amounting to 440 pesos. He said that there was no *carta dotal* (dowry letter) but that many interested parties knew of the said agreement and would testify to the truthfulness of his statement. Losing no time, the alcalde mayor immediately interviewed the late Margarita Martín's father who verified Roybal's statement.[85] In the end, the widower received half of the community property in addition to the dowry.[86]

Once the estate was divided, Ortiz's responsibility was to arrange for guardians for all the minors. He appointed don Bernardo Roybal as guardian ad litem of his three children; the father accepted the position and agreed to care for them and their property. Moreover, Ortiz asked a maternal uncle, Marcial Martín, to administer the children's inheritance. When the children reached their majority, Marcial Martín was to return the inheritance, consisting of cows, sheep, and goats (and the natural increases). Ortiz instructed Martín to deliver a number of the livestock each year to Roybal for the maintenance of the children. In exchange for his services, Martín received three horses, two oxen, a bull, two calves, and some furniture. To ensure that the minors received their goods from him, Martín was required to name a bondsman.

Perhaps if Margarita Martín had left a will, she would have named her husband as guardian of all her children. As it happened, however, Ortiz sought guardians for the Padilla children elsewhere. Carlos Fernández agreed to care for his sister-in-law, Bárbara Padilla. Ortiz listed all of Bárbara Padilla's belongings, which were to be given to her when she reached her majority. Fernández named Bernardo Roybal as his bondsman. Ortiz selected another maternal uncle, José Martín, to be guardian of the two Padilla sons. Martín named Margarita Martín's father as bondsman.

The skill and trustworthiness attributed to alcaldes mayores undoubtedly fluctuated as the post changed hands. In 1760 Bishop Tamarón criticized the alcaldes mayores: "'some,' he said, were 'poor men whom the governors install as alcaldes mayores, individuals who have not prospered in other offices or who have been ruined in trade; or deserters from studies by which they did not profit, who become paper shufflers and swindlers. Such are usually the qualifications of these alcaldes mayores, a career aspired to by useless or ruined men.'"[87] Yet the inventories reveal that many dealt with the task with a keen understanding of the laws, taking care to ensure that the heirs received their just share.

If an alcalde mayor did not understand the requirements of the laws and performed his duties inadequately, the governor was there to guide him. In 1783, in the jurisdiction of La Alameda, Alcalde Mayor don Nerio Montoya went to inventory the property of the deceased José Durán y Chávez.[88] He quickly gathered the heirs and made inquiries about the dowries brought by Durán y Chávez's two wives. Upon determining the dowries, he separated them, estimated the property, and divided it among the children of the first late wife, the children of the second wife, and the second wife. The report don Nerio presented to the governor was one folio. Upon seeing the folio, Governor Juan Bautista Anza declared the document null and of no value. He stated that due to don Nerio's lack of instruction and practice, the settlement proceedings lacked many of the crucial formalities. He ordered the alcalde mayor to return and to have the widow, under oath, present all of the deceased's goods and properties so that he could do an inventory. In addition, he required the alcalde mayor to enlist the aid of two disinterested witnesses, "with knowledge and conscience," to help him with the valuation of the estate. Finally, the governor directed the alcalde mayor to ascertain which goods were accumulated during the first or second marriages and the amount of the dowries. The information provided by the heirs needed to be verified. Upon his second attempt, don Nerio provided a more complete inventory, including a list of all of the property and a number of interviews.

Questions also arise about the honesty of the alcaldes mayores and whether they took advantage of the heirs, especially widows.[89] Although alcaldes mayores did not receive a salary, they did collect fees for the services rendered.[90] For the inventory of Margarita Martín, Francisco Ortiz collected 265 pesos, or 5 percent of the inventoried estate, as directed by law.[91] In most cases, the officials collected much less since most estates were smaller. Perhaps some of these men took advantage of a situation to line their own pockets, but, in most cases, there were so many interested parties, such as children, spouses, and parents, that the opportunities to steal were limited. In the case of Margarita Martín, for example, those who benefited from the truthful division of the estate included the son-in-law and the widower. Moreover, the uncles and grandfather of the Padilla children were present to make sure that the latter received their inheritance.

Informed about inheritance and dotal laws, New Mexicans vigilantly guarded their rights. When Francisco de Silva filed suit against his father-in-law, Nicolás Durán y Chávez, for failing to pay the promised dowry, Silva stated that he had executed the suit with the knowledge "that it was just and a natural, divine right that the father divide the inheritance among the legitimate children."[92] As the suit dragged on and the two men answered each other's accusations, Silva apparently sought the advice of a procurador. It was not uncommon for New Mexicans to seek such legal expertise.[93] Seven days after Silva's first remarks about the divine right of the dowry, he elaborated and quoted dotal laws from a book by Villalobos.[94] Numerically listing the relevant laws, Silva summarized that fathers owed their children their support, which extended to dowries. Furthermore, if a promised dowry was not delivered, the father-in-law was expected to pay interest. By visiting a procurador, Silva expanded his rudimentary knowledge of the dowry laws, thereby strengthening his argument against his father-in-law.

Although some New Mexicans knew the laws more intimately than others, most had rudimentary knowledge regarding the laws of inheritance. Juana Ortega, for instance, petitioned the alcalde mayor in 1750, maintaining that she had not received her maternal inheritance. She submitted her grandfather's will showing that her mother was indeed the heiress of the lands that Juana Ortega claimed were part of her maternal inheritance.[95] In 1781, Teodora Ortiz contended that her husband had fraudulently listed her possessions as his own in his will. In her petition she said plainly: "No one can dispossess me of the just rights I have towards the property that I brought into the marriage . . . nor half the property we acquired during our marriage."[96] Knowing these basic rights allowed New Mexicans to protect themselves from inept and greedy officials and from their own relatives.

In contrast to the state's systematic oversight in matters of property division, the state had the ability to affect family life arbitrarily. In 1727, in the pueblo of Zia, Alcalde Mayor Ramón García Jurado banished Juan Galván from the town for three months for cohabitating illegally with Magdalena. Absolved by the governor, Galván returned from Santa Fe and resumed his affair with Magdalena. For punishment, the alcalde mayor put him in the stocks. Galván's mother, Juana Hurtado, yelled at García Jurado, asking him whether her son was an Apache to be placed in the stocks and to miss mass. The alcalde mayor ordered her to stay out of the situation. She responded "indecorously," enraging the alcalde mayor who told her to "shut up" and not to be "shameless" or he would beat her. She angrily replied that she would hit him with a stick. In retribution, the alcalde mayor ordered that Juana Hurtado be placed in the stocks so that she would learn respect for the law (*la justicia*). In the subsequent investigation, the alcalde mayor became interested in Juana Hurtado's personal life and asked questions about her living situation. Witnesses provided information that Juana lived with a man and had several children with him. Although the church had lamented the situation, the state did not show an interest until Juana acted disrespectfully to the alcalde mayor. There is no way to determine whether the alcalde mayor's interest in Galván was based purely on his illegal cohabitation or whether the alcalde mayor had another bone to pick with the man. Nevertheless, the alcalde mayor's interest in his mother's personal life became aroused only after she interfered with the state official.[97] People who broke both civil and ecclesiastical laws regarding family life could live their lives with little interference from the state. Yet if the state took an interest in their lives for whatever reason, the state might begin an investigation exposing behavior that ran counter to church and state laws regarding family life. In most cases, it is most likely that the state intervened in intimate family matters only when a family member or a member of the community filed a complaint about someone's behavior. Once the magistrates became involved, they began a thorough investigation. Nevertheless, the citizens set the agenda, deciding what was proper behavior and at what point the state should intervene.

In the year 1751, the alcalde mayor of the pueblo of Sandia went to the home of Alejandro Mora after hearing from various people that Mora was mistreating his Indian servant (criada).[98] That *"varias personas"* felt compelled to complain and request a civil investigation highlights numerous aspects of community, state, and family. First, community members took an interest in the fate of Mora's criada. They knew that Alejandro Mora mistreated her and believed that the local officials should step in and stop his uncommon behavior. Obviously, the community recognized that Mora had stepped over a line, in regard to the treatment of domestic servants. His misconduct warranted intervention.

Not surprisingly, Mora rejected this community ethos, countering that he refused to allow the alcalde mayor an interview with his criada. Mora's intransigence led the alcalde mayor to assemble a captain and some nearby citizens to help him in arresting Mora. The citizens seemed more than willing to help, "arriving punctually like loyal vassals."[99] When the alcalde and his assistants arrived to Mora's house, the intractable Mora shouted that he would only come out over his dead body. Unscathed and alive, Mora wounded three men with his knife during the arrest. In the end, they managed to tie him up and take him off to jail.[100]

Mora's cruelty to his eighteen-year-old criada, Juana Miranda, knew no bounds. He whipped her, starved her, tied her up, and threatened to rape her. The nine years she lived with him, she claimed, seemed more like nine thousand years for never having even one hour of peace. She did not have enough breath or voice to speak of all the mistreatments she received.[101] But Juana was not the only victim. Throughout her testimony, Juana stated that Mora committed these cruelties against both her and his wife. One witness testified that Mora's inhumane treatment to his wife was known throughout the region. The witness claimed that the local magistrate and friar had previously reprimanded Mora for the mistreatment of his spouse. Unfortunately, these actions had little effect, and Mora's misdeeds continued unabated. He even threatened his wife by saying that neither the governor nor the king could stop him from killing her if he so desired.[102]

In this Mora had a point; he could have killed her if he had wanted. The community and judiciary previously tried and failed to curb his sadistic ways. Still, in September 1751, Mora sat in jail accused of abusing his wife and Indian servant; there he stewed for fourteen months. The role of the community in this case cannot be overstated. The community complained repeatedly to the local state and church officials. When the warnings given by those officials did not change Mora's behavior, it continued to protest until the alcalde mayor from Sandia finally arrived at Mora's house. While Mora sat in jail, the governor placed the criada in another home. Those who employed criadas had certain responsibilities and, by torturing his criada, Mora had breeched these. After eliciting promises from Mora that he would no longer mistreat his spouse, the governor freed him from jail, allowing him to return home to his wife.

To summarize, the state affected family life on a number of different levels. The crown and viceroys tried to implement settlement policies that would build strong, stable Hispanic societies. The building blocks of society were Christian families. In the first century of conquest, for example, the crown required that encomenderos marry. Over the course of the colonial period, as the colony expanded, the state continued to grapple with how best to settle and hold on to territory. During the reconquest of New Mexico, the viceroy insisted that the settlers be married couples only. Able to control the process in Mexico City, the viceroy carried out the policy. Governor Vargas and Páez Hurtado, however, more willing to allow single men and women to come north, recognized that more Hispanic settlers, whether married or single, would help them reconquer New Mexico. Once colonists decided to venture north, they tried to control the process to the greatest extent possible. The Mexican City settlers, for example, chose to migrate in kin groups. Perhaps they believed that, not only survival, but success would more likely be achieved if they had family networks.

One of the state's most consistent and intrusive roles was its involvement in the transmission of property. Governors and their alcaldes mayores carried out the Spanish laws regarding inheritance. Officials acted as arbiters and as defenders of minors. Property holders expected and often demanded the participation of the state in the process. The state also supported the church, providing soldiers and jails. It upheld the church's rules regarding the importance of promises and the sacrament of marriage. Yet the state did not carefully oversee the intimate lives of its citizens. Instead, it waited for community members to bring forth petitions and complaints. Once appealed to, the state actively investigated and prosecuted transgressors. New Mexicans, cognizant of the workings of Spanish laws as they affected daily domestic life, appealed to the state when members breached community standards, but allowed those who lived their lives decently, if not lawfully, to live in peace.

Chapter 3

The Sacrament of Marriage

IN 1719, THE young New Mexican Cristóbal Durán, son of unknown parents, went to his local parish and petitioned the Catholic Church for a license to marry. He said, "with all of his heart he wanted to contract a marriage with Rosa Navarro to whom he had given his word to marry and to no other."[1] Within a week the local friar granted Cristóbal Durán his license and promptly married the young couple. The marriage took place without incident. Not all New Mexicans, however, experienced such a straightforward marriage. In 1761, don Salvador Martínez, in a petition to the ecclesiastical judge, complained that he had asked the parents of doña Simona Valdes for permission to wed their daughter. Twice they refused him, so he asked the judge to intervene and to determine whether the young woman wished to marry him. The judge complied and sent someone to the woman's house, where she confirmed her desire to wed. In the end, don Salvador and doña Simona married.[2]

In most cases, couples easily contracted marriages, as did Cristóbal Durán and Rosa Navarro. Yet there were times when couples encountered hindrances that slowed their marital plans or blocked them altogether. The only arbiter in all of these cases was the Catholic Church until the Spanish Crown promulgated the Pragmática of 1778 (see chapter 2). By employing the strict guidelines laid out by the Council of Trent (1545–1563), the Catholic Church cast local friars in a multifaceted role. On the one hand, friars upheld the laws of marriage with the ability to grant or to deny couples the right to marry. On the other hand, friars assisted parishioners when, like don Salvador, they felt that their rights were under attack. By enforcing the guidelines of the Council of Trent, friars used their role to protect the prerogatives of vulnerable members of society, such as doña Simona Valdez.

To carry out these duties and uphold the church's edicts, however, the friars depended heavily on the participation of community members. Without their input, the friars would have been unable to fulfill their ecclesiastical responsibilities. Acting as petitioners who wanted to marry or as witnesses to the event, New Mexicans were fully aware of the holy nature of marriage and the various rules that governed the marital process. They chose to involve themselves actively and to assist the friars. The friars, therefore, joined those who were marrying, their families, and the community to fulfill the injunctions of the Council of Trent and uphold the sacrament of marriage in New Mexico.

In this chapter, I examine 1,493 marital investigations dating from 1694 to 1800, as well as the available marriage records for the same time period.[3] From these documents it is evident that the church's interest in matrimony was manifold. Most important, it considered the union of man and woman as a holy sacrament. The marriage ceremony required the blessing of and sanctioning by the church and had to be performed by a church representative before God. By controlling the sacrament of marriage, the church increased its power over the parishioners' religious and moral lives and guaranteed its involvement in their everyday lives. In addition, the church gained monetary benefits.

Marriage in the Catholic Church

In New Mexico, the church's representative was the Franciscan Order. Present in New Mexico since the initial conquest, the Franciscans returned with Vargas in 1692 and reestablished their spiritual reign. The Franciscans acted as missionaries intent on Christianizing Indians. The missionary field, known as the Custody of the Conversion of St. Paul, was an administrative unit that remained subordinate to the Province of the Holy Gospel in Mexico City during the colonial period. Usually thirty to forty Franciscans worked throughout the region. In addition to ministering to Indians, the Franciscans served the Hispanic residents. In fact, in the larger towns, Hispanics made up the majority of the flock. Due to this preponderance, on June 24, 1767, Viceroy Croix approved the secularization of Franciscan missions at Santa Fe, Santa Cruz de la Cañada, Albuquerque, and El Paso.[4] Secular priests, however, did not replace the Franciscan friars in the Hispanic towns until 1798.[5]

A father *custos*, who exercised near episcopal powers as prelate over all New Mexicans, directed the friars' activities and acted as their delegate in business with the governor and other civil authorities. As a representative of the Bishop of Durango, he also fulfilled the role of ecclesiastical judge ordinary, with jurisdiction over matrimonial cases. In addition, the custos was the local agent of the Holy Inquisition and investigated various moral cases including bigamy.[6] The Franciscan friars and the custos also involved themselves in the marriages of New Mexican residents.

Ecclesiastic involvement by the Franciscans varied, depending on a number of factors. Throughout the eighteenth century, friars came to the frontiers of the Spanish Empire from either New Spain or Spain, bringing with them their ideas and customs about the marriage ceremony. They remained in New Mexico for an average of seventeen years. They usually began their tenure at the age of thirty-five and retired in their fifties.[7] Although service in New Mexico was lengthy, their term in a given mission was approximately two and one-half years. Historian Jim Norris points out that this constant relocation led to the friars' inability to master native languages and hence diminished their capacity to Christianize Indians.[8] Regular transfers most likely affected their relationships with the Hispanic residents as well. Friars were less likely to know their parishioners intimately. Each friar's relationship with his flock undoubtedly had an impact on the marriage process.

Men and women wishing to wed in the Catholic Church had to follow its guidelines. First, the couple needed a license, which the church would grant only after a friar conducted a marital investigation. Second, the church required a fee for its services. The Bishop of Durango don Benito Crespo, who visited New Mexico in 1730, made up a schedule of fees used by the church throughout the eighteenth century. Crespo explained that he created the list "because everyone said that the fees are so high and exorbitant that there was no fixed schedule except the will of the father ministers, even though this land is the poorest I have seen."[9] When Fray Francisco Atanasio

Domínguez visited New Mexico forty-six years later, he reported that Crespo's fee schedule was still in use and recorded it:

> Nuptials: For a marriage of Spaniards, 16 pesos 4 reales; arras and candles, with the specification that the arras of any marriage must be thirteen coins of large or small denomination, and that if the marriage be elsewhere than in the principal Church, the fees are to be doubled. For a marriage of free mulattoes, 6 pesos; arras and candles. For a marriage of mulatto or negro slaves or service Indians, 5 pesos, arras and candles.[10]

Domínguez found that New Mexicans did not necessarily follow the schedule per se, paying what they could or pledging that they would pay at a future date. When fulfilling their promises, they often paid with goods such as chile or seeds.[11] He noted with dismay that people of Santa Fe were selfish and greedy, displaying malice toward the Franciscans.[12]

Domínguez also left a thorough account of the common objects of trade and their monetary value.[13] A few examples shed light on the costs incurred by the marrying couple: a fanega[14] of wheat or maize was worth four pesos; a cow, twenty-five pesos; a fowl, four reales; a female donkey or horse, one hundred pesos or more; a pound of chocolate, two pesos; a pair of shoes, two pesos; twenty eggs, one peso; and a fat pig, twelve pesos.[15] Depending on a number of factors such as whether people had a good or bad harvest year or whether the animals were healthy, the cost of marriage could be exceedingly high for a number of the parishioners in a land known for its poverty.

The friars in Santa Fe, Santa Cruz de la Cañada, and Albuquerque depended on these fees from their parishioners for their living. By the time Domínguez arrived in New Mexico in 1776, the friars in the Spanish villas lived solely from the obventions (fees from marriages, burial and baptisms) and first-fruits, which were livestock, wool, grains or other harvest bounty donated by their parishioners. Prior to the secularization of 1767, all friars who served in New Mexico received their stipends, known as *sínodos*, from the crown. The 300 pesos allotted to each friar arrived in goods such as chocolate, beeswax, habits and paper.[16] Bishop Tamarón, who visited New Mexico in 1760, believed that the crown could save money by eliminating the sínodos sent to the friars serving in the Spanish villas. He argued that the revenue from obventions and first-fruits would be sufficient to maintain the priests and estimated that the pesos from obventions in Santa Fe amounted to 3,000 pesos, and that those in Albuquerque and Santa Cruz de la Cañada amounted to 2,000 pesos each.

For all of the practical benefits of marriage that accrued to the church, its interest was also supremely religious. Marriage was a holy sacrament conferring grace. The Council of Trent, which Pope Pius III initially convened in 1545, reiterated, clarified, and canonized the sanctity of marriage and specified how Catholics should unite in Holy Matrimony. The Catholic Bishops wrote:

> Christ also, who hath instituted and perfected the venerable sacraments, hath by his passion merited the grace which gives perfection to natural love, confirms the indissoluble union, and sanctifies those who are united. Which the Apostle Paul intimated, when he said, "Husbands, love your wives, as Christ also loved the Church, and delivered himself for it," presently adding, "This is a great sacrament, but I speak in Christ and in the Church."[17]

The church believed that women and men entered into a blessed union and that they had to abide by the laws governing marriage.

The marital process began when a man and a woman promised to marry one another. As mentioned above, the couple required a license. The prospective bridegroom petioned the local friar who granted the license after a marital investigation. In most cases, the friar opted not to conduct a formal review, most likely because the friar or those he trusted knew those marrying and whether they could do so without lengthy and time-consuming inquiries. If a possible issue existed, the friar commenced an investigation, which was known as a *diligencia matrimonial*. During this process, the friar interviewed the petitioners and the witnesses named by the petitioners in order to determine whether there were any impediments to the marriage. Meanwhile, on three consecutive feast days, a friar read the banns, a public announcement that a marriage would take place in the petitioners' respective parishes. If no one came forward to question the legitimacy of the marriage, the couple could marry.

By following these steps, the church hoped to determine beyond doubt that the couple could marry legitimately in accordance with church doctrine. The friars, as evidenced in the marriage books, quickly carried out the requirements of the Council of Trent and married couples without delay. In Santa Cruz de la Cañada, on January 27, 1727, Fray Manuel de Sopeña married Lazaro de Atiensa and Gertrudis Martin in front of two witnesses. The friars probably carried these investigations out by word of mouth consulting with trusty, knowledgeable parishioners. In a few cases, such as if the *contrayentes* (those who were contracting to marry) lived in different parishes, the friars had to take extra steps to determine whether they were free to marry. In 1775 two brothers from the Santa Fe parish wanted to marry women in the Mission of Santa Clara. The friar Joseph Gabriel de la Quintana read the banns in Santa Fe and then sent the certification that they were single and free to marry to the friar of Santa Clara.[18] Because the men lived in or near Santa Fe, the friars wanted to assure that those who knew them, those who would know about any previous promises or entanglements, had news that the two men were to marry. The vast majority of marriages, however, occurred in a straight-forward manner.

In the eyes of the church, all baptized people who petitioned to marry were worthy of the sacrament if they met the criteria listed by the Council of Trent. When evidence of an impediment existed, the friars began lengthier marital investigations that often delayed the couple marrying. Throughout the colonial period, during the diligencias, the friars posed the same questions to one couple after another regardless of the sex, race, age or social status of the petitioners. When variations did occur between investigations, they seem to have been the result of the friars' particular styles.

Catholic New Mexicans entered into the marriage process with apparent compliance. The diligencias matrimoniales reveal that men and women who wanted to marry willingly provided the necessary information. In fact, in almost every interview, the men and women said they were marrying to serve God and that they wanted to marry according to the laws of the Council of Trent or the Holy Church. In a typical petition dated February 10, 1697, Ramón García Jurado stated, "To better serve God, our Father and to save my soul, I am making a covenant to take the state of matrimony with doña Antonia de las Heras."[19] He offered the needed information so he could marry in the good order of "our Holy Mother Church."[20] Did this formulaic language, typical of the diligenicias matrimoniales, mean that the applicants truly understood and believed in the sanctity of the union they sought to contract? At a time when being Catholic was an ingrained part of people's lives, New Mexicans probably married with the understanding that the union they created was blessed and indissoluble.[21] Regardless, it is likely that in the course of applying for a license, the friars informed the applicants of the proper formula. In this way, at the very least, the applicants learned that the church viewed marriage as a holy matter.

Men provided information about themselves and the women they were to marry. Men would say where they were from, where they presently resided, whether they were legitimate children, whether they were widowed, and why they wanted to marry. The men usually offered similar information about the women. In this initial petition, participants were supposed to tell the church whether they knew of any impediment to the marriage. If one existed, they explained its nature and asked for a dispensation. The information the men offered in most instances differed little over the course of the eighteenth century. After 1750, however, most participants identified themselves racially as Spanish, Indian, mestizo, or coyote, a practice that had been uncommon in the first half of the eighteenth century.

The friars expected the men and women to answer the questions with honesty. In 1709 Fray Antonio Camargo initiated an inquiry into the lives of two petitioners after obtaining extrajudicial information that the man and woman were related to one another. In his initial petition Juan Márquez failed to mention that he was related to Josefa de Apodaca, his prospective bride. Father Camargo thought the omission serious, stating that Juan Márquez proceeded with little fear of God and did not seek to live by his conscience and act justly as one should when serving God.[22] In a case seventy years later, when Father Domínguez reviewed an impediment, he discovered that the purported bride, Gertrudis Martín, had lied under oath when she stated that she knew of no impediment. In fact, a relationship of affinity in the second degree existed because she had had illicit sexual intercourse with her fiancée's first cousin. He called her perjury reprehensible and returned the case to El Paso where an ecclesiastical judge ruled that Gertrudis Martín had lied in her sworn statement and was not to be granted a dispensation. He ordered that she be placed in a safe and secure home for an indeterminate time until matters could be resolved.[23] The omissions and lies in the original petition cost the couple precious time in their pursuit to marry. Close to three years later, on January 9, 1781, when Domínguez no longer presided, an acting bishop granted the couple a dispensation.[24]

Once a friar deemed the couple eligible to marry, a ceremony took place. As outlined in curates' manuals, the ceremony involved two parts: the marriage and the nuptial mass.[25] The marriage could take place in a home, but the mass was to occur in the church. Priests performed marriages throughout the year, but during two seasons they did not conduct the nuptial blessing: the Advent season until after the Epiphany and the Lenten season until after the Octave of Easter.[26] In Santa Fe on April 23, 1737, Fray Joseph Antonio Guerrero, for example, married Joseph Miguel de la Peña and doña María Francisca Rael de Aguilar, but did not perform the nuptial mass. The couple returned to the church where Fray Manuel Zambrano gave them the nuptial blessing on May 7, 1737.[27]

For the ceremony, the priest donned a surplice and a white stole. He had a basin with holy water, an aspergillum, and a plate for the rings. As he described the sanctity of matrimony, the *novios* (the bride and bridegroom) stood, the man on the right and the woman on the left. Instituted by God, marriage conserved the human race and was one of the seven sacraments. It bestowed grace upon those who entered the state with a clean conscience. It helped the couple to overcome life's difficulties, griefs, and the annoyances of old age. It was an escape from fornication with others since the husband and wife had each other. Finally, the married couple instructed their offspring in the Christian faith.

The priest admonished the man to pity his wife as the more fragile vessel. He was to treat her as a companion and not a servant. He was to engage in honest activities to support his house and family and to eschew idleness, the root of all evil. The friar exhorted the bride to be subject to her husband in everything, to despise superfluous ornaments and be modest, to guard the home with great diligence only leaving it if necessary and with the husband's permission, and to be chaste. He concluded by telling them to love and admire one another more than anyone else, excepting God.

After imparting this message, the priest once again asked if there were any impediments. He then asked the bride and groom, in turn, if they wanted each other as legitimate spouses. The novios exchanged their vows in the vernacular. Once both agreed, he took their right hands and said that they were united in holy matrimony. He blessed the ring which the husband placed on the ring finger of the wife's left hand.

The priest then performed the nuptial mass in which he veiled and blessed the couple. (In the cases of widows remarrying, priests were forbidden to perform the mass and to veil them). A script in the manuals also directed the proceedings. The couple stood outside the church door where there was a plate that held the arras (thirteen coins) and the rings. The friar counted the coins then blessed them and the rings. After the novios exchanged rings, the priest had them stack their hands with the husband's open palms resting on hers. The arras dropped from his hands into hers, a symbol of their marriage. She received them letting them drop onto the plate below. Within the church, the priest then conducted the nuptial mass. At one point, as the couple kneeled at the altar, he covered the shoulders of the man and the head of the wife with a white and pink veil. If it was the custom, he also tied them together with the *yugo*, a band or strap. He then blessed them and reminded them to be loyal to one another, to be chaste during religious fasts and festivals, to love one another, and to fear God. After sprinkling them with holy water, he took the wife's right hand and gave it to the man. He once again reminded the husband that he gave him a companion and not a servant and to love her as Christ loves the church.

In New Mexico, most friars celebrated both the marriage and mass in the church on the same day. Whether they followed all of the other instructions is not known. A number of variations in the marital ceremonies most likely occurred. Friars, coming from distinct regions in Spain and New Spain, most likely brought customs with them and carried their own manuals that offered varying instructions. It is impossible to know whether New Mexicans were receptive to newly introduced rituals or insisted on marrying in the manner that their parents had. Different regions in New Mexico might have established their own traditions. Most husbands, for example, did not have the arras or rings to give. Instead the church kept coins and rings to use during the marriage ceremony.[28] The marriage books provide few clues as to the exact nature of the ceremonies performed.

It is likely that the novios donned their best clothes on their wedding day. Perhaps jewels sparkled at the *novia*'s neck and wrists and a beautiful veil covered her head. We do know that the novios' families participated as did the community. Throughout the century, the friars, in the marriage books, marked down the date, the names of the couple, and the names of the required two or three witnesses. In some cases, the male and female witnesses appear to have been related to the bride or groom. Other friars only called upon men to be witnesses. And, at times, the same men, often the sacristans, witnessed ceremony after ceremony. Some friars also asked parishioners to be the padrinos of the novios during the ceremony as well. In the autumn of 1734, when the mulatto slave, Esteban de Estrada, married the free Indian, Juana Mata de Espinosa, not only did three individuals witness the union, but "many people" also took part.[29] Often friars marked down that "many others" came and witnessed the ceremony. Marriage was a community affair, an occasion when the community came together to help celebrate the joining of two people.

Impediments: Obstacles to Marriage

As previously noted, after the man petitioned to marry, the friars began the investigation to determine whether the couple was at liberty to marry. They interviewed the contrayentes and the witnesses provided by the bridegroom. In a typical interview, the friar began by asking the petitioner whether it was his or her free will to marry. The idea of marrying of one's own free will was central to Catholic Church doctrine. The Council of Trent reiterated that the sacrament of marriage could only occur between two people who had consented to marry one another. Ideally, even parents were not allowed to interfere with their children's marriage choices. In 1703, Fray Francisco Jiménez asked María Archuleta whether her desire to marry Miguel Martín was the result of being threatened by her mother, brothers, or one of her relatives with death or another punishment. In the interview with the bridegroom-to-be, Father Jiménez repeated the same questions to Martín. He also asked each witness whether the petitioners were being threatened with death to contract the marriage.[30] Although Jiménez's queries were more zealous than most friars,' the majority of friars did want to determine whether the contractors felt that they were being forced to marry and asked similar questions.

The church clearly wanted to ensure that the participants were at liberty to marry, and for this reason, the friars took a keen interest in the personal history of the people who came forward to petition for marriage licenses. During the course of the investigations, friars tried to ascertain whether the petitioners were widowed, already bound by a promise to marry someone else, had given a vow of chastity or religion to the church, and finally whether they were already married. According to Catholic doctrine, marriage could only take place between one man and one woman. Bigamy violated the core principles of a Christian marriage – that it was monogamous and indissoluble.[31] In the early eighteenth century, the Holy Office of the Inquisition in New Mexico attacked social problems such as bigamy.[32] Indeed one can find more rigorous inquiries into the personal histories of the petitioners in the first half of the eighteenth century than in the second half of the century. During this time, as well as in the late seventeenth century, bigamy was conceivable and attainable since a large number of people who petitioned to marry were from distant places. Santiago Grolet for example, was from La Rochelle, France. He was fortunate in that two fellow Frenchmen were able to testify that he was "single, not married, nor betrothed to any other person."[33]

When widowers and widows petitioned to remarry, the friars, wanting to determine that their spouses were indeed deceased, depended on the witnesses to confirm or to disprove the information provided by the participants. In the vast majority of cases, two male witnesses testified for the man and two different male witnesses testified for the woman. During the first half of the eighteenth century, the petitioners provided witnesses who could tell the friars how the deceased spouses had died and where they were buried. In an interview in February 1719, Pedro Fresqui said that his deceased wife, Micaela de Archuleta, was buried in the church in Socorro and that he had personally attended her burial. To corroborate Fresqui's testimony, the friar interviewed two witnesses who said that they had seen the burial of Micaela de Archuleta.[34] Eyewitness accounts were especially important when the body of the deceased spouse was not recovered or the spouse had died outside the region. On November 17, 1697, Juan de Archiveque reapplied for a license so that he could marry Antonia Gutiérrez. His previous application, dated April 3, 1696, had been denied, and Archiveque presumed the denial was a result of insufficient evidence about the death of Antonia Gutiérrez's first husband. In his new petition, Archiveque included two letters, one from a priest and one from Juan Páez Hurtado, a high-ranking government official, affirming that Antonia Gutiérrez's first husband had been killed in Zacatecas sometime during 1694.[35] By the 1760s, friars paid less attention to the whereabouts of the burials of deceased spouses. Since, by then, most petitioners were from New Mexico, the deaths of previous spouses were most likely common knowledge, information known by the community and the friars.

A person's qualification also depended on whether he or she had promised marriage to another person. Upholding and supporting a promise to marry was an important church tradition.[36] During the medieval period, people saw little difference between a promise of future marriage and an immediate intent to marry. Several influential medieval canonists held that if couples consummated their relationships after they became engaged, their marriages became legal. The church rejected this doctrine as official policy in the fourteenth century; in the popular mind, however, the belief that marriage began when sexual intercourse followed a promise to marry persisted for generations. Due to this ecclesiastical tradition, church officials deemed the spoken promise to marry as a serious and binding commitment worthy of enforcement.[37]

Indeed, in almost every marital investigation in New Mexico, the friars asked the participants as well as their witnesses whether either the man or woman had promised marriage to someone else. The diligencias matrimoniales reveal that very few people had outstanding marriage promises impeding their marriages. Yet the process gave the witnesses the opportunity to offer information that just might postpone or cancel the proposed marriage. In September 1705, Alonso Maese, witness for the petitioner Antonio Sambrano, volunteered that Sambrano had tried to marry a young woman in Bernalillo. Another witness also testified that Sambrano was engaged to the woman in Bernalillo. When the friar asked Antonio Sambrano about the young woman, he swore that "he had not given a promise and that it is true that carried away by his fragility he had liked her not knowing that they were related. And when he found out that they were, he took measures to separate himself. And this is the truth."[38] Perhaps the friar believed Sambrano, or knowing that Sambrano was closely related to the woman in Bernalillo, he decided not to look more closely into the alleged promise of marriage.

One's familial relations played a decisive role in whether a marriage could occur. Antonio Sambrano was wise when he decided to discontinue his relationship with his relative. Catholic laws and traditions, derived from Mosaic and Roman laws, prohibited men from marrying closely related women. During the colonial period, if prospective brides and grooms shared ties of consanguinity and/or affinity, an impediment to their marriage usually resulted (see fig. 1).

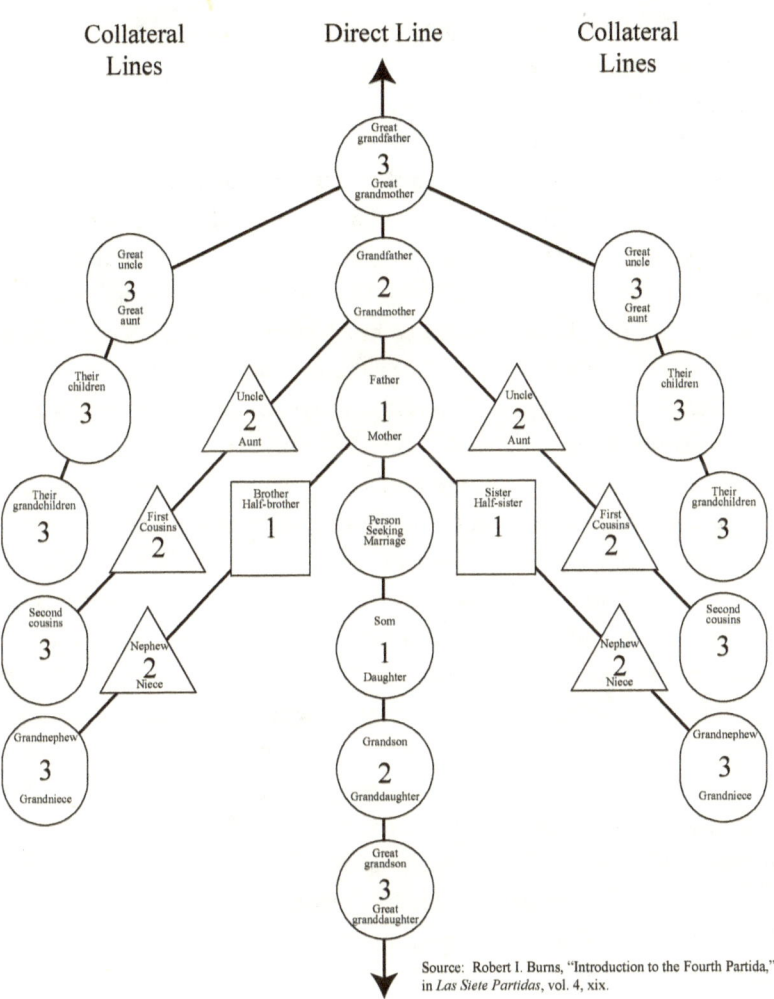

Figure 1. Tree of Consanguinity.

Consanguinity is a relationship between people of the same blood. In other words, people who descend from the same stock or directly from one another are related by consanguinity. To determine consanguinity, one examines the stock, the line, and the various degrees of the relationship. The stock is the common ancestor from whom people mutually related derive their origin. Brothers and sisters share the same stock, namely their parents; cousins have a common grandparent.[39]

The line is the series of people descending from a common ancestor. When people descend one from another, the line is considered direct. Mother and daughter share a direct descending line if it is considered from the common ancestor to the person in question (mother to daughter). It is ascending if the relationship is computed from the person in question to the ancestor (daughter to mother). The line is collateral when people come from a common ancestor but do not descend one from the other (brother and sisters, uncles and nieces, aunts and nephews). The collateral line is equal when the relatives are equally distant from the common stock (first cousins) or unequal when the distance is not the same (aunt and nephew).[40]

To determine the degree of consanguinity, one measures the distance between people related in the same line. The number of generations in the direct line (omitting the common ancestor) determines the degree. For example, there are two degrees between grandfather and grandson (grandfather, father, and son). The degree can also be determined in the collateral line. When the distance of both relatives from the common ancestor is the same, the number of degrees is measured by the number of generations affecting either one. Therefore, first cousins are related by two degrees in the collateral line. When, in the collateral line, the direct degrees are unequal, there are as many degrees as there are generations in the line of descent. Consanguinity between an aunt and nephew is to the second degree.[41]

Affinity is a relationship between people deriving from marriage or from spiritual relationships. Carnal relations also formed the basis of affinity, whether licit (under the realm of marital relations) or illicit (extramarital). Affinity constitutes a diriment impediment to subsequent marriages between a man and blood relations of his wife, and vice versa. Affinity, according to the code of Canon Law (1077), does not beget affinity. In other words, the consanguineous relatives of the husband can contract marriage with the consanguineous relatives of the wife. The impediment of affinity extends indefinitely either ascending or descending in the direct line. In the collateral line, it extends only to the second degree. The terms and methods used to describe and compute relations of consanguinity are also used in explaining affinity.[42]

During the Council of Trent, the church declared itself free to determine the limitations on marriage due to consanguinity and affinity. It reinstated the decrees inherited from the Fourth Lateran Council of 1215, during which

Pope Innocent III declared that an impediment to marriage existed when people were related by consanguinity in the fourth degree (i.e. third cousins).[43] The Council of Trent (1563) limited illicit affinity to the second degree in the collateral line. It upheld licit affinity to the fourth degree.[44] And it reestablished that baptism and confirmation created bonds of affinity.[45]

In the petition and during the diligencia matrimonial, the contractors of the marriage were supposed to reveal if and how they were related. If they were related, the contractor petitioned for a dispensation. In general, priests and friars in the colonies were at liberty to confer dispensations more than their fellow priests in Spain.[46] In New Mexico, the friars granted dispensations as they arose in the first half of the eighteenth century. By the latter part of the century, the Bishopric of Durango, attempting to wield greater control over the Franciscan Custody, increased its involvement in granting dispensations. Bishop Francisco Gabriel de Olivares, however, recognized the expediency of having a local official to grant dispensations and returned the power to the ecclesiastical judge in 1798.[47] The friars, ecclesiastical judges, and the bishops reviewed approximately 154 impediments originating from northern New Mexico. In most cases, the friars approved the dispensations.

In 1718, Ramón de Medina, a soldier at the Santa Fe Presidio, asked for a dispensation. Aware that his intended bride had had sex with his first cousin, Ramón knew that they were affined. The friar granted the dispensation, and the couple married.[48] In another case arising in 1788 and included in documents sent to the bishop of Durango, one of the friars involved in the case provided a genealogical chart explaining the young couple's family relations (see fig. 2). When Mateo and Catalina became engaged, they did not know that they were related.[49]

Once again witnesses played a determining role in the investigation, verifying whether the petitioners were in fact related to the degree they proclaimed. Typically, the two or three witnesses could provide detailed information about how the would-be spouses were related. In 1767, Juan Antonio Montaño, in his petition to marry, asked for a dispensation. He said that he and Antonia Rita Chávez were related by third degree consanguinity in the following manner: "My grandfather was Juan Montaño and he had Nicolás Montaño, my father. My grandfather's sister was Juana Montaño, and she had José Chávez and he had María Chávez, mother of Antonia Rita

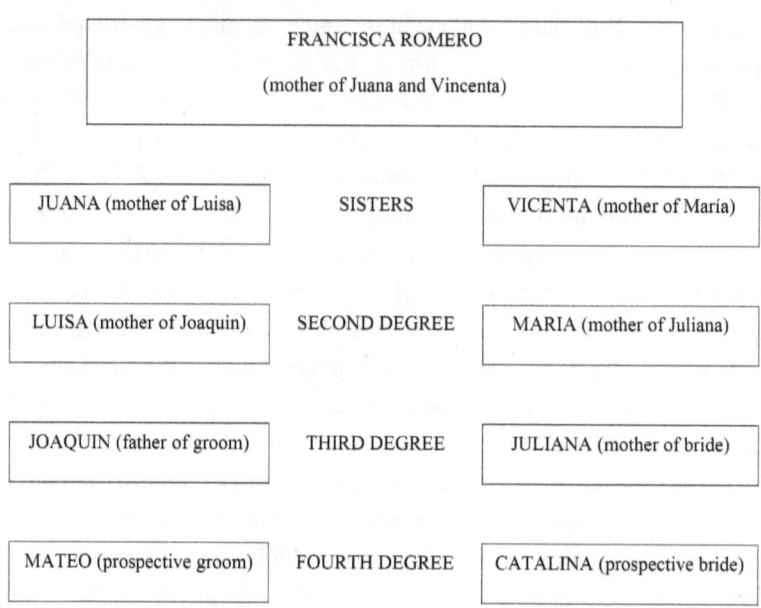

Figure 2. Genealogy of Mateo and Catalina.

Chávez, contractor."[50] All three witnesses explained how the young couple was related in the same detail that Juan Antonio Montaño employed.

The dispensation process yielded practical benefits for the friars and their parishes. Penance given to the contractors often involved some type of donation to the church. Upon granting a dispensation in 1707, the ecclesiastical judge, Miguel Muñiz, ordered the soldier, Melchor de Herrera, to give six books of wax to the Santa Fe Church and six more to the church in Santa Cruz.[51] In 1716, Juan Antonio Baca's penance was to work personally for twenty days in the construction of the Bernalillo Church. In addition, he had to donate four thousand adobe bricks. His intended bride had to sweep the church.[52] Often, the couple paid a fine, such as twelve pesos.[53] The types of penance changed, depending on the particular friars and the shifting needs of their parishes. Nevertheless, the friars could not depend on the income generated from these dispensations. Years could go by with nary an impediment recorded. In the 1780s, as more and more impediments made their way south to Durango, the penance became more religious in nature. Often the contractors would have to kneel at the altar with their arms outspread, recite the Stations of the Cross, and ask God to bless the Catholic Church, the Pope, and the Spanish monarch.[54]

In most instances, the church officials granted the dispensations. In the majority of cases, the cousins were not first cousins, making easy the friars' support of the petitions. Even so, when the friars revealed their motivations for granting requests, they clearly wanted to facilitate the marriage process and to help the poor, often dishonored women. In their eyes marriage was the best possible solution: women received honor, protection, and support.

In 1704, the ecclesiastical judge explained that Josefa Javier was poor and that her parents were too far away to provide her the necessary succor. For these reasons he granted her and Luis García a dispensation.[55] Nine years later, Francisco Durán y Chávez applied for a dispensation because he and Juana Baca, his intended bride, were related in third degree consanguinity. Durán y Chávez claimed he was moved to marry so that he could serve God and protect the poor, virgin woman. Fray Juan de Tagle made the necessary dispensation but attached a condition. He required that Durán y Chávez provide a dowry of 300 pesos for Juana Baca and that he provide wax for the church.[56] Forcing a man to provide a dowry for his wife appears to have been an exceptional move on the part of Tagle. Yet Tagle recognized that a poor woman with a dowry from her husband was better protected than a woman without one. Since Durán y Chávez claimed his main reason for wanting to marry Juana Baca was to protect her, Tagle made the young man live up to his words.

Another prenuptial case sent to Durango in 1795 reveals some of the friars' deliberations over the granting of dispensations. In Santa Fe on April 12, 1795, José Pascual García de la Mora, aged twenty, petitioned to marry Rosalía Saturnina García de Noriega, aged eighteen. When interviewed, José Pascual admitted that he had engaged in sexual relations with the married sister of his intended bride. The adulterous, illicit sexual relation created a bond of first-degree affinity between the young couple, a reason to prohibit the marriage. On the other hand, he stated that he and Rosalía had been intimate and that she was pregnant, a reason to grant permission to marry.[57]

Three friars involved in the case conducted a secret investigation. They believed that the bishop should grant the dispensation and listed the reasons why they supported the couple's request to marry:

1. Rosalía García de Noriega had suffered shame and dishonor.

2. Neither of the petitioners was free to marry anyone else because of their mutual promise and actions.
3. The husband of the sister, who had a bad reputation, was ignorant of what had taken place, even though married to her. Were he to learn of it, there would be a scandal and a divorce would result.
4. It was impossible to know what would happen to the child Rosalía García de Noriega was carrying at the time of its delivery.
5. She was poor, living in sin, her father was dead, and her mother had no way to support her.
6. It would be difficult to find someone else to marry her under the circumstances.
7. The couple was well intentioned and in love.

In Durango on June 18, 1795, the capitular vicar granted the dispensation. To avoid any protests perhaps, the bishop ordered that the couple be married in great secrecy and that the banns be dispensed. As a penance, the couple was to recite the rosary daily and to receive communion and confess monthly.[58]

This remarkable document reveals that three friars harbored deep concern for the well-being of all the parishioners involved. To begin with, they conducted their investigations in secret, hoping to lessen the "shame and dishonor" Rosalía already suffered. The friars also chose to protect the two adulterers, knowing that if the affair were revealed to the husband and community at large, the wronged husband would divorce Rosalía's sister. They seemed to think that a divorce and scandal would be far more damaging to all parties than the adultery already committed. Moreover, they honored the love of José Pascual and his desire to support, protect, and marry Rosalía. In addition, it is evident that the friars deemed the marriage promise worthy of enforcement. In fact, they stressed that the promise precluded the young couple from marrying others. And finally, the friars concern for the unwed pregnant woman and the unborn child shows that they cared for the most vulnerable and least powerful members of the parish.

The Banns, Marriage Promises, and Community Involvement

After couples received a dispensation or if the marital investigation concluded without incident, the friars read the banns on three consecutive feast days.⁵⁹ Feasts were days for expressing religious joy. Proclaimed by the Apostolic fathers, the earliest feast day in the Christian calendar was the Lord's day, Sunday. Some of the other early feast days included Easter, celebrated as early as the second century, and Christmas, celebrated in the fourth century. Eventually, Marian feasts and others honoring saints became commonplace.⁶⁰ By the eighteenth century in New Mexico, there were numerous feasts such as the Circumcision of the Lord, Epiphany, the Apparition of Our Lady of Guadalupe, the Purification of Our Lady, the Incarnation, Our Father St. Francis and All Saints.⁶¹

During the reading of the banns, the community at large became aware of upcoming nuptials. Surprisingly, three feast days often occurred on consecutive days or within a week. This meant that a marriage and an investigation could take place within a week's time if there were no impediments. For example, Fray José Ignacio Sánchez read the banns for a marriage on May 27, May 28, and May 29, 1798, declaring that it was the feast of Pentecost.⁶² In 1794, Fray Cayetano José Ignacio Bernal read the banns on April 30, May 1, and May 3.⁶³ In July of 1795, another friar read the banns on the twelfth, nineteenth and twenty-fifth.⁶⁴ Perhaps due to the brevity of the process, people came forward infrequently to disrupt the proposed marriages. But when people did approach with information about the bride or groom, the friars investigated the claims to determine whether an impediment existed.

The existing evidence indicates that the friars took the allegations extremely seriously. They spent time investigating the claims, listening to witnesses, and, in a few situations, incarcerating the men and sequestering the women. The willingness to begin an investigation, its intensity and thoroughness, and the readiness to follow through, probably depended on the abilities of each particular friar. In cases of broken marriage promises, for example, friars could relentlessly pursue errant men and force them to uphold the promise. Yet most friars seemed to weigh the benefits of making men fulfill their responsibilities. Beyond jailing men for the course of the investigations and imposing fines, friars declined to punish men further. If they had carried out more punitive measures, such as exile, they might have risked the displeasure of the state and the community. Although both the state and the community supported the church's aim to hold men accountable, they did not necessarily want to lose men who contributed to the safety and economy of the society. In the end, the friars' decisions on whether to uphold a marriage promise ultimately hinged on the choices of the men and women. These Franciscans apparently respected the final judgments of the young men and women, wanting to avoid forcing anyone to marry against his or her will. They ranked an individual's free will more important than a promise, perhaps recognizing that compelling men and women to marry people they disliked might lead to unworkable, bad marriages, and further disturbance to local life.

On April 17, 1702, Fray Manuel Moreno received a note asking him "to impede the marriage of Ventura de Esquibel." The correspondent wrote, "It has come to my notice that he wants to marry the daughter of Lucero and that one bann has been read. I have urgent motives to impede it."[65] The note was from Juana Luján. On the following day, the friar interviewed Juana Luján and discovered that Ventura de Esquibel had promised to marry her. With the promise of marriage given and accepted, Esquibel took Juana Luján's honor—that is the couple had sexual intercourse. In the interview, Luján revealed that Governor Rodríguez Cubero was Esquibel's patron and that he opposed a marriage between her and Esquibel. Luján feared the governor's threats, yet she made very clear that she wanted the marriage to be stopped. On the following day, however, the friar received from Juana Luján another note, in which she declared that she wanted to rescind her objections to the impending marriage. She wrote that she had written the previous note without the knowledge or permission of her parents, who advised her to drop the matter. The friar, however, did not drop it.

Indeed, as a result of the second missive, the friar immediately deposited Juana Luján in the house of Captain Sebastián de Vargas. After hearing her first earnest entreaty that the young lover be made to uphold his word, the friar probably had difficulty believing that she had willingly composed the second letter. The friar saw it as imperative that Juana Luján be removed from the presence of those who wanted to influence her. Without further ado, the friar began an investigation into the matter to discover whether an impediment existed. At this point, the situation was no longer in the hands of Juana Luján; it became an ecclesiastical matter.

Temporary custody, known as *depósito*, was a tool that the friars employed in prenuptial disputes to protect a woman from interference or from dangerous relatives or other persons. The church could also place a woman in a depósito after she eloped to ensure that she had married of her own free will.[66]

There is no evidence of any elopements in New Mexico. Another tool the church employed to expedite marriages, if relatives or others threatened to meddle, was the dispensation of the banns, a practice the friars used infrequently. In the case of Juana Luján, the friars were indeed safeguarding her from the influence of her parents and possibly from the threats of the governor.

To ensure that it remained an ecclesiastical matter, the church hierarchy took a keen interest in the case. Fray Antonio Guerra, the custodian and ecclesiastical judge of New Mexico asked Fray Manuel Moreno to send him the information. The ecclesiastical judge then reassigned the case to Father Muñiz. The friars wanted to make sure that the governor did not involve himself in the case. When Father Muñiz interviewed Ana Luján, cousin of Juana Luján and cook at the governor's palace, he cautioned the witness not to divulge any information to the governor. The friars apparently enjoyed cordial relations with Rodríguez Cubero but considered this business to be an ecclesiastical case outside the governor's jurisdiction.[67]

At first, when the friars received the missive from Juana Luján, their initial interest involved the broken marriage promise. According to the friars, Esquibel was not at liberty to marry a woman when he had already made a promise to wed another. But as the case progressed, the friars contended with other important ecclesiastical issues. Namely, they wanted to know whether Juana Luján acted of her own free will. When Father Muñiz interviewed Juana for the second time, after she had been deposited, he spoke of the two letters that she had sent and asked by which did she stand. She claimed that it was the first and that she still wanted Ventura de Esquivel to honor his word.

When Ventura de Esquibel asked the daughter of Antonio Lucero for her hand in marriage, he was still affianced to Juana Luján. He admitted that he lied under oath because he did not think he owed anything to Juana Luján due to her bad behavior. He stated that when they slept together after the marriage promise, he discovered that she was not a virgin. The friar asked him to say once and for all whom he elected to marry and to answer without fear of his patron. Ventura said that he did not fear the governor but that he truly desired to marry Bernardina Rosa, whom he considered "doncella y española," a Spanish, young, virgin woman.

The friar then called Juana Luján forward for one last interview. He read Esquibel's entire interview to her. By listening to the interview in its entirety, she understood that Esquibel thought she was a loose woman, a liar, and unworthy to be his wife since she was of mixed blood. Most likely, the treacherous words of Esquibel hurt her deeply. She defended herself, however, and provided witnesses and evidence to prove that Esquibel's accusations were false. Nevertheless, Luján chose to release Esquibel from his promise. She no longer desired to wed a man who did not want to marry her. She also feared making the governor an enemy. On May 3, 1702, Ventura de Esquibel married Bernardina Rosa, the daughter of Antonio Lucero.

In the end, the church did not force Esquibel to honor his word to Juana Luján. Upon deciding that she did not want to marry Esquibel, she asked that the church make him pay her a dowry. In this matter, the church granted Luján her wish. The friar required that Esquibel pay Juana 200 pesos, in addition to covering the costs of the investigation that amounted to 78 pesos. This was a great deal of money.

There is little doubt that the friars took the matter seriously. They investigated the impediment immediately and spent nine days interviewing a number of different witnesses. They also exerted their dominion over this ecclesiastical matter by depositing Juana Luján and telling the witnesses not to fear reprisals from the governor. In the end, however, why did the friars decide that Esquibel could marry another woman when he had promised to marry Juana Luján? Did they choose not to press the issue because of her final decision? In the beginning of the investigation, the friars wanted to protect the free will of the young woman. Did they continue to honor her free will by standing by her choice? Or did the friars succumb to pressure from the governor, patron of the fickle Esquibel?

New Mexican friars seem to have accepted the idea that men and women could release and be released from a marriage promise if some type of compensation was agreed upon. Other reasons that men and women could unilaterally break a promise to marry included the contraction of an incurable and/or contagious disease, dismemberment, a reversal of fortune of the intended bride or groom, entering religious life, or either person having sexual relations with someone else.[68] In 1697, Nicolás de Espinosa came forward and asked for a license so he could wed Josefa de la Cruz. He decided to interrupt the process when he found out that his intended bride was having a "bad friendship." Once he determined that the rumors were false, he re-petitioned to marry Josefa de la Cruz.[69]

Women also asked the church for support in forcing men to uphold their promises to marry them. In the middle of winter 1736, Inés Griega, resident of La Cañada, presented to the ecclesiastical judge a petition in which she stated that Marcial Martínez had deflowered her two years earlier after promising to marry her.[70] After hearing his continual excuses that he was too poor to marry her just yet, she decided that, because she was pregnant, the time had come for him to uphold his pledge. She sought the church's assistance.

The ecclesiastical judge, *bachiller* don José Bustamante, wasted no time in making inquiries. The judge sent the contents of Inés's petition to Marcial Martínez, stating that he expected a response within three days. Martínez's reply stated that Inés Griega's reports about him were lies. The judge then made the contents of Martínez's reply known to Inés and required that she respond within two days. She did so. This time Inés provided the names of witnesses who could vouch for the validity of her claims.

Bustamante ordered the witnesses interviewed. The first witness, Juan Tomás Martín, swore before God to tell the truth. When asked when he knew of Martínez's promise to marry Inés, he responded that her mother had told him that the two were engaged. With regard to whether the two had consummated their relationship, Martín said that, while passing Inés's house one day while her parents were absent, he saw, through a window, the couple engaged in the carnal act. On one other occasion, the witness found the couple alone in Inés's house while her parents were once again away for the day. The next two witnesses did not know whether a promise between the couple existed, but they both believed that an illicit relationship between the two did occur. At one time, Inés's parents asked the witness, Antonio Montoya, to keep an eye on her while they were away. When he tried to fulfill his duty, Montoya could not find the young woman. Finally, he tracked her to the house of Martínez, where, he supposed, she was having her wheat ground since there were mills in that house. But when he tried the door, it was locked from within. Montoya decided to hide himself behind some seedbeds. He stayed in his spot from about ten or eleven in the morning until four in the afternoon when he finally observed Marcial Martínez leaving his house. Shortly thereafter, he saw Inés Griega leave with her wheat broken but not ground, implying that her activity had had little to do with grinding grain.

With the evidence gathered from the three witnesses, the judge opted to incarcerate Marcial Martínez. Dating from the sixteenth century, when the crown granted Spanish-American church officials the right to request royal assistance, the ecclesiastical authorities did indeed have the power to jail a person for breaking church laws. This power was key to the church's successful endeavor to control the marital process and chastise recalcitrants intent on breaking ecclesiastical rules.[71]

It is hardly likely that the judge used this powerful tool lightly. This case transpired in the winter. The judge ordered Marcial Martínez to be placed in prison where he spent his first night on February 7. Undoubtedly, the prison was a frigid place for a person to spend winter nights. In fact, when Marcial responded to the witnesses' accusations, he complained to the judge that he wished to be unchained due to the cold.[72]

Although Marcial sat in a freezing cell, he firmly maintained his innocence and repudiated the witnesses' statements. He insisted that the assertion of Inés's mother – that he was engaged to her daughter – was false since he and Inés were blood relatives. Marcial also said that he was absent when the witnesses spied him with Inés. Perhaps fortunately for Marcial, the judge did not have to investigate Marcial's declarations. At this point, Inés Griega decided that she did not want to wed Marcial Martín. To remind the judge that she stood on moral high ground in relation to Marcial, she reiterated that Marcial had promised to marry her and it was under this promise that she lost her virginity. She also stated that she had provided proof of these assertions by naming witnesses. Although Marcial should marry her, she stated, "I have said once and many times that I do not want to marry the said Marcial. He should pay me seventy pesos which is very reasonable."[73] Inés chose to accept money over a marriage with Marcial.

The judge supported Inés's choice. Marcial claimed that he was very poor and could not pay seventy pesos. His family agreed to pay thirty-five pesos to Inés. The court verified that the Martín family made the payment. Why did the judge let the matter rest at this point? Why did he not interview Inés once again to ascertain whether she made the choice not to marry Marcial Martín of her own free will? Maybe the judge believed that Inés had made this decision for herself and was upholding her free will to decide whom she would marry. Perhaps the admission made by Marcial that he and Inés were blood relatives chilled the friar's resolve to pursue the case any further. The friars did not mention the fate of the child. Whatever occurred, the existing evidence demonstrates that the friars investigated whether a man had broken a promise to marry.

In the end, it is hard to determine why the friars made the final decisions they did and what they thought about the cases before them. In some prenuptial cases, the friars revealed that they wanted to help protect poor and often pregnant women by facilitating the marriages and granting the desired dispensations. When they found out that contractors had lied in the marital investigations, they voiced their disgust. They tried to follow the rules set forth by their church, and by doing so, they helped protect those with little means of defending themselves

Over the course of the century, the friars of New Mexico tried to uphold all aspects of the marital process as outlined by the Council of Trent. Community members, as the witnesses, were willing participants in the marital process. Perhaps they relished sharing their knowledge with the friars about how and whether the couples were related. As neighbors, they took a lively interest in the affairs of their friends and friends' families. Friars made the most of the witnesses' knowledge of these intimate details, using the acquired information to approve or to deny the petition. The friars, the couple who wanted to marry, the witnesses, and the community members listening to the banns entered into the marital process and supported the dictates of the Council of Trent. In the end, they all came together to celebrate the nuptial mass in the church. A marriage was not only a matter between a man and a woman and their respective families, but it was also an affair that touched the community.

Chapter 4

Sexuality and Courtship

IT WAS A cold night in Santa Fe on December 24, 1762, as people dressed and prepared to attend mass. The tolling bells summoned parishioners to celebrate the birth of Christ. As they bustled in, candlelight illuminated the church. Blas López in all likelihood, however, sought the shadows, for he had something to hide. Beneath his capacious, winter cloak was a woman.

On the same night after mass, Gertrudis de Armijo arrived at home but feared entering because she heard strange noises. A neighbor summoned a soldier to search her house. Upon entering he immediately returned with Blas López in his custody. "Here is the noise from your house," the soldier said. Gertrudis de Armijo asked López why he had scaled the walls of her house. But López left without providing an explanation, leaving Gertrudis de Armijo talking to herself.

Gertrudis did not let the matter rest. Instead she began to interview her neighbors. She found out that Blas López had attended mass with someone beneath his cloak. Another neighbor, Lucas Moya, told her that he had returned home to retire and had encountered Blas López in a corner of his home. He asked López why he was there, and López responded that he was there to sleep with some boys. But when López rose to leave, Moya discovered that he was not with any boys. He was with the young woman, Gregoria Tenorio, daughter of Gertrudis de Armijo.

This unusual case exists because Gertrudis de Armijo went to the governor and filed a civil and criminal complaint against Blas López. The incident offers insight into the lives of two young New Mexicans, their interactions and their relations with their families and community.[1] This case and others raise questions about the cultural meanings of sexuality of young men and women during the colonial period. How did López view his sexual adventures with Gregoria? What were his aims? Did Gregoria view the relationship differently? When Gertrudis de Armijo filed her complaint, her daughter was seventeen years old and Blas López twenty-two. As young men and women became adolescents, following the customs of their parents, many started to view their peers as potential mates. They began to interact with each other sexually, ranging from flirtation to sexual intercourse. They entered into a game of seduction with one another, though most men and women did not take the risks that Blas and Gregoria did. The rules to this game, both written and unwritten, guided the youth of New Mexico in their quest to find lovers and spouses.

Courtship and sexuality are understudied in the colonial period. Often historians discuss sexuality in terms of honor and shame (*vergüenza*). Honor was a male attribute. Honorable men esteemed honesty and loyalty, concerned themselves with their reputations, acted with manliness, and exerted authority over their families. In this interpretive scheme, men enhanced their honor by sexually conquering other men's wives, sisters, or daughters. Women, on the other hand, experienced vergüenza if they failed to maintain their sexual purity or display discretion around men. As heads of the household, men secluded their women, if possible, to maintain the women's purity, and by so doing they secured their family honor and preserved their symbolic value.[2] Ultimately, the court of public opinion decided whether men and women acted with honor.[3]

By beginning the study of courtship and sexuality within this framework, all behavior on the part of young men and women can be understood according to the terms of seduction by which the man seduced, and the woman succumbed and was victimized. If marriage did not follow seduction, the man's virility was nevertheless enhanced, while the woman was dishonored and shamed. This simplistic binary approach contains many drawbacks. First, it reduces the complexity of sexuality: men were not always the sexual aggressors and women not always the sexual victims. It also eliminates the importance of love and friendship in courtship. Many relationships between young men and women endured after the initial seduction, suggesting that the relationship contained more than conquest and submission. Moreover, by concluding that all seductions without marriage led to the women's dishonor and downfall distorts the complexities of interpersonal relations. Nonvirgin women often went on to marry other men who viewed them as honorable enough to marry. It follows, therefore, that the community's consideration of a woman's reputation was not always dependent on whether a woman had kept or lost her virginity. Finally, the idea that the seclusion of daughters was the ideal behavior for families implies that parents who did not sequester their daughters had failed somehow. Although historians allow that women worked and could not be sheltered all the time, they maintain that segregation was the ultimate goal and that meetings between young men and women were chance, secretive, and unsanctioned by parents.[4] Instead evidence suggests that parents granted youth some autonomy when they began courting, despite the ideal of seclusion.

Historical Influences

Although much of the courtship process and the intricacies of sexuality remain hidden, the historian can decipher the historical influences that helped construct sexuality during this period. Before turning to these influences, however, a definition of sexuality is in order. Often we think of sexuality as a driving, instinctual force, rooted in the biology of the human animal.[5] Fixed and universal, most people experience some type of sexual awakening with puberty and many eventually experience reproduction. Jeffrey Weeks argues, "But biological sexuality is only a precondition, a set of potentialities, which is never unmediated by human reality."[6] In other words, the essentialist framework that defines sexuality as biological and universal denies the historical construction and culturally specific aspects of sexuality. Sexuality, therefore, is constituted in a historically specific period by a number of different forces. In colonial New Mexico, the church, the state, families, communities, and the economy all contributed to the sexuality experienced by young Hispanic men and women.

Not surprisingly, the church involved itself in the intimate lives of people, codifying sexual behavior. The Latin doctors of the early Catholic Church, such as Augustine (354–430) and Jerome (340–420), knew from personal experiences the weakness of the flesh, analyzed the sins of sexuality and its manifestations, and debated the subject with each other.[7] These debates led to an explicit examination of sexual deviance. During the twenty years of the convention of the Council of Trent, theologians produced catechisms and confessionals that outlined Catholic dogma regarding male–female relations. The central precept of acceptable sexual behavior was straightforward enough: physical love was only appropriate when it occurred between a married couple. The church deemed all other sexual activity as deviant and sinful. Through confession and penitence, the bishops and parish priests were to instill the social and personal mores advocated by the Catholic Church.[8]

According to Catholic theology, God endowed human beings with reason, free will, and a sense of responsibility. He made people subject to His law, which is known to people by the dictates of conscience. People must act according to these injunctions. Thus when people do sin and transgress God's laws, they do so knowingly and willingly. Sin deprives a person's soul of sanctifying grace, leaving the person in a "state of habitual aversion from God."[9] To achieve grace once again, the penitent must confess his or her sins to a priest, who will absolve the person and restore the friendship between God and the confessant.[10] Hence, those who sinned, who thought about sex, or who engaged in immoral sexual relations needed to confess to a priest and repent. Michel Foucault believes that confessions concerning the sins of the flesh increased following Trent and during the Counter Reformation, that the Catholic Church "attributed more and more importance in penance—and perhaps at the expense of some other sins—to all the insinuations of the flesh: thoughts, desires, voluptuous imaginings, delectations, combined movements of the body and soul; henceforth all this had to enter, in detail, into the process of confession and guidance."[11]

This process of confession and guidance resulted in a population that had to take its innermost thoughts and actions and relay them to someone else. Foucault writes, "The Christian pastoral prescribed as a fundamental duty the task of passing everything having to do with sex through the endless mill of speech."[12] Sex was "put into discourse." The discussion and knowledge of sexual sins, this discursive element, existed in eighteenth-century New Mexico. The custody's library contained a number of religious texts discussing issues of sexuality and included *Despertador de Noticias de los Santos Sacramentos* published in Mexico City in 1695.[13] In this confessional, the author Fray Clemente de Ledesma explained and expounded the Seventh and Tenth

Commandments: thou shalt not commit adultery and thou shalt not covet thy neighbor's wife.[14] He wrote that, if a priest were to understand these commandments, he must know the seven distinct forms of lust.

The first form was simple fornication, defined as a sexual act with a single woman or a widow. The second act, known as *stuprum* in Latin, was a sexual act with a virgin. The third was adultery, sex with a married person. The fourth form was incest, which was defined as sex with a consanguineous relation or with someone related by affinity. Fifth on the list was a form of lust known as sacrilege, which occurred when people engaged in sex in a sacred place. Sixth was the act known in Latin as *raptus*, a man abducting a woman from her home and having sex with her. Lastly, Ledesma listed the many acts that ran against nature: bestiality, sodomy, masturbation, and any other sexual acts that did not include sexual intercourse between a man and a woman.[15]

In addition to the confessional, New Mexicans learned of the crimes of lust from the pulpit. One friar, propounding a sermon on lust, declared, "It is from the heart that we must displace this monster of sensuality.... it is the cause of sudden deaths, infectious disease, and numerous maladies of the liver."[16] Forewarned by the church, most Catholics likely knew of the sexual sins. Indeed, in both ecclesiastical and civil cases, very few people, if any, claimed that they were ignorant about the sinful nature of their sexual crimes.

For example, the church's success in educating its parishioners about the sins of lust is evident when people admitted that impediments to their marriages existed. In 1695, Pedro Madrid, "to relieve his conscience," admitted to his first cousin, Cristóbal de Gamboa, that he had had illicit sex with Antonia López. Cristóbal de Gamboa, who petitioned the church to marry Antonia López, understood that illicit sex created an impediment to his marriage. He and Antonia López were now related by second-degree affinity. Even Antonia López, an "*india doctrina*," (Indian neophyte) comprehended the complex web of affinity created by illicit sexual relations. She related that initially she did not know how closely related the two men were. When she discovered the fact, she terminated the relationship with Pedro Madrid and immediately relieved her conscience in front of witnesses.[17]

A case from 1731 reveals that New Mexicans understood the nature of unorthodox sexual behavior and that it was part of the colonial discourse.

After some goats had damaged his seedbed, the thirty-year-old Santa Fean, Manuel Trujillo, began tracking the culprits, hoping that they would lead him to their owner. After cresting a hill and descending into a valley, Manuel Trujillo saw two Indian men committing the *"pecado nefando,"* the abominable sin of anal sex, at the side of an arroyo. In a fit of extreme anger, Trujillo began hitting the men with the reins. He reprehended the two, saying that they were committing a great offense against God the Father. Trujillo immediately went to the authorities and denounced the two Indians "so they could be punished as they deserved."[18]

More historical evidence describing colonists' sexual transgressions exists in the more populated areas of central Mexico. Historian Asunción Lavrin finds that the self-motivated confessions of people who had broken ecclesiastical norms is a strong indication of their ultimate acceptance of church dogma, but that the historical realities of conquest and the subsequent process of colonization put pressures on Catholic laws and led to a social reality of consensual unions and illegitimacy. She concludes that a strong tension between norm and practice characterized the sexuality of the colonial population.[19]

In addition to educating their parishioners about sexual deviance, the friars punished those who grossly overstepped the norms of sexuality. In most cases, the friars tried to facilitate marriage, granting dispensations to couples whose sexual relations with each other or others had created ties of affinity.[20] In one exceptional case, however, the ecclesiastical judge forbade a marriage because of the woman's sexual exploits. On February 7, 1717, Antonio Martín petitioned to marry the twenty-year-old widow, Gertrudis Sánchez de Oton. After hearing the *amonestaciones* (banns), Juan Martín, first cousin to Antonio Martín, came forward to confess that he had engaged in an illicit relationship with Gertrudis Sánchez. He was twenty-three years old and only wanted to relieve his conscience. Two days later, Juan's father and another cousin came in to relieve their consciences. They too had had sex with the young widow. The ecclesiastical judge denied Martín's petition, instructing the local friar of Santa Fe to admonish the young woman charitably.[21]

The church was not the only institution to influence the lives of New Mexicans; the civil arm of the state also played a role in defining sexuality and the range of acceptable behavior. In general, it upheld the church's goals to control family formation.²² Regarding the process of betrothal (*esponsales*), the *Siete Partidas* states that bishops could compel betrothed persons to complete their marriages.²³ Since the church in New Mexico lacked the agencies or instruments to compel recalcitrant suitors to fulfill their marriage promises, the church turned to the civil authorities for help with matters of enforcement.²⁴ Citizens dissatisfied with the church's response to their complaints could also directly appeal to the governor in cases of broken marriage promises. When citizens appealed to the governors and their subordinates, the magistrates carried out the letter and spirit of the law. But, in most cases, civil authorities did not initiate cases against or persecute those who lived outside the societal norms. Their role was less intrusive and more reactive.

For instance, the state rarely scrutinized the courtship process, intruding little on the sexual relationships of unwed couples. That position ran counter to the actions of authorities in colonial New England, who regularly intervened in the lives of young couples. Fear of prenuptial pregnancy was the root of this concern and intrusion. When a pregnancy did occur, authorities pressed for marriage to assure legitimacy and financial support for the child.²⁵ When pregnant women refused to name the fathers of their children, the New England authorities commonly asked midwives to extract the fathers' names during the throes of childbirth.²⁶ The authorities punished fornication because they did not want to support illegitimate children with community monies. They also believed that such immoral behavior denigrated the sanctity and importance of marriage in society.²⁷

New Mexican officials showed less concern for the fate of children born to unwed mothers. The state neither supported foundlings nor gave aid to mothers in need. No laws obliged men to support their illegitimate children.²⁸ In most cases, the state showed little inclination to press men to meet their responsibilities. Throughout the eighteenth century, in cases of broken marriage promises when a child was involved, the state asked the man to make a one-time monetary donation nominally for the woman's lost virtue. This attitude began to change, however, by the beginning of the next century. In two cases from 1805, the women asked the men to promise regular monetary donations to help raise the children until they were three years of age. At that point, the fathers were supposed to take the children and raise them, acting as legitimate fathers. The fathers in both cases agreed to the terms.²⁹

In the following case a young woman had promiscuous sexual relations for years before the governor became involved. Even then his initial involvement was not due to her illicit sexual behavior but to the alleged misconduct of her father. In the winter of 1766, Governor don Tomás Vélez Cachupín received a letter from Fray José Eluterio Junco y Junquera accusing Manuel Martín of incest. The governor lost no time in apprehending the suspect and investigating the matter. The governor also placed Martín's daughter, the alleged victim, in deposit. During the questioning, the alcalde mayor discovered that the daughter, Melchora Martín, had four children with four different fathers. The shocked governor wanted the matter investigated further to determine whether the fathers were single while they had had affairs with Melchora Martín. Had they committed the sin of simple fornication or that of adultery as well?[30] He was concerned with the men's immoral behavior and not whether they were providing financial support to the children. Once the alcalde mayor interviewed the men and discovered that they had not committed adultery, the governor turned his attention back to Melchora.

In the end, the governor found the accused man, Manuel Martín, innocent of the charges brought against him. Nevertheless, Vélez Cachupín wanted to determine how such moral turpitude had transpired and decided to interview the witness himself. In his interview with Martín, the governor asked him how he had consented to such "scandalous excesses" without punishing Melchora. The father replied that he had punished his daughter from the first, whipping her and cutting off her hair. Yet she remained impenitent and continued her excesses. Governor Vélez Cachupín decided to keep the woman in deposit in the house of the ecclesiastical judge until he decided she should be released. At this juncture, the governor felt some responsibility to cure the woman of her sexually deviant behavior, but Melchora Martín had delivered four children, and the state had done nothing to curb her conduct. The governor only involved himself after Father Junquera incriminated Manuel Martín.

The governors' unwillingness to entangle themselves in the personal problems of their subjects had to do with the demands of governing a frontier. Governor Vargas confronted a precarious situation at the time of the Spanish reconquest of New Mexico in 1692. Many Pueblos resented the return of the Spaniards, and, in 1696, again revolted. After the Spanish quelled the uprising, Pueblos and Spaniards established peace and combined their forces to defend themselves against nomadic Indians who harassed and attacked their settlements. Governors regularly rode out on raids, leaving them little time to devote themselves to monitoring their subjects.[31]

In this environment of conquest and recurrent warfare, the most complex impact on Hispanic men's and women's sexuality was the ransom of captured Indians and their subsequent adoption by Hispanic families. The colonists engaged in trade with nomadic Indians at trade fairs (*rescates*) or through small-scale bartering (*cambalaches*) and often purchased slaves known as *indios de rescate*, or "ransomed Indians."[32] Upon purchase, the owners baptized the captives, who were often children, and reared them in their own homes, calling them genízaros and/or criados. In exchange for their labor, the genízaros received a Christian upbringing. The criados frequently remained in the families for as long as ten to twenty years, until they became tithe-paying citizens.[33] Of course, the situation varied depending on the relationships between the criados and their owners. Some criados remained with their captors for life; others formed families and lives of their own.

Many genízaros, kidnapped from their Indian families, were children. Yet Hispanic families also bought young Indian women and brought them into their homes. These women often suffered sexual abuse at the hands of their captors. Between 1732 and 1800, friars at Santa Cruz de la Cañada baptized 192 Indians born to infidel parents.[34] Unfortunately for historians, friars did not always provide the ages of those whom they baptized. In 109 cases, they merely indicated they were baptizing *párvulos*, or children.[35] Not infrequently, however, the captured Indians were adults. In six cases, friars identified Indian women as adults ranging in age from thirteen to twenty years. On April 8, 1798, Father Bibián de Ortega baptized María Rosa de la Trinidad, a thirteen-year-old Apache girl.[36] It is possible that the seventy-seven baptized people not explicitly classified as párvulos were in fact adults. Females were about 58 percent of this group.

Although the crown had outlawed Indian slavery in 1542 and laws existed to protect servants from mistreatment, the genízaros, forcibly cut off from their societies and families, proved vulnerable. At the time of the reconquest, Viceroy don José Sarmiento Valladares and a council formed by him decided on the proper treatment of captives: they should be given a Christian education, work in their masters' houses, be treated well, and not be sold as property.[37] When governors found evidence of abuse, they removed the criados and placed them in other homes. In 1763, two criadas from Albuquerque complained to Governor Vélez Cachupín that their respective masters had failed to indoctrinate them and had put them to work as shepherds. Manuela, criada of Isabel Chávez, was pregnant by Domingo Chávez (possibly a cousin of the master). Upon examining the two young women's knowledge of Christian doctrine, the governor found them to be ignorant. He also decried the masters' lack of Christian charity; they had placed the criadas in the dangerous countryside, exposing them to sin as was abundantly evident by the pregnant Manuela. Frequent raids by nomadic Indians rendered the countryside dangerous. The governor sent the women to new homes where they would learn Christian doctrine and Spanish customs, where they would be fed and dressed, and where they would work in the home instead of the countryside.[38]

Homes, however, did not always prove to be safe havens for criadas. For instance, men, intent on sexually using Indian women, often found their most helpless victims within their own homes. Isolated in private houses and not afforded the same protection as daughters or wives, servant girls had little hope of defending themselves from the brothers or fathers with nefarious designs. Fray Pedro Serrano recognized the genízaras' sexual vulnerability from the time of their violent abduction through placement in a Hispanic's house. In 1761, in a requisition to the Viceroy Marqués de Cruillas, he wrote that the Indian captors raped the young female captives before selling them to the Christians. Afterward, the abductors boasted to the Spaniards, "Now you can take her, now she is good."[39] The implication was that the captive women who had been raped would be more obedient and more open to sexual advances than otherwise. Unprotected women working in the homes caused young men to feel they had license to fulfill their sexual need with these women because they were Indians who lacked vergüenza.

Traditionally in colonial society, while elite men believed that their daughters and sisters deserved respect and needed to be guarded, they perceived women of color and of the lower classes to be less sexually pure and less deserving of protection. In fact, some Spaniards contended that they were entitled to sexual access to women of color. On two separate occasions, Spanish men, brought before the Inquisition in New Spain between 1538 and 1566, declared that having sex with an Indian was not a sin. The other said more precisely that it was more sinful to approach a Spanish woman than an Indian woman. Another man—accused of penetrating a virgin slave in 1571—said that his was a pardonable sin. These men believed that their crimes against Indian and slave women were less grave than attacking Spanish women.[40]

Two centuries later on the California frontier, Spaniards continued to view Indian women as sexually exploitable. Soldiers seduced women, frequented Indian prostitutes, and, in some cases, raped them. In the atmosphere of war and conquest that prevailed in California, marriage between Spaniards and Indians occurred infrequently.[41] Historian Steve J. Stern concludes that, in late colonial Mexico, elite men believed that they could sexually assault lower-class women through powers of intimidation or persuasion. He concludes, "In effect, a man of power dared the subaltern woman he cornered to resist him and dared her subaltern mate (if she had one) to resist him, in full knowledge that the power advantage discouraged open defiance."[42]

In eighteenth-century New Mexico, a less rigid class and racial hierarchy diminished the tensions Stern describes. Moreover, Hispanic villagers depended on their Pueblo neighbors to help fight their common enemies. As a result, Hispanic men did not risk angering neighboring Pueblo men by taking advantage of their wives and daughters. Second-generation genízaro women proved less vulnerable as well. Their respective families and communities protected both groups of women, whereas Plains Indian servants proved most susceptible to the sexual advances of men. Nevertheless, not all genízaras de rescate (genízaras of the first generation) became victims of sexual abuse. Raised within Hispanic houses, they learned to adjust and negotiated a degree of agency within captivity.[43] Native women, for example, sought to create bonds of kinship with members of the captor society. Some women might have initiated sexual relations to achieve these ends. In addition, captive women integrated themselves economically and played important roles as interpreters, translators, and envoys for Spanish military leaders. All in all, these women achieved some measure of security and comfort for themselves as well as for their descendants.[44]

Still, given the very nature of being forcibly subjugated and unprotected, some women did suffer abuse before achieving any security and comfort. The frequency of illegitimate children delivered to Indian servants attests to their sexual vulnerability.[45] On April 12, 1733, in the parish of Santa Cruz de la Cañada, Fray Manuel de Sopeña baptized the baby Manuel. Two weeks later another friar, José de Eguía, baptized the baby Marcos. In both cases the friars marked the fathers as "unknown" and the mothers as Apache Indians. Manuel's mother, María, was a servant in the home of Antonio de Salazar and the other mother, Isabel, was the servant of Cristóbal Tafoya. Between 1732 and 1800, friars identified thirty-four criadas who bore illegitimate children, listing the fathers as unknown. This number represents an undercount of criadas who gave birth. Many parents opted not to identify themselves. The friars registered 377 mothers as unknown. All these mothers were not necessarily criadas, but criadas might have chosen to remain anonymous to shield their children from being labeled offspring from adulterous unions. Moreover, the criadas might have been safeguarding themselves from a nosy friar or a belligerent master. Of the 377 babies, the friars identified the race of only nineteen: eight Indians, two mestizos, two coyotes, and seven Apache Indians.[46]

María Lucero, the criada of Miguel Lucero, took her child to be baptized on July 18, 1777, in Albuquerque. She was one of seventeen criadas known to have borne illegitimate children between the years 1706 and 1783. As was the case in Santa Cruz, many parents chose anonymity. Close to 19 percent of the mothers listed were unknown. Of the 482 babies baptized in Albuquerque from 1706 to 1783, friars listed the race of one hundred children and identified fifty Indians, fourteen coyotes, six mestizos, and two genízaros.[47] The racial identification of these children born of "unknown parents" provides a rough indication that at least 15 percent of the mothers were unmarried Indian women.

In most cases, the friars did not know or did not name the fathers. Who were the fathers of these illegitimate babies? In the case of suspected incest mentioned earlier, Manuel Martín admitted that he had fathered Melchora with "*una india pura genízara de rescate*" (a pure, ransomed, Indian genízara) before marrying. A moment later, under the inquisitive gaze of the governor, he changed his story, saying that he had actually engendered his bastard daughter after being married to someone else for three years. Martín also revealed that Melchora's mother had delivered another baby, whose father he did not know. Even if Martín, as the head of the household, was not the father of the servant's second child, he had failed as a protector, leaving her open to sexual advances by other men.

In the home, then, some men learned that sexually conquering certain women was tolerable behavior. Young men, in all likelihood, observed the actions of their fathers and patterned their conduct after them. If men abused their servants, sons could come to learn that these actions were acceptable. Young men heard competing discourses: on the one hand, the church's objections to sexual impropriety of any kind and the state's willingness to remove servants who suffered from excessive abuse; on the other, the colonizer's boast that Native women were available for sexual conquest. The result was a varied population where not all men sought to conquer and abuse Indian women. Moreover, captive women sometimes established bonds of kinship, implying that not all sexual relations contained coercive elements.

Some young men admitted that they were uninitiated in the ways of love and sex, pointing out their innocence to church, state, and family authorities. These data belie the idea that all men were seducers who conquered and deflowered, intent on proving their virility.[48] In 1714, Nicolás Durán y Chávez admitted that he had given a promise to marry to Juana Montaño de Sotomayor and they had engaged in sex, but that he had been a "boy" at the time and did not really know whether she was a virgin.[49] In 1725, another young man accused of deflowering a woman described himself as "fragile and miserable."[50] Even if these men used this tactic to get out of their promises, their behavior still highlights the fact that men experienced sexuality diversely and that they went through different stages of sexual awakening.

Female children learned other lessons at home. Parents taught young girls sexual propriety. In colonial Spanish societies, married women had to remain faithful to their husbands to maintain their honor and that of their families. A woman obtained honors and dignities when she married, and the greatest honor was that the sons she had with her husband were considered legitimate and inherited the father's property. A woman would, therefore, honor her husband and protect the family name.[51] Until they married, young women also learned that they should preserve their virginity, which connoted an unsullied life and respect for the moral canons of the church.[52] When they guarded their reputations, women retained their honor and protected the honor of their families.[53] In the end, women maintained their honor if the community perceived them as chaste.[54]

Did the loss of one's virginity mark the end of an honorable life in New Mexico? Depending on the time, place, and situation, the meaning of honor changed in the Spanish empire.[55] In New Mexico, the communities determined someone's behavior as honorable based on a number of variables. The appropriate behavior for young men and women differed from the acceptable, honorable behavior of married men and women. The actual meaning of honor, never easy to define, becomes more evident in the prenuptial cases.

Prenuptial Relationships

Many young people in New Mexico took an active part in choosing partners, meeting with one another and spending time together. Elite families in many parts of Spanish America protected and isolated their daughters to preserve their sexual purity, but this strategy proved unrealistic for most New Mexican families. Only families who owned several servants could effectively seclude their daughters. Most daughters participated in the family chores—washing clothes, tending fields, or milling wheat—reducing a family's ability to isolate them.

Work began at a young age with adults sending children off to do chores and tasks. In the process of daily work, young men and women often encountered each other, sometimes with consequences beyond the control of their families. In spring 1719, Catarina Villalpando sent her sister on an errand. When the girl returned and told her sister of an altercation with the fifteen-year-old boy who lived next door, Catarina came out and yelled at him, calling him an "Apache dog." The twenty-five-year-old woman was not going to remain aloof while her younger sister was harassed. She and her sister had work to do and she would not let that boy interfere.[56]

In addition, young women and men often met at church or at family gatherings. Miguel Chávez, whose daughter had a sexual relationship with José Antonio Salazar, was a friend and a compadre of Salazar's father.[57] It is not surprising that the young couple knew each other and developed a relationship. Blas López and Gregoria Tenorio, another pair, and cousins related in the second-degree consanguinity, most likely met at a gathering of family and friends. On these occasions, young people made acquaintances and formed friendships. Some couples eventually managed to find time to nurture their relationships away from guardians' prying eyes. At the time of mass, Gertrudis de Armijo had no idea that her daughter was hiding beneath Blas's cloak.

The ages of Gregoria Tenorio (seventeen years old) and Blas López (twenty-two years old) were the approximate average ages of the women and men who married in eighteenth-century New Mexico. The majority of women who married did so during adolescence, between the ages of fifteen and twenty. During these years, young women began to take more interest in the opposite sex, seeing them as possible lovers or potential husbands. Men who married at López's age followed and foreshadowed the footsteps of numerous New Mexican men who married in their early twenties (see figs. 3, 4, 5, 6, and 7).

After meeting and getting acquainted, many young people began a courtship that often ended with a promise of marriage and a *prenda*. The prenda was a gift, sometimes a ring or a rosary, that the couple exchanged as a symbol of a promise to marry. In 1750 the lieutenant governor, don Bustamante y Tagle, interviewed Tomás Gallegos and asked him whether he had deflowered Margarita García Jurado. Gallegos admitted that he had "a friendship of words, palpitative embraces, and little kisses with her but that he had not arrived to the act of carnal copulation." He stated that he had done these things because of the great love he felt for her and his desire to marry her. He ended the relationship and married someone else, however, when he heard that Margarita was flirting with other men.[58]

When young men and women courted and promised to marry, they expected fidelity from their betrothed. Tomás Gallegos was not the only man to break off an engagement. In 1697, Nicolás de Espinosa ended his engagement when he heard that his girlfriend was having a "bad friendship" with another man. When he discovered the rumors were false, however, he decided to marry her after all.[59] Although both the church and state frowned upon broken engagements, young men, especially, demanded fidelity from their intended brides once a promise had been made. Even secondhand rumors were enough to warrant ending an engagement, for whispered words and innuendos impugned a young man's honor and cast doubts on his ability to control his bride-to-be.

Once engaged to marry, some couples decided to consummate the relationship. Although the church did not support the practice, many lay people believed that a promise followed by sexual intercourse was equivalent to a sanctioned marriage. The idea that a betrothal equated an actual marriage dated back to the *Siete Partidas*. The fourth law states: "There is no difference or distinction, so far as the validity of a marriage is concerned, between one contracted by words relating to the present time, and the other which is consummated by the husband having carnal union with his wife. This is the case because consent alone, made by words relating to the present time, is sufficient to render the marriage valid."[60] Indeed, most men and women fulfilled their promises and married. The cases that exist, however, reveal what transpired when the couples failed to marry. What becomes evident is that men and women had different expectations. Usually women seemed willing to have sexual relations as part of a continuum that led to marriage. Men, on the other hand, seemed more desirous of initiating relationships with little intention of honoring promises. Sex was the desired result and marriage a trap. Exceptions existed on both sides, of course, but the overall breakdown shows that men and women viewed sex differently.

The case of Blas López of the commodious cloak and Gregoria Tenorio, recounted at the beginning of this chapter, illustrates men's and women's differing interpretations of courtship and sex. When the alcalde mayor of Santa Fe interviewed Gregoria, she admitted that she had gone to mass under Blas López's cloak, that they had returned to Lucas Moya's house and finally that she had helped Blas into her home through a hole in the roof. Her explanation was that when Blas came to get her, he had said that they would be together and that he wanted to marry only her, not the woman from La Cañada. Made aware that he refused to marry her, she now believed that his pleas for her hand in marriage were false. While Gregoria was being interviewed, Blas López sat in a cold jail cell. He was imprisoned for two and a half months. Throughout his incarceration, he denied any wrongdoing.[61]

This was not the first time that the couple's business had come before the authorities. To rid himself of the case, Governor Vélez Cachupín forwarded it to the ecclesiastical judge, don Santiago de Roybal. Returning the case, the judge stated that three years earlier in 1760, Gregoria accused Blas López of deflowering her with a promise of marriage. Roybal had ruled the accusation false and further declared that the couple shared bonds of kinship. Moreover, Blas López had promised to marry Matildea Herrera of Santa Cruz de La Cañada. Indeed, the church had already read the banns, and nothing impeded their marriage save López's incarceration.

For three years, then, Gregoria and Blas López had shared some type of relationship. Gregoria used all the means at her disposal to marry her cousin but, for whatever reason, Blas did not want to marry her. His motivations for pursuing the relationship seem clear enough: with Gregoria he found a willing partner in his sexual escapades. On that Christmas Eve night alone, he took numerous risks to fulfill his sexual desires.

In another case in January 1766, Miguel Chávez of Albuquerque went to the ecclesiastical authorities to complain that José Antonio Salazar had raped his twenty-two-year-old daughter and impregnated her after a promise of marriage. When the friar interviewed María Rosa Durán y Chávez, he asked whether "with this man she had dealings and illicit communication, yielding her body in offense of the majesty of God our Father." María Rosa responded that she had engaged in an illicit relationship with José Antonio Salazar but that she had yielded her body to the young man because he had promised marriage. Swayed by his words, she had believed that he would carry through with his intention.[62]

Unfortunately for María Rosa, José Antonio Salazar, age twenty-three, vehemently refused to marry her, even if the authorities "quartered him or put him into shackles up to his neck."[63] Obviously, the young man did not like the woman and believed that prison, where he presently sat, was preferable to a life with María Rosa. But when the friar asked him how many times they had illicit copulation, he answered "*como quinze veces poco más o menos*" (about fifteen times a little more or less).[64] Another witness indicated that the relationship between Salazar and Chávez had begun the year before.[65] Salazar never admitted to making a pledge, but if he had made her a promise, he clearly had no intention of honoring it. Like Blas López, Salazar also scaled the walls of his lover's house to reach her and intended to have sex with her without the benefit of marriage.

These young people in New Mexico, then, established relationships and engaged in sexual activity. Although the young men might have seen these relationships as sexual and lied to achieve these ends, the women, active participants themselves, were not necessarily blameless victims. In the year 1777, Juana Padilla went to the ecclesiastical authorities and declared that she had had sex with Gregorio, alias "*El Satebo*," after he had promised her marriage and after she had given him a prenda. She complained that she was now pregnant and that El Satebo would not realize his promise to marry her. El Satebo admitted that he had had sex one time with Juana Padilla. Unlike López and Salazar, El Satebo neither courted the woman nor developed a close relationship with her over time. Indeed, he swore that he by no means promised the woman marriage and believed her to be a "woman of the world with children." When questioned about the prenda, he exclaimed that she had given him a rosary because he did not have one. She had told him to take it "so that the devil will not take you," but had never said that it was a prenda. When asked if he would marry her, he responded that his intention had never been to marry her. Upon hearing this, Juana Padilla said that, since he did not want to marry her, she would be content with 150 pesos. In response, El Satebo said that he would not pay, firstly, because he had never offered anything, and secondly, because he was poor. In the end, the authorities asked him to pay her two black shawls.[66]

The judges usually interviewed numerous witnesses, but in this case the ecclesiastical judge seemed unwilling to pursue the matter any further. Apparently, the judge believed that El Satebo, age twenty-four, spoke the truth and that Juana Padilla, age forty, was trying to entrap the young man. Far from being victims, women could also actively pursue men and use sex as a tool to achieve their ends, namely marriage or money.

In the cases of Blas López and José Antonio Salazar, the parents petitioned the authorities to remedy their daughters' dishonorable predicaments. Yet the timing of their involvement suggests that they were unaware or unwilling to involve themselves at an earlier stage in their children's relationships. Gertrudis de Armijo must have known of her daughter's entanglements with Blas López spanning at least three years. It is more difficult, however, to discern when Miguel Chávez became cognizant of his daughter's relationship with José Antonio Salazar. Nevertheless, he was not guarding his daughter sufficiently to prevent her from meeting men. In February of 1705, Juana de Valencia, mother of Juana Rodríguez, knew that Sebastián Luján had deflowered her daughter in September 1704. Initially she did not complain about Luján's behavior on the assumption that he would marry her daughter. When she discovered he intended to marry another, Juana de Valencia appealed to both the civil and ecclesiastical authorities for the punishment of Luján.[67]

Evidence suggests little or no parental involvement in the incipient stages of relationships. Instead, young people sought the support of their peers, relying on them as messengers, witnesses, and confidants. In 1702, Ventura de Esquibel turned to a fellow soldier and asked him to send a message to his love, Juana Luján. The soldier passed the message onto another woman who then relayed it to Juana Luján. She, in turn, sent a message and a ring through the intermediaries to Ventura. Their oral missives were passionate, each claiming that they kissed the other's hands.[68]

José Antonio Salazar, also confiding in a friend, told him that he had taken María Rosa Chávez's virginity but that he would not marry her. The friend said that Salazar was interested in marrying another woman. The friar recognized that friends might provide more evidence, so he interrogated another witness about whether he knew María Rosa Chávez. The witness said that he knew her because they had been raised together. He stated that he and María Rosa's cousin had observed the couple together.[69] Regrettably, the document ends here. Nevertheless, these peers, privy to the relationship, understood more about it than did the parents.

Blas López depended on his peers to corroborate his story. The alcalde mayor interviewed Blas on many occasions, and each time Blas denied any wrongdoing. During the first interview, he claimed that no one was under his cloak during mass and that he was with Antonio Madril, his twenty-two-year-old friend. Unfortunately for Blas, Madril denied being with him on December 24.[70] In another interview, Blas asserted that he had carried his little sister beneath his cloak and that Baltasar González, also age twenty-two, was a witness to the fact. González, however, said that Blas's claim was false; he had not been to mass that night.[71]

Madril's and González's reluctance to help Blas López suggests that peer complicity went only so far. Blas López's behavior seems to have exceeded the bounds of the community's sense of decency. Blas was engaged to another woman when he brought Gregoria Tenorio to mass. By bringing her there under his cloak, Blas committed numerous lustful sins, including sacrilege. The peers' flat refutations to corroborate Blas's story attest to their disapproval.

When men and women engaged in sexual relations outside of marriage, they ran certain risks. For women, the most obvious consequence was pregnancy. By having sex with or without a marriage promise, women chanced a future of pregnancy and raising their children as single parents. Between 1731 and 1800 in Santa Cruz de la Cañada, 20 percent of all births (881 out of 4,327) were illegitimate.[72] Similarly, between 1747 and 1800 in Santa Fe, 20 percent of all births (1,025 out of 5,140) were illegitimate.[73] In contrast, between 1706 and 1786 in Albuquerque, 32 percent of all births were illegitimate (825 out of 2,589).[74]

If women were persuaded that marriage would follow intercourse, they probably did not fear the consequences of becoming pregnant. Because natural children (those born to unwed parents who could marry if they chose) would be legitimated once their parents married, there was actually no need to rush the marriage. Any number of circumstances, such as financial hardships, Indian attacks, or a death in the family could lead to the postponement of marriages, even in those cases in which the couples already had children.

There is little way to prove that married couples had had children together before their nuptials. The friars neither listed that information in the diligencias matrimoniales nor returned to the baptismal records to make formal notes that children were now legitimate.[75] In addition, many parents who baptized their children chose anonymity; instead of writing the names of the parents, friars wrote, "*padres no conocidos*," or unknown parents. In Santa Cruz de la Cañada, between the years 1731 and 1800, friars wrote "unknown mother" for 9 percent of the baptisms and "unknown father" for 13 percent.[76] Similarly, in Santa Fe, between the years 1747 and 1800, friars wrote "unknown mother" for 8 percent of the baptisms and "unknown father" for 15 percent.[77] In Albuquerque even more parents failed to identify themselves. Between 1706 and 1786, friars designated approximately 20 percent of mothers and fathers as "no conocidos."[78] There are instances, however, in which the mother gave her name but did not identify the father. Tracking the number of children whom mothers baptized demonstrates that some mothers married after that first child's baptism. On May 22, 1784, Fray Sebastián Antón baptized Sebastiana Martín's natural daughter, María. Over a year later, in July 1785, Sebastiana Martín married Juan Pedro Mascareñas. The couple had two more children who received baptismal waters in 1786 and 1793, respectively.[79] It is likely that Juan Pedro Mascareñas was María's father.

Given that the illegitimacy rates were so high, it is easy to assume that many couples engaged in sex without worrying about possible pregnancies. Did young men and women have access to contraceptives? No evidence exists to suggest that they had knowledge of contraceptives; indeed, few options existed. *Coitus interruptus* (onanism) was most likely their only choice. Whether youth understood the benefits of onanism remains difficult to assess. Contemporaries in the British American colonies used the method as did couples in France.[80]

Although no known evidence of birth control exists for colonial New

Mexico, early evidence does indicate that women went to midwives in search of potions to restore their menstrual cycles. In a broken-marriage-promise case from 1736, the ecclesiastical judge interviewed the forty-nine-year-old midwife, Josefa de Medina. Medina reported that, four months previously, the mother of the complainant called on her for a *remedio* (cure) that would make her daughter's menstruation start again. The midwife did not provide the desired remedio because the young woman in question was already four months pregnant.[81]

Catholic theology complicated knowledge, practice, and dispensation of contraception. Church theologians debated the moment of ensoulment, the point in time when the fetus obtained a soul. In 1661, Paul Zacchias, physician to Pope Innocent X, believed that the human soul was infused at the moment of conception. In the late eighteenth century, the Italian theologian, Alphonsus Liguori, citing St. Thomas, believed in the forty-day, eighty-day rule: the male fetus was infused with a soul after forty days, and the female soul, after eighty.[82] The ecclesiastical judge did not express any particular concern with Josefa de Medina's testimony. Perhaps New Mexicans believed that either forty or eighty days marked the start of a pregnancy.

In any event, Medina's remedios did not necessarily have the wished-for effect. At this time, there was no foolproof, effective, and safe potion to induce an abortion. If a pregnant woman's menstrual cycle began to flow again, miscarriage was the likely cause.[83] Nevertheless, the young woman's mother knew that the midwife had some type of potion (whether effective or not) that could help her unwed daughter, and she tried to procure it.

In addition to risking pregnancy, women jeopardized their reputations as virginal, honorable women. Did loss of virginity lead to an irreparable loss of honor? How did the community perceive women who had lost their honor? The evidence regarding youths' and the community's sense of honor comes from a handful of broken marriage promises and one case of character defamation. These cases reveal that honor was a complex notion, complicated, at times, by issues of race. Beneath the many layers, however, a few similarities among cases help uncover local perceptions of honor.

When a man promised a woman marriage, had sex with her, and then refused to marry her, the woman in question lost her *honra*, meaning her virginity and her reputation as a maiden. Historian Ramón Gutiérrez writes that the New Mexican woman was considered shameless and her shamelessness dishonored the family as a whole. He states, "The verdict of public opinion or the family's reputation and honor depended on the father's riposte. The absence of a response to an affront was dishonorable and socially negative. If a man admitted his weakness and humiliation and did not contest the defilement of his property and of his honor, he became a cuckold in the community's eyes."[84] In most cases, however, women acted on their own initiatives, bringing their suits before the civil and/or ecclesiastical authorities.

The idea that only fathers or brothers could defend the honor of their female kinfolk is unsubstantiated in the evidence from colonial New Mexico. Of the thirteen cases involving loss of honor, eight women came forward to petition the governor or the ecclesiastical judge (see table 3). After hearing the banns about her lover's upcoming nuptials to another woman, Juana Luján complained to the friar that the groom had already promised marriage to her. She did so of her own volition without any involvement from her parents. Indeed, once her parents discovered what she was doing, they advised her to withdraw her suit.[85] In 1725 Manuela de Armijo filed a complaint against Juan Lobato for deflowering her after a promise of marriage. The ecclesiastical judge immediately placed de Armijo in deposit. When the judge interviewed her, he stressed that she should speak the truth under threat of excommunication "and that she answer truthfully what he asks her without fear or advice from her father nor another person, instead answering freely, fearing God." He then asked her whether the complaint she filed was hers, springing from her own motives or whether she was counseled and induced to file it. The judge reported her response was, "It is hers because it is the truth and it is a just demand."[86]

Instead of waiting for their fathers or brothers to defend them, these women filed suits to recover their honor and, if they perceived it to be lost, their reputation. These women expected ecclesiastical and civil authorities to hear their suits and help them to achieve their goals. The courageous, eloquent, sixteen-year-old Juana Luján explained why she had dropped her initial suit but was again pressing it against Ventura de Esquibel: "She said that her motives were because she did not want to have complaints with the governor. She had heard that the governor was maligning her character (*crédito*) by spreading rumors that she had had illicit relationships with various men. All of it is false and she can offer proof. After considering that she was a poor, unprotected woman, now without her reputation, which she had had before this suit, she did not want nor does not want to release him from his word."[87]

That Juana Luján and other women acted on their own to defend their honor, in some cases soliciting the help of attorneys or relatives, was not unusual. The historian Sonya Lipsett-Rivera also finds that women in late-colonial New Spain actively protected their honor and social standing.[88] In addition to using legal channels to defend their honor, some employed gossip or violently attacked those who sought to impugn their reputations. Moreover, if women became pregnant, they might try to hide the fact and even resort to infanticide to conceal their shame and to protect their families.[89] According to Lipsett-Rivera, these women worried about how their communities perceived them. In New Mexico, on the other hand, women did not see their lost virginity and pregnancies as reasons to hide from their fellow citizens. Indeed, as a pregnant spurned lover, Juana Luján believed her reputation was intact and did not see herself as discredited until after the governor spread malicious rumors.

What role, then, did the public play in these cases? When women came forward to challenge the men who had broken their promises, they did so in a public forum. Why would they expose themselves to more public scrutiny, especially if they were not pregnant? In most cases, they had conducted their courtship in the open; these relationships were not secret affairs. In fact, women depended on witnesses to corroborate their stories. That tactic suggests that women did not perceive their actions as dishonorable. In their opinion, men's actions, not their own, deserved censure. When Inés Greiga complained about the behavior of Marcial Martínez, she presented witnesses who knew of her sexual relations with him. She hoped to use their knowledge of her lost virtue as a means to force Marcial to marry her. This strategy runs counter to the idea that the appearance of virginity and modesty was tantamount to honorable behavior. In 1702, Pedro de Montes de Oca, the messenger of love and prendas between Juana Luján and Ventura de Esquibel, testified that when he had heard the news of Esquibel's upcoming nuptials to another woman, "he felt the desire to come and declare what he knew, as he was now doing with pleasure."[90] Instead of spurning the "fallen woman" and supporting his fellow soldier, Montes de Oca backed Juana Luján in her suit to make Esquibel honor his promise. Montes de Oca knew that the couple had exchanged prendas and that Esquibel was acting dishonorably. In sum, given that courtship was public, women believed that they acted from a position of strength and honor and that more public exposure would not damage their cases. In fact, the public's knowledge of their amorous relations counted as evidence that women used to force the men in question to fulfill their promises.

Women might have also wanted a public forum so that they could protect themselves against people within their own families. The idea that the importance of honorable behavior rested alone in the public eye denies the complexity of family relations. In spring 1767, María Manuela de la Luz Romero, a resident of Albuquerque, went to great lengths to repair her damaged reputation. She claimed that a "damned coyote" named Mariano Baca, hailing from a "low sphere and [burdened] with depraved manners," was publicly proclaiming his wish to marry her. When various people told her of the man's declarations, María Manuela, overcoming the "veil of modesty," paid a visit to the ecclesiastical notary, José Hurtado de Mendoza, accompanied by Bárbara Benavides, the public midwife of the Atrisco valley. María Manuela "earnestly" requested the notary to witness a gynecological exam that would verify her virginity. Mendoza agreed and attested that it was "infallible that she was a maiden." She committed all of these actions because she was worried about what her father would say when he returned from his trip. She said that once he heard the news, she did not know what else, besides the civil and criminal complaint she was filing, would satisfy him.[91]

This case further highlights how race and class added to the subtleties of honor. Although María Manuela went to great lengths to prove her sexual innocence and, in the end, received a satisfactory outcome from the governor, questions remain about the case. To begin with, Mariano Baca admitted that he had deflowered María Manuela with a promise of marriage, having previously testified as much before the ecclesiastical court in Albuquerque. Indeed, four female witnesses corroborated Baca's story. (The records of the ecclesiastical case are not extant.) No further witnesses came forward to attest one way or the other. Instead the case relied on the biting words of the "*doncella honesta y recogida*" (honest and retiring maiden) and the imprisoned coyote, each represented by a *defensor* (legal advisor). The odd circumstances of the case (the gynecological exam, the lack of witnesses, and Mariano Baca's position [why would he lie?]) indicate that María Manuela's concern for her reputation had much to do with the social position of Mariano Baca. She had crossed a race and class line that she believed her father saw as critical to upholding his position of honor in the community.

Moreover, women's first concern was not always their lost honor or their reputation. Juana Padilla seemed motivated to file suit against El Satebo for monetary gain or, had she succeeded in her suit, matrimonial security.[92] Other women seemed more concerned with basic survival. Juana Montaño hired a defensor to present her suit to the governor. She had been involved with Nicolás Durán y Chávez for seven years, was the mother of his children, and wanted Durán y Chávez to honor his marriage promise. Montaño's father was deceased, and she lived with her mother. The defensor said that Montaño wanted Durán y Chávez to fulfill his promise so that her children could be legitimated and that she could live in God's grace; she probably also feared for her and her children's well-being.

The best way for women to regain lost honor was for the men to realize their promises and marry the women, yet the church and the state seemed unwilling to force men to do this. Moreover, some women, during the course of the investigations, came to believe that marriage with an unwilling groom was not worth the aggravation. María Rosa Chávez, whose father, Miguel Chávez, had filed a suit to force José Antonio Salazar to honor his promise to his daughter, could not help but notice Salazar's reluctance to marry her. (He was the young man who claimed he would rather be drawn and quartered than marry her.) In her interview she said that initially she supported the suit to make him fulfill the word he had given her, "but now seeing the scorn he felt towards her, it has erased her desire. In this fashion, she does not want to marry José Antonio." When the friar asked whether, upon admitting this to her parents, she would change her mind, she replied, "On the contrary, not now or ever will she want to marry."[93]

Initially, Juana Luján wanted Ventura de Esquibel to honor his promise, but she also released him from his promise when the friar read her his testimony in which Esquibel claimed he wanted to marry the Spanish maiden and not Juana Luján. She surmised that if Ventura de Esquibel was forced to marry her, their married life together would be bad. Once she relented, she immediately demanded that he pay her a dowry: "since Esquibel acknowledged his obligation to her, he cannot deny recompensing her with a sufficient dowry so that she can marry."[94] She asked that Father Muñiz represent her suit for compensation since she feared that a civil representative would not want to press her suit for fear of displeasing the governor. She also wanted the money paid to her before Esquibel married. She figured that it would be harder to collect her payment after he was wedded. She concluded that "she did not ask for the dowry from charity but for justice."[95]

The settlement known as a dowry, in theory, allowed a nonvirgin woman to compete in the marriage market, as she would have done had she preserved her virginity.[96] With the data available, it appears that the dowry had an impact on whether the woman in question subsequently found a husband. The two women who received the largest settlements (200 pesos) later found husbands. Nevertheless, the cases available cannot be used to suggest a pattern to support whether the dowry generally had an impact one way or the other. Undoubtedly, the settlement (probably paid in goods) came in handy, especially if the woman was with child (see table 3).

In the end, when the cases were over and women's past and present exploits were exposed, did these women suffer irreparable loss of honor? If restoration of honor was solely determined by being able to find a husband, then the answer is no. Perhaps no case damaged the reputation of a woman more than did the investigation into the life of Juana Rodríguez. When the twenty-four-year-old Sebastián Luján filed his petition to marry Juana Teresa Trujillo, perhaps he knew that the investigation would not go smoothly. The friar asked him whether he had promised to marry another, and Sebastián replied that he had not made such a commitment but that, on his way to give testimony to the friars, a woman had accosted him and had told him that he owed her daughter her honor (la honra). He defended himself, saying: "He had not given her a promise of marriage. Even though he had had a friendship with Juana Rodríguez he had not found her a virgin nor had the friendship been laboring under a promise."[97]

Influenced by her parents, the fourteen-year-old Juana Rodríguez immediately filed an impediment.[98] According to Juana, Sebastián and she had often played together. But on this occasion he wanted to "enjoy her as a woman." She resisted; he said that was a signal she was not a virgin. Finally, after assuring her that he would not leave her for lost, he deflowered her. With her ear to a crack in the door, the fifteen-year-old María de las Nieves heard what transpired and testified that there was shouting and hitting. When Sebastián Luján finally left, the witness found Juana crying and wiping the blood off of herself. Juana Rodríguez also admitted that on a subsequent occasion she had spent the night with Sebastián. Although she was filing the impediment, she did not want to marry him, for she feared him. She wanted a dowry instead.

Sebastián Luján offered a different version of the events. He had had sex with her, but he did it neither with violence nor under a marriage promise. Moreover, he had found her without "the flower of her body." Regarding the testimony of the two young women who had described a rape, he replied that the mother of Juana Rodríguez was capable of influencing the witness, María de las Nieves.[99] To corroborate his account that Juana Rodríguez had not been a virgin, he named a number of witnesses who knew her character. One young soldier said he had seen Juana Rodríguez with two different men and had seen her hugging one of them. Another witness said he knew that she had an amorous relationship with Cayetano Fajardo. On different occasions he saw them "play, titillate and give each other kisses." Yet the relationship ended one night when Juana Rodríguez told Cayetano that she wanted to marry Francisco de Perea, who had promised her marriage and taken her virginity. Since that night, their relationship had been on again, off again.[100] The friar summoned Cayetano Fajardo who verified the account.

By the end of the investigation, the sexual peccadilloes of Juana Rodríguez proved too much; she did not receive even a small dowry. Her impediment collapsed, and Sebastián Luján and Juana Teresa Trujillo married on February 24, 1705. Having had sexual intercourse with at least two men and various sexual encounters with Cayetano Fajardo, all now exposed to the public, Juana Rodríguez's honor seemed damaged beyond repair.[101] Yet a mere five months later, she married the twenty-four-year-old Antonio Velázquez. Ironically, Juana de Guadalupe filed an impediment to block their marriage, claiming that Velázquez had promised her marriage and had deflowered her.[102]

There is little evidence to help illuminate why such an apparently disgraced young woman was able to find a willing husband so soon after she filed the impediment. Perhaps Juana Rodríguez was extremely beautiful and desirable. Perhaps her mother connived to find a young man who would overlook Juana's sexual indiscretions. Although Juana Rodríguez's family was not wealthy, in other situations, some young men might have been swayed to marry if the women were favorably endowed. The most likely scenario is that the community overlooked, to some extent, Juana Rodríguez's faults because she was so young and because the community and families allowed young people some latitude in the courtship process.

Evidence from other documents supports this contention. In 1750, in her last will and testament, María de la Candelaria González appointed her son executor of her estate. This was not an odd move, for many parents looked to their children to become their executors. What was anomalous, however, was that the young man did not receive any goods because he was not a legal heir. The bulk of her estate went to her two legal daughters whom she conceived with her lawfully wedded husband. This husband had been willing to marry María de la Candelaria even though she had an illegitimate son.[103]

Juana Luján also found respectability after Ventura de Esquibel left her deflowered and pregnant. When she dictated her will in 1762, she was wealthy and venerated in her community. The will reveals that the matriarch had three children out of wedlock. Yet the illegitimate status of her children did not hinder her from acquiring land and wealth, nor did it prevent her from marrying Francisco Martín.[104] She also endowed her daughter and saw that she married well. Not surprisingly, Juana Luján took the dowry of 200 pesos provided by Esquibel and used it wisely, turning herself into a wealthy woman whose estate was appraised at her death at 6,000 pesos.[105] Not lost forever, honor could be regained.

Men also assumed risks when they dallied with women with no intention of marrying them. Depending on the women with whom they became involved, the hazards varied. Men who associated with women like Juana Luján, who could defend themselves or who had parents to intercede on their behalf, incurred the most retribution. Sexual entanglements with "women of the world with children" held less danger. In the eyes of some men and, to some degree, the community, such women had little honor. Melchora Martín's father tried to hold the four fathers of his grandchildren accountable, but his efforts proved fruitless. Nonetheless, El Satebo, who dallied with a "woman of the world," believed that the payment of two black shawls to Juana Padilla was onerous. Finally, men who tried to cross a color or class barrier, perhaps risked the most.

To begin with, the church and state, in some cases, imprisoned men during the investigation. Of the fourteen cases, men suffered imprisonment in seven (in two cases, their fate remains unclear). The governor incarcerated Mariano Baca for nine months, the longest term of imprisonment, a sentence most likely imposed because Mariano Baca was a coyote. There is no question that being jailed was a distasteful experience, especially in the cold winter months. In addition, imprisonment, particularly long-term incarceration, could be financially stressful, even ruinous. In fact, Nicolás Durán y Chávez succumbed and agreed to marry Juana Montaño, asking that the marriage be celebrated as soon as possible so that he could be released from his confinement.[106]

In addition to being imprisoned, the state or church imposed fines and punishments. In some cases, the fines were hefty and possibly caused financial hardship. Nevertheless, it seems likely that the authorities recognized which men could bear the burden; men who came from families with means or had connections to the governor (like Ventura de Esquibel) might have paid more. In two cases, the presiding governors banished the men: the governor banished Blas López from Santa Fe for three years, and the governor banished the coyote Mariano Baca from Atrisco (he did not name a time period, so it was probably an open-ended banishment). Such harsh punishments forced these two men to forgo any number of relationships with friends and families. Furthermore, Blas López's inability to enter the capital city might have caused financial repercussions.

By pledging marriage and then severing their promises, men risked offending the community. Blas López sought corroboration and support from his friends but received neither, leaving him with little hope of winning his case. Perhaps Blas López's disregard and lack of respect for the community's sense of dignity (he committed sacrilege by entering the church with Gregoria under his cloak) provoked a particularly harsh sentence. The state also upheld the importance of a promise. During the investigation of the rape of Margarita García by Juan Lobato, it came to light that previously another man had promised Margarita marriage. Lieutenant Governor Bustamante y Tagle had the man arrested for breaking his word (at this time he was married to another woman). Upon releasing him, the lieutenant governor made him pay for the cost of his stay in jail and admonished him for breaking his promise, telling him to change his ways or else he would be punished again.[107]

Whether men encountered difficulties in their search for brides after these cases remains ambiguous. Some men, like Ventura de Esquibel, were already engaged to other women during the investigation and then carried through with their marriages once the friars lifted the impediments. It is likely, however, that some of the men earned bad reputations. In 1725, when Manuela de Armijo accused Juan Lobato of deflowering her after a promise of marriage, the eighteen-year-old Lobato tried to extricate himself by saying that he had promised another woman marriage. When the friar interviewed the named woman, Francisca de Silva, she denied that a promise between them existed or that she even knew Lobato.[108] Within two years both young women were married, but there is no evidence that Juan Lobato ever married.[109]

In summary, as men and women matured, the church, the state, their particular circumstances, and their families inculcated them and influenced them with ideas about their sexuality. The main thrust of the church's teachings was that all sex, both in thought and in deed, outside the marriage bed was sinful. The state reinforced these notions, helping the church with enforcement and also fully investigating complaints made to the governor. In addition, parents tried to teach their children Christian morals and customs. In the case of young women, this meant guarding their virginity and maintaining their reputation.

Although some lived by the rules and preserved their sexual purity and social reputation, many young men and women negotiated or violated these guidelines. They sought the company of other young men and women. With the assistance of their friends, they began relationships and courted. They made their own decisions about whether they would have sex and, if they chose to do so, then had to live with the consequences. The consequences of their actions varied.

In general, the community accepted the idea that young people courted and expected the men to honor their promises. Community members monitored the relationships, perhaps offering protection to young women while noting people who could not be trusted. In some cases, witnesses came forward to help the young women and confirm their stories that relationships had existed and promises had been exchanged. Because the public knew the stories behind women's lost honor, they reserved harsh judgment and allowed young women to resume their places in the community. Some of the men and women eventually found acceptable marriage partners. Others, however, overstepped the public norms, and peers and community members denied them their support.

Chapter 5

Marriage

WHEN COUPLES STEPPED before a friar to unite in holy matrimony, they participated in a ritual that had changed little over the years. Although the ritual remained static, the marital process did not. Before a man petitioned the church for a marriage license, he had already taken many steps that might have begun with courtship, led to a betrothal, and ended with a discussion of his betrothed's dowry. A common occurrence throughout the eighteenth century, the process, in many respects, remains obscured in the historical record. What role did parents play? Did children reject parents' intervention or accept it? How did young people come to select certain mates? Historians Patricia Seed and Ramón Gutiérrez—in their studies of marriages in Mexico City and New Mexico, respectively—come to different conclusions regarding parental intervention and control.[1] Seed, examining the colonial period from the fifteenth century to the early nineteenth century, finds that young people married for love in the early period but that the trend reversed itself at the end of the period with parents becoming increasingly involved in manipulating marriages. Gutiérrez, on the other hand, argues that aristocratic parents exercised greater control over marriages in the early part of the eighteenth century. By the end of the century, however, their authority lessened, and marriage for love increased. Historian Silvia Arrom discusses the failings of both theses, arguing that Gutiérrez's evidence is so scarce and anecdotal that the change remains difficult to perceive. Seed's argument loses its potency due to the discrepancy in available cases:

389 cases exist for the period 1574–1689 and forty-nine cases for 1779 to 1821 (although the population increased dramatically during the latter period). Arrom suggests searching for alternative sources to ascertain whether Seed's and Gutiérrez's theses warrant further investigation.[2]

Although data for New Mexico remain comparatively scant, a number of sources reveal that the marital process throughout the eighteenth century remained a complex affair with few trends supporting either Seed's or Gutiérrez's contentions. Actions by New Mexicans regarding the selection of spouses can be better understood on a continuum. On one end, young women and men selected their own mates, and on the other end, parents dictated who their children would marry. To control the process, parents had access to certain tools: dowry, gossip, and the ability to appeal to state and ecclesiastical authorities. Often these tools proved ineffectual, curtailing parents' ability to dictate the terms. Children, on the other hand, armed with knowledge of ecclesiastical law, could elicit the help of the church. More than likely, in most cases, the process did not involve conflict but negotiation. The dispensation cases reveal that many young people married to enhance their basic survival, an aspiration both parents and children could agree on.

The Benefits of Marriage

Those who married saw the institution as being beneficial. They automatically assumed a role of honor within the community by entering into marriage. Further, upon marrying, they entered a Christian moral order and demanded and expected respect. Historian Richard Boyer, in his studies on central Mexico during the colonial period, finds that people, from the powerful to the powerless, believed that marriage linked them to the moral economy of society.[3] Marital status was also an important dimension in people's social identity. In every marital investigation, witnesses readily identified the contrayentes' status as single, widowed, or engaged.

Most youth who married followed in their parents' footsteps. Even those raised in unsanctioned families—whether that meant being raised by a single parent or by unmarried parents—often chose to marry and, therefore, to break with the pattern set by their parents. In New Mexico, of the 1,156 men who provided information about their parents in their marital investigations, 55 men (about 5 percent) revealed that they did not know their fathers.

Of the 1,314 women, 67 claimed that they did not know their fathers (5 percent).[4] Others claimed that they were natural children and knew who both their parents were. At the time of their birth, both parents could have married. During the century, 43 men (nearly 3 percent) and 33 women (slightly more than 2 percent) identified themselves as natural children. These numbers are likely an underestimate: many contrayentes did not provide information about their parents, probably in order to hide their illegitimacy. Subterfuge is evident in many diligencias matrimoniales. Regardless, many of the younger generation chose to break the pattern of their parents who had not wedded.

By marrying, parents conferred legitimacy on their offspring. The importance of legitimacy was twofold. First, in regard to property, legitimate heirs inherited their parents' wealth. When making their wills, parents followed laws that allowed one-fifth of the estate to be given freely to anyone and the remaining four-fifths, known as the *legítima*, to be divided among the forced heirs. The legitimate children received the legítima before any other beneficiaries.[5] An illegitimate heir, no matter how beloved, could only receive a fifth of a father's or mother's estate if the parents had legitimate heirs.[6] Although many people in New Mexico owned very little property, their possessions were precious, and the importance of passing these on to children was great.

Second, legitimate children began life as honorable members of society. As set out in the *Siete Partidas*: "Honor and exceeding great advantage result to children by being legitimate, as, for this reason, they share the distinctions of their parents; and they can also receive any order or sacred office of the church, as well as other secular honors."[7] Historian Ann Twinam's work on illegitimate children who were born of the elite classes and who desired a royal grant of legitimacy attests to the fact that illegitimacy could taint a person's reputation and lead to humiliation as well as thwart professional and political aspirations.[8] A preoccupation with legitimacy did not seem to exist in New Mexico to the extent it did elsewhere in colonial Spanish America. This attitude, most likely, was the result of a less rigid caste system, a tiny elite class, a large number of illegitimate children, and the lack of professional mobility in either government or church positions. Nevertheless, an absence of evidence illustrating the importance of honor conferred upon legitimate children does not mean that it should be discounted in New

Mexico. On two separate occasions in Santa Cruz de la Cañada, mothers went to the great trouble of creating legitimate parents for their illegitimate offspring.[9] Why would these women find couples willing to pose as the legitimate parents at the baptisms if they did not believe that something symbolically important was at stake? The importance of property and being the donor or recipient of land, tools, and weapons, perhaps, is the greatest clue that legitimacy mattered to men and women when they decided whether to marry.

Another important, perhaps vital, benefit of marriage, though less visible in the documents, was the assurance of having a life-long partner to help cope with the travails and hardships of life on the frontier. Marital partners strove to survive and to raise their children amid Indian attacks, droughts, freezing winters, sickness, and other calamities. Husbands and wives shared the chores, responsibilities, and joys of life. Vicente de Armijo was fortunate in his choice of a wife. On his deathbed in November of 1743, he referred to his wife of forty years as "beloved and dear."[10] Of course, some couples experienced discord, as well, making their lives hellish.[11] Available evidence offers little insight about the feelings between couples. Nevertheless, marriage survived and flourished during the colonial period.

Although some eschewed marriage for various reasons, most adults aspired to marry. The decision to marry and whom to marry preoccupied young people and their families. The existing evidence suggests that both parents and children played an active role in the decision-making process. As with courtship, community members took a lively interest in marriages. To achieve their goals of finding suitable marriage partners, parents and their offspring fought with each other, used their property to entice marital partners, and employed gossip.

The Role of Parents and Family Members

The dispensation cases and most marital investigations hide the role that parents or family members played. Little strife was recorded most likely because in most cases children married partners of whom the parents approved or those whom the parents chose in the first place. Parents raised their children to value what they valued. Young people probably agreed with their parents that the best candidates for marriage were those who had prospects and property and who advanced their families' positions in some way. In a practice known as endogamy, people married into their own social and economic groups, rarely breaking social norms. Moreover, parents taught their offspring to disregard first and second cousins as potential mates, which resulted in a low incidence of close-cousin marriages.

In a recently formed colony, parents and their offspring might have employed marital strategies that improved their chances of economic security. To do this, they might have eschewed tactics that they would have practiced in their home city, rejecting endogamy in favor of exogamy. Many of the settlers from Mexico City, for example, came from the artisan class. Though these skills proved essential in governing and developing a frontier society, the inhabitants quickly figured out that to thrive they would have to marry outside of their group of Mexico City artisans.

An examination of the marriages of Mexico City settlers reveals that when the time came to marry, these "new" New Mexicans opted to select "old" New Mexicans as mates. Why did these colonists, who mostly settled in Santa Cruz de la Cañada, choose to marry those who had lived in New Mexico prior to the Pueblo revolt? Perhaps because the New Mexicans had land grants on which they could establish farms to sustain themselves. Also, there was little chance that the two groups shared any kinship ties. Economic opportunity, in addition to compliance to the church's marriage laws regarding consanguinity and affinity, proved to be a strategy for which many residents of Santa Cruz de la Cañada opted.

José Antonio Esquibel and John B. Colligan provide detailed genealogies of these settlers in their book *The Spanish Recolonization of New Mexico*. When it came time for the children of the original settlers to marry, the majority (74 percent) married spouses whose families originated in New Mexico. Perhaps more telling, the parents (or adult settlers) also chose to follow this strategy when they remarried (or in a couple of cases married for the first time). Miguel de la Vega y Coca married his first wife in Mexico City in order to be accepted as a colonist. This wife died sometime before May 1697 soon after arrival to New Mexico. Two years later, he elected to marry doña Maria Montoya, a native of New Mexico. The two raised eight daughters. Six daughters married into families from New Mexico. One daughter married a man born in Mexico City; the other married the Spaniard, don Bernardo de Bustamante y Tagle.[12]

As evidence elsewhere in Spanish America shows, however, some young people did choose partners deemed unsuitable by their parents and peers.[13] Although there are few prenuptial cases in New Mexico, the tensions evident in a handful of diligencias matrimoniales and broken-marriage-promise cases reveal parental involvement in all aspects of the marital process. As seen in the previous chapter, many parents allowed their children some leeway in selecting their mates and only became concerned when they feared that the desired outcome, namely marriage, would not be achieved. Yet the range of familial participation varied. Some parents selected the spouses and depended on their children's compliance. Even siblings expected a say in the matter. On the other hand, many citizens knew that they had a right to choose their own marital partners. If young people were willing to stand up for themselves, parents had little choice but to yield to their wishes.

In 1715, Sebastiana de Jesús, the sixteen-year-old daughter of unknown parents, seemed visibly reluctant to marry Gerónimo de Ortega when she went before the friar to answer questions about her upcoming nuptials. She spoke of the differences between her desires and those of her adoptive mother. When the friar asked whether she married of her own free will, she replied that, when the mother who raised her, Lucía Ortiz, first asked her about the marriage, she had said no, but she then agreed to marry so that she would not anger her mother. Her disinclination to marry increased when she heard that Gerónimo de Ortega's father was wearing the habit of mercy, a form of penance imposed by the Inquisition.[14] The friar, uneasy about the girl's responses, interviewed her a second time to determine whether she wanted to marry, and this time, she agreed. Gerónimo de Ortega and Sebastiana de Jesús became husband and wife, united in holy matrimony.[15]

This event in 1715 reveals much about parental involvement in the marriage process. The most obvious detail is that Lucía Ortiz pressured her daughter to marry against her wishes. Although Sebastiana had negative opinions about her prospective partner, she still felt a strong sense of filial duty and succumbed to her mother's mandate. At the same time, community opinion mattered to Sebastiana for her resolve wavered upon hearing about Gerónimo's father. The mother, Lucía Ortiz, on the other hand, was less concerned about the transgressions of her daughter's future father-in-law. As an adoptive mother, she did not have the same resources available to her to settle a better match. Finally, Gerónimo's father failed to intercede in the affair. As a penitent, he was in no position to dictate to his son who he should or should not marry. The bridegroom and mother-in-law were the active negotiators.

Some *diligencias matrimoniales* reveal that young couples did not always know their future spouses. In 1703, the fifteen-year-old María de Archuleta claimed she only knew her prospective husband, the eighteen-year-old Miguel de Martín, by sight.[16] Obviously, others had negotiated their marriage. The number of arranged marriages remains hard to pin down because the majority of friars did not pose a question about whether the couple knew one another. The vital questions for the friars were whether the people married of their own free will or by force. María de Archuleta agreed to the match and was not forced to marry even though she did not know Miguel de Martín. It was a valid marriage in the eyes of the friars. The friars took their cues from the prospective brides and grooms. If Sebastiana de Jesús had emphatically stated that she did not want to marry Gerónimo, the friar's response might have differed. As it was, Sebastiana's vacillation gave the friar pause, but in the end he did not deposit Sebastiana. During the second interview, her answer, that she was willing to marry, satisfied him. In 1777, when the friar asked the sixteen-year-old mestiza, Josefa Domínguez, whether she wanted to marry, she responded that she did not want to marry Antonio Martín. The *alcalde ordinario*, Lorenzo Madrid, and her mother had arranged the marriage. Josefa said, "Placed in liberty, she did not wish to marry and that she had not given a marriage promise to Antonio Martín or to any other man." The friar ceased the investigation at that point. The marriage never took place.[17]

Other children, unwilling to submit to their parents' demands, undertook subterfuge or relied on ecclesiastical law to control their own marriages. In a marital investigation conducted in 1714, Sebastián González declared that, out of fear of his father, he had run from his home to marry elsewhere.[18] In another case from 1710, José de Armijo stated to Fray Lucas Arévalo that he wanted to marry María Blásquez against her parents' wishes. He asked Fray Lucas to intervene because the parents were impeding the match. The friar complied and placed Blásquez in deposit, where she admitted that she did indeed want to marry Armijo. After a few days, when Fray Lucas allowed her to return home, she claimed that she no longer wished to marry. Armijo appealed to the friar again, arguing that by their actions Blásquez's parents were breaking tenets of the Council of Trent.[19]

Fray Lucas recognized that he lacked the knowledge concerning the particulars of the case and passed it to Ecclesiastical Judge Fray Miguel Muñoz who immediately redeposited María. While being interviewed, María said that her resolve to marry vacillated when her godmother visited; the godmother had cried that her decision to marry would be her parents' deaths. María Blásquez relented on the condition that her parents not excessively intervene in her future affairs. The parents, however, replied that they would exercise more control over her prospective marriage plans. Faced with that harsh reality, Blásquez decided that she did want to marry José Armijo after all.

When interviewed, Armijo declared that he already considered himself married since Father Arévalo had witnessed them join hands and vow to marry. The ecclesiastical judge quibbled with Armijo over this point (at that juncture the license had not been obtained) but agreed that the marriage should be celebrated. And in the end, José Armijo and María Blásquez wed, despite her parents' reservations.

The attempt by Blásquez's parents to control their daughter's marriage ended in failure. Despite her meddlesome parents' disapproval of Armijo, María Blásquez had been able to foster a relationship with him. Armijo, on the other hand, acted without his parents' guidance. Instead, the twenty-six-year-old Armijo sought support from his older brother in his bid to marry. The brother, Antonio de Armijo, had witnessed the betrothal with Father Arévalo and was able to testify to the fact. With his knowledge of ecclesiastical law, his prudence in having witnesses to his betrothal, and his perseverance in the face of Blásquez's parents' intransigence, Armijo achieved his goal—marriage to Blásquez.

Other family members joined in the marital negotiations as well. Young María de Archuleta's parents were dead at the time of her marriage in 1703. Perhaps she lived with guardians and they arranged her marriage, or maybe an older brother acted as matchmaker. The evidence suggests that siblings, like Antonio de Armijo, involved themselves as frequently as did parents. In 1702 Antonio de Esquibel confronted his brother, Ventura de Esquibel, and told him that if he married Juana Luján, he would curse him. Ventura responded that, "he did not care about his brother's curses, that his soul came first, and he did not want the devil to take it." The pressure from Antonio de Esquibel and the governor proved too much, however. Ventura de

Esquibel rejected Juana Luján and instead married Bernardina Rosa Lucero, a woman he did not know.[20]

In another case from 1707, Alonso García and María de la Rosa Manzanares of Albuquerque had been living together without the benefit of marriage and had two children together.[21] For an undisclosed reason, María de la Rosa's brother, Félix de la Candelaria, concluded that the couple ought to marry. Close to midnight, he went to the convent to tell the friar that the young couple was in his house, imploring the friar to come and witness their exchange of a vow to marry. Upon agreeing, the friar, Pedro de Mata, called for two more witnesses. When everyone reached the house, they observed the couple taking each other's hands and promising to marry.

Félix de Candelaria considered the matter urgent perhaps because, as a soldier, Alonso García's time at home was short. Moreover, the brother also might have recognized that his sister and her children, as a soldier's widow and orphans, would receive some compensation if Alonso were to die. Whatever his reasons, the brother deemed that his place was to intervene in his sister's affairs.

The Dowry and Gossip

Parents not only sought to influence their own children; they had to entice others to marry their offspring. In this effort, they used the available tools such as the dowry, paternal and maternal inheritances, and gossip. An overall strategy does not appear in the documents, however. Parents' success rate in affecting their children's marital plans hinged on numerous factors, such as their disposable wealth, the number of children they had, and their negotiating skills. Ultimately, their success depended on the cooperation of their children.

Historian Alida C. Metcalf, who studies frontier families in colonial Brazil, reveals how planter families, using the dowry, manipulated the Portuguese inheritance laws to maintain large estates of land and slaves. Since one daughter and her husband received preference, sons agreed to fend for themselves, either achieving success in the expanding frontier or becoming part of a less wealthy and less prestigious class.[22] No comparable overarching strategy existed in New Mexico. There are few surviving dotal letters revealing the negotiations between fathers and their future sons-in-law. Wills and settlements, however, provide evidence that some women did indeed bring dowries to their matrimonial homes. In an examination of 104 wills and settlements, 17 documents display evidence of dowries while 82 make no mention of dowries. In 5 wills, the testators were not married.

The dowry was a specific amount of property that a father or mother, who was able, bestowed upon a daughter when she married. In New Mexico, most dowries consisted of livestock including ewes, sheep, cows, and horses. In 1783 the widow of Sergeant don José Durán y Chávez, testified that her mother had endowed her with two pregnant cows.[23] In addition to livestock, dowries included land, household furniture, and servants. When Miguel de Archibeque wrote his will in 1727, he noted that his in-laws had endowed his wife with twenty cows, a team of oxen, a plowshare, and an Apache woman.[24] In his 1768 will, Ramón García revealed that his wife had brought to their marriage 250 ewes and shares in two ranches.[25]

Although the husband administered the dowry, it remained the woman's property and could not be alienated without her permission. Ramón García sold the shares in the two ranches, keeping a record of the money he received. On December 4, 1733, in the village of San Felipe de Albuquerque, the soldier, Lorenzo Griego, sold a piece of land he had acquired as a dowry from his wife Casilda Jaramillo, who had placed the land at his disposal.[26] If the marriage ended, the husband had to return its value to the woman. The husband also had to identify the property in his will, and it was to be passed on to the woman's heirs or to be returned to her parents. In one case from New Mexico, the husband held on to the dowry, using the property to help raise his children.[27] To protect the dowry, the husband had to pledge his own property and could not alienate, gamble with, or dispose of the dowry, accepting legal responsibility if he did so.[28]

Ideally, the dowry's function was twofold: a pecuniary beginning for the couple and financial security for the widow. For many newly married couples, the dowry afforded the means of setting up a household. Nicolás Ortiz, writing his will in 1742, said that he had begun his married life with no property of his own. All he had earned was through his labor. Upon marrying, Ortiz and his wife had a place to reside, however, because she brought a house and cultivable lands as her dowry.[29] Undoubtedly, this dowry yielded a nest egg that helped to support them and, later, their three children. When the invalid soldier, José Antonio Griego, wrote his will in 1785, he remembered that he had been extremely poor. His wife, though, had brought three hundred ewes to their marriage as a dowry. The couple went on to have fifteen children. In this case as well, the dowry had provided the young couple with enough property to begin their wedded life.[30] In another situation, Francisco de Silva never received the dowry promised by his father-in-law, Nicolás Durán y Chávez. Silva complained that he had counted on that contribution so that he could feed his family.[31] Often petitioners exaggerated their situation to make government officials more receptive to their pleas. If Silva spoke in earnest, however, it seems likely that he would have waited to marry until he was better able to care for a family.

The dowry also gave a woman the means of supporting herself in case of widowhood. If a husband died or went bankrupt, the law protected the wife's dowry, placing her property beyond the reach of the husband's creditors.[32] For this reason, husbands whose wives had received dowries elaborated on them in their wills. And in the settlement cases from New Mexico, the state officials tried to ascertain whether the widows in question had brought dowries to their marriages.

With these financial benefits, a dowry was a potential incentive used strategically by parents to secure an acceptable marriage for their offspring. Unfortunately, diligencias matrimoniales provide limited information on this practice. When Miguel de Arichibeque married in 1716, his wife brought a dowry to their marriage. Did this dowry affect the marital negotiations? Did the parents offer the dowry to Miguel de Arichibeque as a way of cementing close family ties, or did they offer it to protect their daughter from future poverty? At the time Arichibeque married, his mother was dead and he was one of two legitimate heirs to his father's property. In other words, he had some property and might receive more. It is difficult to gauge the importance of the dowry in the marital negotiations without knowing the exact worth of the husband's and parents' properties.

Methods of endowing daughters by New Mexican parents differed from parental use of the dowry elsewhere in Latin America. In contrast to the practice in colonial Brazil, New Mexican parents tried to endow all daughters as best they could, not favoring one over another. If parents had promoted one child's material fortune over another's, the costs to the favored child—resentment and alienation—might have been too high. On a frontier where people depended on their kin's help, promoting harmony among siblings proved a valuable strategy. In a suit filed in 1736, Jacinto Sánchez, married to the legitimate daughter of don Pedro Chávez and doña Juana Montoya, complained that his wife had yet to receive her dowry. He cited the law, canonical and derived, that all parents must endow their children. Sánchez knew that don Pedro Chávez had amply provided dowries to his other three married daughters and that his wife had been shortchanged. Shortly thereafter, don Pedro Chávez died and his estate was divided, revealing that all four daughters, once Sánchez's wife received her full share, had been endowed equally.[33] There could be little finagling of the law when so many members of the community were cognizant of the law—that all legitimate children should receive their equal share—and, moreover, knew the details of the dowries and how much each daughter had received.

Yet the division of Chávez's estate also shows that parents' best intentions could often be thwarted by circumstances beyond their control. Don Pedro Chávez, as a young man, had prospered. He was a militia captain, and, when he married, his young wife brought an Indian woman as a dowry. With this Indian woman's help, the young couple increased their animal holdings. By the time doña Juana died, they had at least 350 cattle and about 1,000 sheep.[34] With this wealth, don Pedro was able to endow his daughters. After his first wife's death, don Pedro married Gertrudis Sánchez who brought neither wealth nor a dowry.[35] It was at this point that his misfortunes began. He became mentally unstable and an unreliable breadwinner. As a result of these ill-fated events, Chávez's prosperity eroded. For this reason, his daughter, Jacinto Sánchez's wife, had not received the full amount of her dowry. Don Pedro and Gertrudis had four children, and three were living when he died. It is likely that the children from Chávez's second marriage never received dowries, as did their half-sisters.

Perhaps, fathers negotiated dowries with young men, fully knowing that they could not deliver the promised goods. Or perhaps fathers gave their word and then discovered that it was too great a burden to relinquish the pledged amount. To Francisco de Silva's complaints about the absence of the promised dowry, his father-in-law, Nicolás Durán y Chávez, responded that he was still alive and had unemancipated children.[36] He was loath to part with the sheep that he used to feed his family.

Moreover, parents not only endowed daughters; they also gave their sons property when they became emancipated or married. Ramón Gutiérrez states that this property, known as the patrimony, "was the material resource a father had to apportion among his children at strategic moments to maximize their reproductive success."[37] He argues that aristocrats favored the eldest son at the time of his marriage, giving him a disproportionate amount of premortem parental property. In this way, the family could attract a suitable wife who would maintain or enhance the family's public rating. Furthermore, the family property would remain largely intact. There is little evidence in the New Mexican archives to support this claim, however.

Doña María de Cabrera did not favor an elder son over her other children. On April 2, 1712, the widowed mother and her son-in-law went before officials to partition some of her lands. Upon her daughter's marriage, Cabrera decided to give her daughter a dowry, declaring that she was legitimately entitled to certain lands. The mother, after estimating her property, divided the lands in equal parts among the seven children and gave her daughter a parcel of land as her dowry.[38] In another example in 1783, don José Durán y Chávez's mother gave property to all her children when they married, not favoring one child over another. Don José's widow testified that upon giving them fifty sheep, the mother also gave her other heirs an equal share.[39]

Captain Andrés Montoya, legitimate son of Captain Antonio Montoya and doña Manuela Hurtado, wrote his will in 1740.[40] He indicated that he had already granted some farmland in La Cieneguilla to his sons and sons-in-law. He wanted some land to be set aside for his unmarried children. He stipulated that the land should be comparable in quality to the parcels he had given to his other children (it must possess the same goodness and quality, "*bondad y calidad*"). If it were of a lesser value, he wrote, then more land should be assigned to them. In his will, Captain Montoya did favor one son, Francisco, who had sold the land his father had given him at the time of his marriage. He bestowed on this son another piece of land, saying it came from part of his fifth. Assignment of the fifth, however, does not signal a patrimony in which one son received favored treatment to enhance family honor. Montoya explained in his will that Francisco had no land to farm. Francisco was likely struggling to feed his family, and the father sought to ease his son's suffering. If anything, Montoya strove to treat his children equally, bequeathing land equally to each of them to the best of his ability.[41]

When Juana Luján dictated her last will and testament in March 1762, she included a document recording the dowry that she had given to her daughter, Luisa, in 1721. Luisa's husband, Juan Esteban García de Noriega, received goods valued at the large sum of 2,500 pesos. The generous dowry included lands and a rancho in Santa Cruz de la Cañada, 200 pesos in coin, over 200 domesticated animals, and over 150 household items including jewelry, clothing, and furniture.[42] Luisa's brothers, on the other hand, received very little while their mother was still alive. Juana gave her son, Juan, goods valued at 351 pesos. When her son Francisco married, she had given him goods worth 587 pesos. The official inventory of Juana's estate found that each heir was to receive 1,880 pesos. Luisa's dowry, however, exceeded her legitimate portion by 620 pesos. To ensure equity in the inheritance, the state required Luisa to relinquish some goods to her mother's other heirs.

Unmistakably, Juana favored her daughter by granting her such a large dowry and giving her sons relatively less property (although still a generous amount compared to what others received at the time). Not only did the daughter get so much more wealth, but she and her husband had over forty years to enjoy the benefits of the dowry. It is not surprising to discover that Juana Luján granted her daughter such a large dowry to secure a suitable marriage. After Ventura de Esquibel treated her so poorly, she wanted to ensure that her daughter suffered no such disgrace. Bestowing such a large sum also points out that the landed and prosperous used their wealth as they saw fit.

The well-to-do don José Maldonado, for example, stated in his testament that he had given what he could at the time of his children's marriages.[43] When his son Gaspar married, don José granted him thirty-seven pesos. Upon her marriage, the daughter, Francisca Antonia, received seventy-two pesos and the son, José Miguel, accepted eighty-five pesos from his father. The differences in these sums seem to reflect José Maldonado's varying fortunes over the course of his life. At the end of his life, he wanted to make certain that each child shared in his estate equally. He thus provided the records of the gifts his married children had received, guaranteeing that these amounts would be subtracted from their inheritances. When he mentioned that he wanted some of his land divided amongst his heirs, he expressed his desire that Antonio, a minor, should be apportioned the best land since he had not favored Antonio with any gifts during his lifetime. The historical record reveals no discernible pattern of the wealthy giving patrimonies to benefit the eldest male heir over the other heirs. Instead the record shows that most parents wanted all of their heirs to gain from their material fortunes and strove to fulfill the letter and the spirit of the inheritance laws.

The promise of a dowry or gift did not always entice the chosen mates to comply with an arranged marriage. Men did not always take the dowry into consideration when they married. Nicolás Durán y Chávez's will, written in 1768, reveals that his wife, Juana Montaña, did bring a dowry to their marriage.[44] The dowry, consisting of twenty-five head of livestock, did nothing to tempt Durán y Chávez to marry, however. He and Juana had had a relationship for seven years before he agreed to marry her, and then only because he was imprisoned and wanted to get out of jail.[45] Of course, Nicolás might have been waiting to marry a woman with a larger dowry, but at the time of his trial, he was involved with no other women.

Another case also discloses that a man's decision to marry did not always rest on material goods. When the Sergeant don José Durán y Chávez died in March of 1783, a question arose about the dowries his two wives had brought to their respective marriages. The point was an important one, and Governor Juan Bautista Anza wanted proof about the dowries.[46] In the inquiries carried out by the alcalde mayor of Bernalillo, it came to light that the first wife, María Antonia, had not brought a dowry, for she was destitute. In fact, Durán y Chávez's mother, Gertrudis Sánchez, claimed that her daughter-in-law had been a poor girl of unknown parentage.[47] Another witness called her an Indian servant.[48] And one more testified that all she had when she married was a skirt, a shirt, a grinding stone, and a little locket that she wore.[49] When María Antonia died after three or four years of marriage and after bearing two sons, don José Durán y Chávez married the legitimate and endowed Elena Gurulé.

Surprisingly, Elena Gurulé's parents had raised both Elena and the deceased wife, María Antonia. Why did don José choose an illegitimate servant as his wife instead of an endowed, legitimate daughter? At the time of his first marriage, he was a poor man, bringing nothing but the "cloak on his shoulder."[50] Elena Gurulé's dowry, amounting to 231 pesos, would have been a welcome income to one so humble. When he married the second time, don José's mother gave him fifty head of sheep. Whereas when her son had married initially, she had given María Antonia some cloth, stockings, and some shoes.⁵¹ Perhaps Gertrudis Sánchez had more readily approved of the second marriage and had willingly given her son goods that would help him and his second wife establish themselves. It is more likely, however, that Gertrudis Sánchez gave her son his patrimony when she was able. Nevertheless, don José Durán y Chávez, who rose to some prominence during his lifetime and accumulated wealth amounting to over 2,000 pesos,⁵² chose initially to marry an unendowed servant when he might have been able to marry Elena Gurulé.

A man could also give his bride a gift, known as the arras, which, like the dowry, would belong to her and also be protected from his creditors upon his death. The husband, however, could not allocate more than 10 percent of his property to arras. This restriction existed to guard the property of the children, as in the case of a widower seeking remarriage.⁵³ There is little if any evidence of New Mexican men giving arras to their brides, however.⁵⁴

Parents with little property to bequeath had other tools at their disposal. At times, they used gossip to draw others into their schemes. In 1736, when Inés Griega and Marcial Martínez became involved with one another, Inés's mother, Antonia Maese hoped that the two would marry.⁵⁵ To achieve this end, Antonia Maese began spreading the word that Marcial had promised to marry her daughter. Marcial tried to extricate himself from the relationship, claiming Antonia Maese could not have said that they were engaged because he was closely related to her daughter. Perhaps Antonia Maese had hoped for a dispensation. Despite her efforts, Marcial Martín did not want to marry her daughter.

A case from 1705 also highlights the weaknesses of parents in negotiating marriages for their children. Newly arrived to the Kingdom of New Mexico, Sebastián Luján sought to begin his new life with a bride by his side. He asked Juana de Valencia for her daughter's hand in marriage. Juana de Valencia jumped at the chance, but unfortunately for her, she could not find a sheet of paper so that they could draw up a contract. Sebastián Luján, who considered himself too poor to marry immediately, insisted on waiting for the governor's arrival. He believed that they could delay drafting the contract. Juana de Valencia agreed, seeing how poorly clothed he was. To seal their agreement, she gave him a bison hide with which to cover himself.⁵⁶

Sebastián Luján did not recognize the hide as a token, however, and began to look elsewhere for a wife. He had sexual relations with Juana de Valencia's daughter after a promise to marry her, but, once he had learned more about Juana Valencia and her family, he considered the agreement null and void. He claimed that he was "blind, without experience" when he arrived, and now that he had more knowledge of the situation he believed himself to be free to marry another.[57] He asked Juana Teresa Trujillo to marry him instead.

When Juana de Valencia heard the rumor that Luján was to marry someone else, she quickly tried to salvage her unraveling plans by having her daughter claim an impediment to his marriage, by filing a civil and criminal complaint with the alcalde mayor, and by resorting to malicious gossip. The mother and her son accosted Juana Teresa Trujillo on her way home. Juana de Valencia asked the young woman whether she planned to marry Sebastián Luján. She responded that she did not. Juana de Valencia said that this decision was good because he was not her equal in quality (calidad). Although his father was a Spaniard, his mother was a poor castiza, daughter of a coyote from Zuni. She also said that Sebastián Luján was "tied" and that she had already paid him a hide.[58] The mother hoped that by her intercession, Juana Teresa would opt not to marry him, leaving the young, low-quality man to her daughter.

Yet events proved to be beyond the mother's control as Sebastián Luján and Juana Teresa had already engaged in carnal relations. Juana Teresa begged the ecclesiastical judge to require that Sebastián Luján fulfill his word to her or else she would lose her honor, which Sebastián owed her, as well as her good standing, good reputation and good name ("*su honra lo que le deve dicho Sebastián Luján sino, el crédito, buena fama, y buena reputación*").[59] Moreover, witnesses proved that Sebastián Luján had reason to renege on his agreement with Juana de Valencia. Her daughter had had various other amorous encounters as confirmed by her male partners. The weakest aspect of the mother's attempt to resurrect her daughter's marriage plan was inattentiveness to her daughter's wishes: her daughter did not want to marry Sebastián Luján. When interviewed after she placed the impediment, the daughter said that she would rather receive money than marry Sebastián Luján for she feared him.[60]

Community members also played a part in these prenuptial dramas. Neighbors and kin, by listening to and circulating gossip, had an impact on whether a marriage would take place. Mothers who used hearsay to affect a match obviously thought it was a potent tool. In the cases available, the mothers' efforts failed, revealing that gossip cut both ways. Although spreading stories was an effective tool in some cases, it was not fail-safe.

Neighbors were not only recipients of gossip; they participated fully in other points of the process. As previously seen, the church and state depended on community members as witnesses in marriage investigations and dispensation cases. Some community members engaged more fully, coming forward of their own volition to "relieve their consciences" by informing the friars that they knew of impediments that blocked a marriage. In 1729 during the marital investigation of María Gerónima Montaño and widower José Antonio Rodríguez, a witness came forward to relieve his conscience saying that María Gerónima was the granddaughter of José Antonio's first cousin. The witness's information proved erroneous yet it held up the marriage for a year. When José Antonio reapplied for a license, he explained that he and María Gerónima were related by fourth-degree affinity, not consanguinity. They received permission to marry.[61]

Kissing Cousins: Marriage Strategies in the Dispensation Records

In the year 1788, a nineteen-year-old soldier, Mateo García de Noriega, applied to the Catholic Church for a dispensation to marry the twenty-seven-year-old widow, Catalina Aranda Tafoya. The need for a dispensation arose due to the fact that they were blood relatives. Initially unaware of their kin ties, they promised to marry and subsequently began a sexual relationship. When Father Muñoz Jurado of the Santa Clara Mission questioned Catalina, she admitted that they had engaged in sexual relations from July 1786 until about the beginning of February 1787. The couple saw marriage as a means to ending their sinful behavior. Catalina spoke to her mother of her "carnal sins and shame," while Mateo considered marriage an atonement. On January 25, 1788, close to two years after Mateo and Catalina's relationship began, Bishop Tristán granted the couple a dispensation.[62]

Although the diligencias matrimoniales are rich in detail, they provide few clues as to why people chose particular partners. During dispensation cases, on the other hand, friars questioned the couple about why they wanted a dispensation. Mateo and Catalina's case is typical. Love, desire, and sin often led cousins to the altar. Most men stated that they wanted to rescue their cousins from a life of poverty. Others cited *igualdad* (equality) as a reason for marrying cousins. Suppositions about the word *igualdad* often lead to the conclusion that cousins marrying cousins was a strategy that families employed to maintain and to enhance their honor, social status, blood purity, and privileged economic positions.[63] Instead of an overarching plan of familial aggrandizement, however, evidence from dispensations granted to northern New Mexicans between 1694 and 1800 suggests that individuals and their families carried out marriages to enhance their survival, to fulfill their desires, and to uphold their own ideas of honor.

If the marital strategies of a family involved marrying cousins, the ecclesiastical authorities restricted their choices by enforcing rules limiting marriage between those related by spiritual ties or marriage (affinity) or those related by blood (consanguinity). The church even limited marriage between distant cousins, those related by fourth-degree consanguinity. Cousins who wished to marry needed permission from the church. During a marital investigation, the friars asked the prospective groom and bride whether they knew of any impediments that prevented them from marrying. At this point, the groom revealed whether he had blood or spiritual ties with his wife-to-be. If they were related, the groom requested a dispensation. In almost all cases, friars or their superiors in the church hierarchy granted the couples permission to marry, revealing that the church's representatives wanted to facilitate these marriages.[64]

Cousin marriage did occur in eighteenth-century New Mexico, but those cousins who did marry did not have the same grandparents or great-grandparents. There are 1,496 extant marital investigations, of which only 108 marriages involved cousins related by third, third and fourth, or fourth degrees of consanguinity (approximately 7 percent). Twenty-two marriages occurred between those related by affinity. In 28 cases, the couples or friars did not mention the couples' kin ties.

The vast majority of New Mexicans who married chose mates who were not closely related (second degree of consanguinity). Undoubtedly, extended families got together in times of celebration, throwing young cousins together and providing an opportunity to meet young people of the opposite sex. In spite of these circumstances, few close cousins actually married. Instead, they practiced self-regulation, fully aware that first, second, and even third cousins were off-limits. In one case in 1705, Antonio Sambrano petitioned to marry. During the course of the marital investigation, a witness testified that Sambrano was engaged to a woman in Bernalillo. Sambrano, denying he was engaged, explained that "he had not given a promise and that it is true that carried by his fragility he had liked her not knowing they were related. And when he found out that they were, he took measures to separate himself. And this is the truth."[65]

Antonio Sambrano was not the only young man who found himself falling in love with someone who turned out to be a relative. Catalina and Mateo of the capacious cloak also began their relationship unaware that they shared ancestral ties. Of the sixty-nine explanations given in the dispensation cases, six men claimed that they had been ignorant of the kinship when their relationships began. Oftentimes, family associations eroded, leaving the connection a distant memory. In other cases, couples remained unsure about whether they were related due to the often-complicated familial ties resulting from adoption or adultery. Friars often turned to the elderly members of the community, the *ancianos*, for explanations of events that occurred years earlier.

In the year 1779, José Manuel Silva and María Josefa Silveria Sánchez did not know that they shared family connections. Witnesses came forward to dredge up the sexual peccadilloes of a previous generation. In the year 1714, when Nicolás Durán y Chávez married Juana Montaño under the threat of imprisonment for breaking a marriage promise, he claimed that only one of Juana Montaño's children was his own. According to Nicolás Chávez's son, Fernando, his father persisted with this story, telling his son: "Gertrudis and Nicolás, your brother and sister, are not my children. When I married your mother, she already had those two." Gertrudis, José's grandmother, was the supposed ancestral link between José and María. If, as Nicolás Durán y Chávez alleged, she were not his daughter, the couple was not related. However, other witnesses remembered differently, leaving in doubt about whether they were related. In the end, the couple received the required dispensation.[66]

In some cases, people opined that they had limited choices of marriage partners because of the isolated and sparsely populated area in which they lived. When explaining their reasons for choosing cousins, young men bemoaned the fact that they shared common ancestry with almost everybody in the vicinity. Often they cited the Latin term, *angustia loci*, meaning "restricted place." The friars recognized this as a legitimate reason for granting dispensations. In 1796, when Friar Rosete forwarded to Durango the dispensation proceedings of José de Jesús Montoya and Rosa Archuleta, he confirmed that the couple was related to almost all the families of the province in the fourth degree.[67]

Even though friars permitted lack of awareness and angustia loci as justifiable reasons for granting dispensations, the cousins who insisted on marrying, despite its unlawfulness and the necessity for dispensations, acted out of the ordinary. Their behavior implies that they had ulterior motives for marrying, but in fact their motives were often mundane and practical. Of the explanations given, the overwhelming reason for marriage with a cousin was the woman's poverty. Poor women and their families recognized that marriage was a better option than remaining with destitute parents who often had other children. They welcomed proposals from cousins as well as from other men who could afford to marry. In 1762, Urgencio de Jesús Savedra wanted to marry Juana María García Jurado, who was related to him by third-degree consanguinity. As he put it, "being a poor orphan of solemnity and having given her a promise to marry, I ask and entreat you to dispense this impediment."[68] Sixteen-year-old Tomasa Trujillo wished to marry even though she was related to Vicente Romero. She stated that "she wished to live under his protection, with his assistance, subject to his dominion, and because her parents were poor and elderly."[69]

Men who offered marriage to indigent women could not have expected to benefit financially. Marriage with poor women meant that they were starting their lives together without the aid of a dowry. It is unlikely that the sole incentive to propose was poverty. Men perceived that mention of the women's poverty might influence the outcome of their petitions. It follows that men had other inducements as well when they proposed marriage.

One reason men, and women for that matter, married was because they fell in love. After an offer of marriage, couples often engaged in sex. Some of the cousins who sought dispensations saw marriage as a way to avoid embroiling themselves and their families in scandals, and more important, perhaps, as a means to legitimize their offspring. In 1707, nineteen-year-old Luis de Chávez applied for a dispensation, aware that he was related to fourteen-year-old doña Leonor Montaño. He admitted to having had sex with her because he was "fragile and miserable." With understatement, he noted that, if they did not marry, it would lead to notable scandal and inconveniences. They received a dispensation and married.[70] In another case in 1796, Domingo Sánchez acknowledged that he knew he was related to María Guadalupe Baca but was ignorant as to the degree. He said that he had been in love with only her since 1793 and that he had deprived her of her virginity. Their friar, José Cayetano Bernal, forwarded the information to Durango, noting the scandal and angustia loci. The bishop, Francisco Gabriel de Olivares, granted the dispensation.[71]

Nevertheless, the friars frowned on those who used sexual relations as a means to achieve their goals in the dispensation process. José Manuel Silva took matters into his own hands in an attempt to marry his cousin, María Josefa Silveria Sánchez. Under a promise to marry, the couple engaged in sexual relations. Each hoped to achieve something by the act. The young woman believed that Silva would marry her if they had sex. Silva assumed that her pregnancy would help them secure the required dispensation. He did not know that his strategy only angered the church officials.[72] In another case from 1779, Miguel Hermenegildo Baca, aged thirty-three, requested a dispensation because he was related by fourth-degree consanguinity to María de los Reyes Padilla, aged twenty-one. Miguel confessed that he had had sexual relations with María on various occasions, resulting in her pregnancy. He assured the friar that they did not engage in sexual relations to facilitate the dispensation process. Instead, his weakness and his hope of marrying her had compelled him. María de los Reyes admitted that she loved him. She did not wish to lose her honor and she feared that her father would punish her.[73] Whether sex was used as a tool may be beside the point. In the end, the friars and their superiors granted dispensations to those who had engaged in sex.

Love and desire, therefore, played a role in many of the cousin marriages. Other cousins married for practical reasons. Widows and widowers, for example, found that they needed help to raise their respective families and some found spouses among their cousins. Of the 158 marriages between relatives, twenty-seven widowers (17 percent) and eighteen widows (11 percent) sought dispensations. This generally reflects the population in which 18 percent and 11 percent of the petitions to marry were filed by widowers and widows, respectively. In 1761, Salvador García, who was related to doña Margarita Durán y Chávez by ties of fourth-degree consanguinity and affinity, begged for a dispensation. He stated that he had small children and his intended had four children, as well. He promised to love doña Margarita's children, and she vowed to love his children.[74] Salvador García believed that the children would be better off with two parents. By mentioning the children, he revealed a valid reason for cousins, and widows and widowers for that matter, to marry. They received their dispensation.

In some cases, the petitioners provided several reasons why they wished to marry a relative. In 1779, in his petition for a dispensation, the widower, Antonio José Romero, stated that his intended, the widow María Baca, was poor, pregnant, and thirty years old, an age that severely limited her marriage opportunities. And separated from her relatives, she lacked the means to support herself.[75] As in many cases, Romero's plea for marriage did not represent a well-devised plan, but a stop-gap measure to prevent scandal and poverty.

Yet some men, and perhaps their families, seemed to have had more carefully planned strategies. Out of the sixty-nine reasons given, nineteen men cited igualdad as a reason they wished to marry their cousins. Did igualdad reflect a familial tactic, a concerted effort by the couple and their respective families to maintain racial purity, family honor, status, and wealth? Were these cousins part of the elite intent on maintaining their privileged positions? In colonial Latin America, igualdad signified certain qualities such as legitimacy, honor, wealth, property, and power. From the evidence available, however, many who claimed to want igualdad in their marriages did not possess the symbols and trappings of the elite. New Mexicans, depending on a number of factors, interpreted quality on many levels. The term pops up over the course of the century and more often in the last thirty years of the eighteenth century. Even within this thirty-year period, economic changes, in addition to other historical influences such as war, might have shifted the meaning of the word.

When men mentioned igualdad as a reason for wishing to marry a cousin, they often cited other reasons as well. Of the nineteen petitioners who stated igualdad as an explanation for choosing their female cousins, eleven men elaborated and provided additional reasons. Five said that they wished to marry their cousins because of igualdad and poverty. In 1716, Juan Antonio Baca proposed marriage to his cousin, doña María Gallegos. In his petition, he declared that his cousin was a poor orphan and that the entire jurisdiction offered no others who were his equal: "My only desire is to protect this virtuous maiden."[76] Fifty-four years later, in 1770, Juan Antonio Baca, related to doña Bárbara Montoya, asked for a dispensation. He complained that this kingdom held no women with quality of blood. He also presented the fact that doña Bárbara was a poor, abandoned orphan whom he hoped to protect by marrying.[77] In these cases, men worried more about making a match with someone whom they recognized as their equals or perhaps their betters than about the women's poverty. (In the two cases above, the men gave the women the title of doña whereas they did not identify themselves as dons.[78]) In other words, igualdad expressed family honor through blood and not through wealth. The women, on the other hand, might have believed differently. Subsistence and protection might have outweighed the importance of quality.

The idea that families hoped to maintain the quality of the bloodline by marrying distant cousins remains fraught with difficulties. In New Mexico persons of different races had mixed and mingled over the century. In such a small community, most people knew each other's family trees. Those who identified themselves as españoles and dons, therefore, did not try to hide their Indian or mulatto blood and claim limpieza de sangre (purity of blood). In 1768, Ignacio Chávez, español, the legitimate son of don Francisco Durán y Chávez and of doña Juana Baca, wished to marry doña Úrsula Bernardina Sánchez, española, legitimate daughter of don Jacinto Sánchez and doña Efigenia Durán y Chávez. The two shared common ancestry, related by second-degree consanguinity. Ignacio Chávez, for whatever reason, did not want to pay the fine of six pesos and ten reales as penance for having his marriage dispensed. Well informed about ecclesiastical law, Ignacio Chávez reapplied, arguing that their case should be considered in light of the Papal Bull of Gregory XIII, which allowed Indians related by consanguinity to marry. Chávez explained that his grandmother, Juana Baca, received Indian blood from her father and mulatto blood from her mother. Chávez expounded that Indian and mulatto blood also ran through the veins of Úrsula Sánchez, her grandfather being Indian and her grandmother being both Indian and mulatta. Unfortunately for Chávez, the friar did not agree with his argument, concluding that the applicants were only part Indian. Nonetheless, the couple received a dispensation from don Francisco Gabriel de Olivares, who cited angustia loci and the poverty of the applicants. In the end, Chávez had to pay the fine.[79]

Typically, a person of honor was someone who was legitimate, born to married parents. In general, illegitimate children did not inherit from their parents as did their legitimate siblings. Failure to inherit land or material goods put illegitimate youth at a disadvantage when they attempted to marry. To Francisco Durán y Chávez, however, this consideration was of little importance. In 1713, he sought a dispensation to marry doña Juana Baca who was born of unknown parents. He argued that he was moved by his will to serve God and to protect the poor maiden. He feared that her poverty made her vulnerable to losing herself and to marrying someone beneath her (*con desigual suyo*). Five years later, Antonio de Chávez, brother to Francisco, sought a dispensation to marry Juana Baca's sister, doña Antonia Baca (also illegitimate). Antonio feared that if he did not marry her she would disgrace herself in marriage. He also added, "I declare that I am moved by no other thing than charity to protect this poor one and for the great affection I have for her." Francisco Durán y Chávez and his brother measured igualdad on different terms than their contemporaries in Mexico City. Moreover, they were moved by more than one reason when they sought the hands of the Baca sisters.

In seven of the igualdad cases, the men also mentioned angustia loci as a reason for marrying a cousin. If all their neighbors shared common ancestors, one could argue that they were all of the same quality. Just because people were distantly related, however, did not mean that families believed all branches of the family tree were worthy. Depending on how the subjects defined igualdad, a number of different causes, such as marriage to Native Americans, illegitimacy, or infidelity, could have caused the demise of a branch. In one case from 1785, a father emphatically opposed a marriage between his son and a cousin related by third-degree consanguinity. He willingly impugned the honor of his distant relations because he did not approve of his son's choice. The cousin in question, María del Rosario Martín, sent a plea to the friar, Santiago Fernández de Sierra, complaining that Mariano Sánchez had given her a promise to marry. Under the vow, they had had carnal copulation, resulting in her pregnancy. Martín claimed that, in a similar situation, Sánchez's father had impeded another son's marriage. She feared that she too would be left to suffer. When the friar interviewed Mariano Sánchez, he admitted that he owed María del Rosario Martín her honor and that he wanted to fulfill his promise. They received their dispensation and married, the father's plans for his son thus stymied.[80]

In the end, cousin marriages illuminate the numerous strategies individuals and families used to fulfill their goals. What they hoped to achieve in marriage differed remarkably. Even when men cited igualdad as a reason to marry cousins, they interpreted the meaning of the word in many ways. These dispensations reveal that parents did not always have goals to increase familial wealth and honor, nor were they always intent on completely controlling the process. Even when they wished to intervene, they did not always achieve success. Their tools could prove ineffectual, at times. Young people also willingly involved themselves and fought when they thought necessary. The variety of sources available show that the selection of spouses cannot be viewed as a linear process that changed in a single direction over time.

Chapter 6

Domestic Life and Discord

IN FEBRUARY 1704, Ana Bernal, separated from her husband and unable to reconcile with him, sought the intervention of the church. She hired a lawyer (procurador) who presented her suit to the ecclesiastical judge, Juan Álvarez.[1] The judge interviewed the estranged husband, Luis López, who agreed to resume his married life (*vida maridable*) with her. He promised, "to love her as God commands, to assist her to the best of his ability, to treat her well in deed and in word, and to view her with the love required of the matrimonial state."[2] In the end it came down to this: López vowed that he would find land where they could live apart from her relatives.

Luis López cited living near his wife's family as the reason behind the estrangement with his wife, Ana Bernal. To avoid residing near his in-laws, he had abandoned his wife thus breaching one of the most important tenets of the vida maridable—the conjugal household. Both civil and ecclesiastical authorities expected couples to reside together and to set up households separate from the parents. Indeed, Juan Páez Hurtado actually threatened López with penal servitude in the Philippines if he did not comply with the order for them to reunite. The conjugal household constituted the foundation of a marriage.

The available evidence suggests that couples accepted land from whomever offered it belying the idea that only husbands' families provided land when partners married.[3] The separation of López and Bernal indicates that a household's location could have a negative impact on family life. The opposite held true as well; families that resided closely turned to one another for support and love. Yet, in cases of marital abuse, a woman's chances of survival increased when the couple lived near her relatives.

Household Patterns, Nuclear Families

In general, a historical consensus portrays Mexican rural families as extended and urban families as nuclear.[4] Alicia V. Tjarks likens the "broad or composite" family groups of New Mexico to the social structure of the haciendas of northern New Spain.[5] In "broad or composite" families, perhaps, the grandparents, adult children, and grandchildren all occupied a large estate. However, in most cases in the three villas of Santa Fe, Santa Cruz de la Cañada, and Albuquerque, married people established their own homes and lived as nuclear families. Families, in general, began as the conjugal pair and the offspring living together under one roof. Over the course of married people's lives together, relatives, due to a number of various circumstances, moved in with nuclear families and/or moved out, creating complex families whose composition changed over time, expanding and contracting. *Household*, a more inclusive term, includes family members, their servants, and others. Household members also changed over time. During the eighteenth century, when few social institutions existed, the state and the Catholic Church expected families to take on certain responsibilities. A household, therefore, often expanded and included dependents or citizens who became temporary household members. For instance, both ecclesiastical and civil officials incarcerated male prisoners in a cell in the presidio, but no such place existed for female offenders. Instead the officials turned to families and asked them to accept the women into their homes. In 1719, the alcalde mayor (local magistrate) of Santa Fe placed Catalina de Villalpando, accused of hitting a boy over the head with a rock, in the house of the soldier Ventura de Esquibel.[6] For the duration of the investigation, Esquibel's household size was increased by one.

Though the full extent of variations of household and family expansion and contraction might be hidden, the best source for reconstructing household patterns in eighteenth-century New Mexico remains the 1790 census. Viceroy Conde de Revillagigedo II ordered the census to be taken to determine who constituted the population of the vast colony. He sent instructions to New Mexican Governor Fernando de la Concha who in turn circulated them to the alcaldes mayores and the friars who were to carry out the local censuses.[7] Census takers went from house to house and named the head of the household and his family. Among the three villas the enumerators counted 561 households in Santa Fe, 497 in Santa Cruz de la Cañada, and 248 in Albuquerque. Most people lived in households that contained both a husband and wife. Widows and widowers headed the next largest groups of households, with more widows as household heads than widowers (see table 4). Rather than living alone, most single men and women resided with kin. Nevertheless, they did not represent a large proportion of the population. Adults, in most cases, married and established households with their spouses.[8]

By examining the dual-headed households, a pattern can be observed that illuminates household composition relative to the life cycle of men and women in New Mexico. A life cycle begins with birth and then passes through childhood on the journey to life as an adult. Men, for example, assumed many roles during a life cycle: son, brother, cousin, betrothed, husband, father, uncle, and grandfather. In New Mexico, women entered their adult roles at earlier ages than did men by an average of five years (see fig. 5). To reconstruct actual lives, a historian ideally can track various data attempting to follow a cohort's life patterns.[9] With only one census, this task is unattainable. Nevertheless, by dividing men into age groups (<20, 20–29, 30–39, 40–49, 50–59, and >59) the data reveal that men and women lived in complex families at certain times in their lives (see tables 5, 6, and 7).

The major visible trend is that the nuclear family predominated throughout a couples' life together. Complex families existed, as family members moved in and out, following their own paths. In their twenties and thirties, some men and women accepted their siblings into their homes. Perhaps younger siblings temporarily needed a home after their parents died. Siblings who never married often found a home with their married siblings. When their spouses died, parents moved in with their adult children. Alternatively, a widow might have opted to bequeath premortem property to her adult, married children with the result that they moved in with her. In Santa Cruz de la Cañada, not one household contained married children residing with their parents. Overall, only a scattering of mothers moved in with their sons or their daughters, not enough to form a trend.

Although nuclear families predominated, they by no means operated as isolated units cut off from one another. Kin relations, ties between siblings and cousins, proved essential to the survival of families on the frontier. Families interacted intimately with their kin, often on a daily basis. Many young couples set up their households in communities composed of their siblings. Moreover, siblings often inherited property jointly from their parents. This arrangement required them to manage the property together or to come to an amicable agreement about how to divide the property.[10] Very few cases of property disputes between siblings exist, suggesting that siblings worked through their problems before outside intervention became necessary.

Siblings often relied on one another in times of adversity. Although the archival records do not spell out the exact reasons nieces and nephews resided with their aunts and uncles, it appears that family tragedies—death, sickness, poverty—often thrust children into the homes of relatives or others. The smallpox epidemic of 1780 that ravaged New Mexico left many orphans. In Albuquerque, of twenty-four nieces and nephews who lived with their aunts and uncles, ten children might have lost one or both parents to the smallpox epidemic; all were ten years old or older at the time of the census. Thirteen of the fourteen nieces and nephews who resided with uncles and aunts in Santa Fe also could have been orphaned by the epidemic. In Santa Cruz de la Cañada, fourteen of seventeen might have lost parents to smallpox.[11]

Parents, before dying or during times of trouble, turned to their children's godparents to raise their children. During times of joy and renewal, most parents chose to strengthen the bonds they had with their siblings by creating spiritual ties with them. A study of the baptismal records reveals that mothers and fathers often asked their brothers and sisters to be the godparents, compadres, of their first children.[12] State authorities also chose close relatives as guardians to protect children's inheritances and to rear them.

In addition to the death of parents, children took up residence with relatives for other reasons. Perhaps parents sent their children to skilled siblings so that their children could learn a craft, and the families who accepted the children could benefit from extra labor. One enumerator identified a twenty-five-year-old nephew as a weaver who resided in Albuquerque with his uncle, Leonardo Antonio Gutiérrez, who was also a weaver.[13] A range of childcare arrangements and conditions existed with apprenticeship being the most formal. Apprenticeship contracts between parents and the masters described the mutual obligations down to exacting details.[14] Though apprentices undoubtedly did work in New Mexico, the lack of evidence of contracts suggests that the negotiations between parties was more informal. In one case in the Santa Fe census, the enumerator identified a Spanish boy, age fifteen, as an apprentice. His master, thirty-year-old Juan Francisco Montoya, was a silversmith.[15] Francisco de Mascareñas set up an apprenticeship for his nephew Juan to learn the skills of an armorer. Francisco seems to have paid the master Sena a fee for the instruction, implying that Juan did not remain in Sena's home.[16]

Moreover, childless couples might have wanted children to be part of their lives. Corporal Luis Jaramillo and his wife of thirty-three years had three children, "all of whom God saw fit to take to Himself at an early age." Their home was not without children, however. He and his wife raised his nephew. In his will of 1764, Jaramillo instructed that one fifth of his estate, eight cattle and sixty ewes, be set aside for his nephew.[17] The nephew's father was still alive when Jaramillo wrote his will as he was one of the executors. This arrangement benefited all family members: the parents were relieved of one more mouth to feed; their child might receive material benefits from the adoptive parents; and aunt and uncle welcomed a child into their home.

In 1756, in his will, Juan José Moreno recounted that, having had no children of their own, he and his wife had raised their niece as their own daughter. For the "love and affection" he felt for her, he left her the remainder of his property—sixty ewes and all of the niece's clothing. While the girl was to remain with her aunt, he willed that the ewes be taken to the girl's father so that they would increase in number until the time of her marriage. He hoped that she would marry an honest person of good qualities and with his wife's consent.[18]

Nieces and nephews also might have lived with their aunts and uncles if their mothers were not married and did not have houses of their own. The forty-two-year-old widow, María Gertrudis Martín, resided with her two sisters and the sisters' illegitimate daughters.[19] They undoubtedly found that they could better pool their resources by living together.

Grandparents also stood in as parents. At times, from necessity, they raised their illegitimate grandchildren as did Manuel Martín, the man accused of incest. When the governor ordered that the local friar correct the dissolute ways of his errant daughter, her children were ordered to remain with Martín.[20] Other grandparents welcomed their illegitimate grandchildren. In 1704, don Tomás de Herrera Sandoval, resident of Santa Cruz de la Cañada, petitioned Governor Vargas for help in obtaining his illegitimate granddaughter from the deceased mother's master, Bartolomé Sánchez.[21] He explained that his son had engaged in sexual relations with the young woman who had become pregnant. Not only was the baby his granddaughter, but his wife and his son acted as the baby's godparents. When the young mother died, don Tomás asked Sánchez for the baby so that he and his family could raise her, but Sánchez refused to comply. The governor assisted don Tomás, and ordered Sánchez to give the baby to her grandparents.

Residential Patterns

A number of variables affected where a couple set up their household. Nicolás Ortiz's wife received a dowry that included a house and cultivable lands. Since Nicolás Ortiz had no property, the couple chose to live in his wife's house.[22] If Ortiz's in-laws had divided their estate among their children, it is likely that Ortiz's neighbors were his wife's kin. A couple, then, ended up residing near the wife's family or the husband's family depending on who received the more desirable property. Captain Andrés Montoya gave land to his sons and daughters, suggesting that, if brothers and brothers-in-law did not necessarily live next to each other, they at least worked the land side by side. At the time of his will in 1740, his unmarried children had not yet received any land.[23] His will intimates that his unwed children would receive land apart from their siblings' land, revealing that the residential patterns of families depended on many variables, such as the number of children to receive land and the location of the land to be divided.

Patterns emerge in the 1790 census data since the enumerators went from house to house and marked down the names of the household heads, their wives and their respective ages. Surname clusters abound in the data; most clusters involved two households. Of 497 households in Santa Cruz, approximately 188 households shared kin ties with their neighbors (37.8 percent).[24] In Albuquerque, out of 248 households roughly 93 households possessed kinship bonds with neighboring households (37.5 percent). Finally, in Santa Fe, of 561 households, more than 235 households had relatives as neighbors

(41.8 percent).²⁵ (See figs. 8, 9, and 10 for examples of surname clusters in Albuquerque, Santa Fe, and Santa Cruz de la Cañada, respectively.)

Some surname clusters reveal that parents bestowed land on both male and female offspring and did not favor one male with a premortem patrimony. Since New Mexicans preferred to live near the land they farmed, the census data suggests that parents, when able, divided their tillable soil among their married children. Those who worked as skilled or day laborers might have had just enough land so that their children could reside near the parents. In Santa Cruz, for example, the day laborer, Pedro Archuleta, aged fifty, lived beside Juan Antonio Archuleta, aged forty-eight, also a day laborer. Another day worker, José Toribio Archuleta, aged twenty-eight, resided next door. Antonia Archuleta, aged forty, wife of the farmer Juan Romero, and her sister occupied the subsequent home. Apparently, the siblings, Pedro, Juan Antonio, and Antonia inherited land from their parents. Perhaps the land did not fully support the Archuletas, forcing them to search for other types of employment besides cultivation. Juan Romero, the brother-in-law, did farm the land. His wife and his sister-in-law, unmarried at age thirty-two, possibly united their inheritances, giving him enough land to sustain them.²⁶

The sixty-year-old farmer from Santa Fe, Vicente Jiménez, apparently divided his land among his children. His twenty-seven-year-old son, Isidro, who occupied the neighboring household, also farmed the land, as did Manuel Antonio, age twenty-four, who resided next door. The three daughters, Teresa, María de la Luz, and Antonia, married men who did not farm (the enumerator did not mark down Antonia's husband's employment), although they all resided in the vicinity. The enumerator described all of the Jiménezes in racial terms as being of color quebrado, mixed race.²⁷ The farmer, Juan Antonio Baca, age sixty-eight, also chose not to favor only one son with a patrimony. His five neighbors all farmed the land. All five were married men named Baca who ranged in age from twenty-two to twenty-seven.²⁸

La Vida Maridable and Patria Potestas

Men and women began married life with certain legal prescriptions that defined their roles as husbands and wives, and fathers and mothers. To begin with, the church and state expected men and women to set up a joint household and begin the vida maridable, conjugal life.²⁹ Bound together before

God, couples established the vida maridable in which they lived together and slept together, and in which the husband maintained the wife. In fact, the law required men to support, protect and guide their wives. In return, wives owed their spouses near total obedience.[30] In 1705, Inés de Aspitia filed a complaint with the church authorities contending that her husband, Cristóbal de Góngora, had failed to make a conjugal life with her ("*que no hace vida maridable conmigo*"). Her absent husband, she stated, acted against human and divine law by refusing to provide her with sustenance and clothing. She begged that the ecclesiastical judge examine her case with merciful eyes and help in the return of her husband.[31] For his part, Cristóbal de Góngora understood his duties to his wife, but felt deeply aggrieved by his wife's actions—he accused her of witchcraft and adultery—and tried to circumvent them by asking for a divorce. On previous occasions, church officials had ordered the couple to live together. Nevertheless, each spouse emphasized that the marriage was unworkable, each accusing the other of failing to fulfill his or her respective role. Each participant sought some type of remedy. The case, only a fragment, ends without revealing whether the judges tried to reunite the two yet again.

Inés de Aspitia, by appealing to authorities, acted within her rights. Women often sought advice and intervention from local church and state officials when they perceived husbands to be shirking their responsibilities. Indeed, civil law allowed women the right to file suit against abusive husbands.[32] Cristóbal de Góngora also knew that the church granted divorces in cases of adultery and ardently tried to procure one. Although divorce did not sever the marriage bond, it permitted the couple to establish separate households.[33]

Another aspect of the vida maridable was known as the conjugal debt. Ecclesiastical law required that men and women engage in marital intercourse—a spouse's due.[34] Serving two purposes, according to the church, marital intercourse controlled unlawful lust and led to procreation. In 1695, Inés Martín, in the only extant petition for a divorce, complained that her husband owed her the marital debt and that she remained in the state she had been in when her mother bore her.[35] She hoped that God would grant her another man who would sustain her and with whom she could have "blessed children." The ecclesiastical judge, Francisco de Vargas, prescribed medicines to the impotent husband and asked the wife to wait for four months.[36]

Inés Martín, like other New Mexicans, expected that childbearing and childrearing would be part of her familial life. As parents, men and women also had to fulfill legal dictates. Known as the *patria potestas* (paternal powers), fathers exercised exclusive authority over their children in return for the nurturing, education, and inheritance they provided their legitimate children. The law also required fathers to support and rear their natural children, but they did not have to leave them an inheritance. Fathers had no legal obligations to other children, namely those born of adultery or incest, and those born to prostitutes or nuns.[37] Mothers fully shared the responsibilities expected of fathers, but the law denied them the patria potestas.

Very few cases relate how New Mexicans fulfilled their parental duties or what parents thought about them. In a custody case from 1732, two guardians vied to raise the young Juan Mascareñas.[38] In this suit, each person expounded on his suitability as a guardian and why the boy should be remanded to him, revealing their ideas on the responsibilities of parenthood. Since Juan's mother's death in 1726, don José de Reaño and his wife María de Roybal had raised Juan. Reaño said that his wife had taught and indoctrinated Juan in all the things pertaining to the Catholic faith. A change in custody occurred in 1730 when Juan's uncle, Francisco de Mascareñas, brought Juan to his house. Two years later, Reaño felt compelled to petition the governor to return Juan to his care "because of the affection and love that my wife has for him, having raised him, and because he came to my house so obviously naked, and because of the affection I have for him." He charged the uncle with neglect, declaring that Juan "experienced hardships like hunger, nakedness, and carrying wood for the Indians of Galisteo Pueblo in exchange for corn." Reaño also accused Francisco de Mascareñas of squandering Juan's property, by eating the boy's sheep and selling his land.[39]

The uncle rejoined that he felt "pity and compassion" for Juan because each time he had visited, he had discovered his nephew "out of don José de Reaño's house, with welts from a leather whip, naked and dying of hunger." Mascareñas had sold some of Juan's sheep, but countered that they went to Bernardino de Sena whom Mascareñas had hired to teach his nephew Sena's occupation. Contrary to Reaño's assertion that he had forced his nephew to carry wood for the Indians, the uncle had instructed Juan to read all day.

The above accusations show that parents who taught their children "good customs," indoctrinated them in the Catholic faith, provided food and clothing, and loved them acted properly. Bad parents, according to their accounts, physically punished their children and assigned onerous workloads. Parents also had to guard their children's property and use it for their children's benefit only. In most cases in New Mexico, when one parent died, the living parent, acting as the guardian, took responsibility for his or her children's inheritance. In this case, the governor, Gervasio Cruzat y Góngora, decided that Mascareñas's sale of Juan's land was prejudicial to the boy. He opted not to name a guardian, however, saying that the boy (approximately fourteen years old at the time) was old enough to feed and clothe himself.

Mascareñas also asserted that he was providing his nephew with an education, implying that some type of instruction to the young was something to be lauded. Few people in New Mexico actually received an education that included reading and writing. Instead fathers and mothers taught their children necessary skills to survive.[40] One father, Felipe Tafoya, who acted as an alcalde mayor of Santa Fe in the 1760s, imparted his skills, which happened to include literacy, to his stepson. The stepson, in turn, became the provincial *protector de indios*, the crown-appointed official who represented Indians in formal litigation.[41]

Marital Harmony/Marital Discord

Luis López agreed to live with his estranged wife, Ana Bernal, vowing to love her and to treat her well both in deed and in words. It is impossible to determine whether he kept his promise. Yet when he wrote his will in 1728, he had been married to his wife, Ana, for thirty years and they had had one child, Antonia López. Together they had achieved much: he had a house in Chimayo, farmland, an orchard, and 136 sheep. He also mentioned a girl that he had raised, leaving her some land for a *milpa* (cornfield) with the permission of his wife and daughter.[42] Apparently, Luis and Ana had mended their differences and forged a long life together as man and wife. Nevertheless, it remains extremely difficult to establish whether or not most couples achieved some type of marital harmony because those details are typically not recorded in sources available to historians. Although some expressed love and friendship during their courtship in the diligencias matrimoniales and dispensation cases, once they married, the working relationships between husbands and wives slip from view. The aberrant cases that do reveal the intimate details of the vida maridable reveal domestic violence and adultery. The New Mexico archives offer only a handful of these cases, making it hard to formulate overarching conclusions about marital relations during the course of the colonial period. Since most New Mexican spouses did not resort to civil or ecclesiastical courts, perhaps one can surmise that most marriages functioned well enough.

Even so, as our only sources, these cases of domestic discord are extremely valuable, giving examples of what constituted *la mala vida*, or hard life, and what means women used to end their suffering at the hands of violent husbands. The manner in which New Mexican women reacted to their mistreatment and the subsequent intervention by their families highlights the divergent interpretations about what constituted a marriage, what degree of violence was tolerated as legitimate, and the various aspects of women's roles as wives. The cases show how some women and their families believed in the governors' restorative justice, whereas others employed different means to curb a husband's excessive mistreatment. Comparison of husbands' behavior also proves illustrative. Although these men allegedly beat their wives in the privacy of their homes, they did not act in a vacuum. Their families, the community, and even state opinion mattered in how men meted out domestic abuse and, in some cases, tried to disguise it. Although most women did not complain publicly of extreme aggression, the available cases expose the range of acceptable conduct in a marriage and how the husbands or in-laws behaved outside the standard norms. The cases also imply that residential patterns played an important role in a woman's hope for survival when faced with violence. The women who had support from kin and community endured and survived. Women without help, living in isolation, fared worse.

When men and women began their married lives together and established their new households, the pressures they experienced must have been great. They had entered a new stage of life in which they had to assume new responsibilities. No longer could they depend on their parents for the sustenance they had once provided and the guidance they had given. Now couples had to support themselves and make their own decisions. The most challenging aspect of married life, perhaps, was the fact that a spouse had to interact daily with and sometimes defer to a new person. Men and women had learned that as husbands and wives they had to perform certain roles. Religious confessionals, available in New Spain at the time, spoke of the contractual nature of marriage and the reciprocity necessary to sustain a peaceful and loving relationship. In Fray Jayme de Corella's view marriage was "a virtual contract . . . in which the husband is obliged to maintain her, and she to obey him in what is rational and just."[43] When a man fulfilled his obligations, the woman's duty was to obey and esteem him. If he failed and mistreated her, she could seek redress. Undoubtedly, in the first months of marriage, couples began the process of finding a way to live together in harmony. Falling far short of the ideal, some couples, when difficulties arose, resorted to aggression.

Two domestic violence cases from the early part of the eighteenth century help to begin a discussion about the roles of wives, husbands, and state officials. Recall the lives of Nicolás Durán y Chávez and his wife, Juana Montaño, residents of Albuquerque. After a relationship of over five years and the birth of children (he denied that they were all his), Juana Montaño complained to the governor that Nicolás had failed to make good his promise to marry her. The governor imprisoned Nicolás who then relented and agreed to marry. The new husband and his mother must have greatly resented the young woman, for in a civil case from 1714, just a few months after her marriage, Juana Montaño pleaded to the governor to rescue her from her husband and her mother-in-law.[44]

After their compulsory wedding, the young lovers and their children went to live with Nicolás's mother, Luisa Hurtado. As life together commenced, tensions grew, and Nicolás began beating Juana, as she told it, and "mistreating her with words," and "treated her indecently" in regards to her apparel by "not giving her even one pair of shoes." Even his mother had mistreated her with many insults. She felt such great distress that she fled to her sister's house nearby. The distance proved too little, for the mother-in-law, with the help of her son and grandson, successfully pursued the runaway wife. Dragging Juana back home by her hair, Luisa Hurtado locked her in the house to await Nicolás who was away at a trade fair.[45]

Upon arriving home, Nicolás locked Juana in the kitchen, whipped her, and beat her with a stick. Juana Montaño believed that she would have died if her sister-in-law, Isabel de Chávez, had not intervened. At another point, Nicolás carried a *coyunda*, a strap for yoking oxen, with which he intended to whip Juana, but again Isabel stopped him and asked if he were a heretic, implying that only a non-Christian would be so cruel. The hardship Juana suffered was so severe that she decided to go to the governor for protection and for a solution to her situation.[46]

On one Saturday afternoon, the twentieth of October, an opportunity to escape arose. Juana received permission from her mother-in-law to visit her sister so that her sister could delouse her. When Juana arrived, the sister and Juana's comadre encouraged her to flee to Santa Fe, saying: "What are you waiting for? It's better to go to the town. Do you want to wait for him to hit you and leave you for dead?" On the way down to the river to wash, the two women exhorted Juana to join them so that "we can show you the ford where you can cross and go." Juana traversed the river and walked all night. After resting a little, she walked through another night and arrived at midday on Monday to the outskirts of Santa Fe. During the last leg of her journey, a man on a mule gave her a ride to her brother-in-law's house in Santa Fe. Her long flight from Albuquerque successful, she sought the governor's aid.[47]

In the second case, on April 20, 1713, near Santa Cruz de la Cañada, Juana Luján, saw her sister-in-law, Catalina de Valdez, peeking out of the top of the *coy* (a partially underground storage building with an entrance through the roof). Oddly, upon reaching the coy, Juana could no longer see Catalina nor did Juana hear any response to her calls. When Juana looked down into the coy, she saw her sister-in-law lying face up at the bottom of the ladder surrounded by shards of a broken water jug. The bloodied Catalina was alive, but she could no longer speak.[48]

Juana Luján called for help. The four women who heeded her summons were shocked by what they saw. Blood, brains, and flesh covered the walls. Bloody handprints marked the walls and the rungs of the ladder. Barely alive, with the crown of her skull bashed, there was little hope that Catalina would survive. Witnesses later said that the gashes were so deep that her brain could be seen. The women carried Catalina to Juana's house to apply the holy oils before she died. Later in the evening when the alcalde mayor arrived to bear witness and to examine her wounds, Catalina was dead.[49]

Catalina's husband, Miguel Luján, and his sister, Juana, claimed that Catalina had inadvertently slipped from the ladder and had fallen onto the broken pottery shards. Governor don Juan Ignacio Flores Mogollón, based on a report of the events, ordered a thorough investigation. The principal investigator, Juan Páez Hurtado, believed that it had not been an accident, but that Miguel Luján had bludgeoned his wife to death.

During the course of the investigation, Páez Hurtado came to understand that Catalina had suffered a prior "accident." In the latter part of 1711, Catalina had asked her husband, Miguel, if he would accompany her to the pueblo of San Ildefonso so that she could visit her mother. Miguel Luján alleged that en route, the horse was startled, and somehow Catalina's petticoats became entangled with the saddle. The mare dragged the young woman leaving her bloodied and unconscious. Miguel immediately left her side to go in search of a priest.[50]

Catalina awoke in her mother's house. "When she came to herself after three days," her mother recalled, "I asked her whether the mare had put her like this or had her husband. My daughter said that, 'it was my husband, Miguel Luján, who has placed me in the way you see me.'" A few days later after the shock had worn off, the mother again encouraged Catalina to tell the truth as to whether Miguel Luján had mistreated her and left her senseless. The young wife denied that he had, becoming very angry with her mother and accusing her of trying to discredit her husband.[51]

Wives and Husbands

In examining these women's histories, perhaps, the most striking differences proves to be how each woman handled her situation. Compared to Catalina, Juana seems almost brazen. Under no circumstances, was Juana going to abide her husband's behavior. Catalina, on the other hand, submitted to Miguel Luján's wrath and, in the end, protected his reputation at all costs. How did two contemporary women from such similar backgrounds come to such radically different ideas about how they should behave as wives? Their contrasting behavior suggests that no single, agreed-upon code of family honor dictated how women should respond. Instead, each woman interpreted the culturally accepted beliefs about family life and acted as she saw fit, whether that entailed remaining silent or seeking the aid of family, friends, the governor or a priest.

Imagine Juana Montaño's distress upon moving in with her new husband and his family. After a long relationship of over five years, she took the extraordinary step of suing Nicolás Durán y Chávez so that he would fulfill his marriage promise. When she finally achieved her goal, and the couple married, she became a respectable wife and her children became legitimate.

Instead of a glorious beginning to this new marital life, however, she found herself a beleaguered victim. According to her statement, Nicolás's family treated her like a servant, her husband failed to provide for her, and her mother-in-law constantly berated her.

What had Juana Montaño expected? To begin with, she had reason to trust that her husband would provide for her basic needs such as clothing and shoes. Indeed, when women married, their husbands legally owed them support, protection, and guidance.[52] In 1714, Governor Flores Mogollón described marriage as follows: "The couple lives together in one house with the husband taking care to sustain and to maintain his wife, assisting her in all that is necessary, his work permitting; and the wife looking after her husband and the house, alleviating his work when possible."[53]

The idea that a husband created the mala vida (hard life) if he did not sustain his wife was a common refrain in domestic violence cases throughout the colonial period in the greater Mexican region. In a case from 1545 in New Spain, Francisca de Tórrez's parents filed a suit complaining that Francisca's husband had denied his wife support and had even gambled away her dowry.[54] In the latter part of the colonial period, women and their families continued to file complaints when husbands failed to provide for their lawful families.[55]

In numerous cases, a husband's failure to provide materially for his wife resulted from his involvement with another woman. Grievances about lack of sustenance went hand-in-hand with complaints about adultery. When women married, they expected their husbands to remain faithful to them and that the fruits of their husbands' labor would benefit them and their offspring only. In 1740, María Magdalena Baca of Santa Fe complained that her unfaithful husband did not give her anything from the soldier's ration that he received from the palace.[56] Isabel de Medina of Santa Fe, in 1765, also complained that her husband was having an affair. She noted that although her husband worked every day, he only helped her with a little bit of corn. She implied that the other woman and her children received the bulk of what her husband's labor produced.[57]

These two women also mentioned that their husbands did not spend their nights with them. One of the foundations of a conjugal home was that the husband and wife resided together. The implication was that the couple would have sex, reproduce, and provide one another with companionship. In

New Mexico, a husband's nocturnal presence also meant that he was present to help defend his family against enemy attack.

Juana also could expect that within her new household she would be afforded a place of respect. When women entered their new homes as brides, they became members of a hierarchical household in which their husbands assumed the role of "the lord and the head of his wife."[58] Legally wives became subject to husbands' authority over all aspects of their lives, yielding control over most of their property, legal transactions, and earnings.[59] Nevertheless, certain legal codes also recognized that when women became wives they received certain benefits. In the *Siete Partidas*, the law states that women obtained "honor and dignities through their husbands, and by reason of them." Moreover, wives, as the mothers of the heirs, "should honor, protect, and preserve their husbands above everything else in the world, and their husbands should treat them in like manner."[60]

In Juana's case, her mother-in-law already occupied the honored place of woman of the house and appeared extremely reluctant to relinquish this spot to her daughter-in-law. Perhaps Juana might have overlooked her mother-in-law's arrogance if she had not been forced to suffer a worse indignity: her husband and his family treated her like a servant. She complained that she had to serve them and had to pick the corn in the milpa.[61] Juana believed this work was beneath her and should be performed by servants. The documents do not reveal whether or not the Chávez household had servants, but it is highly likely that it did. Moreover, any servants were probably Native American captives, their presence creating a racial/cultural hierarchy within the household. Juana found herself performing tasks that she, as the legitimate wife, thought that she should not be forced to do, tasks that equated her with Indian captives.

Juana also thought her husband's actions unreasonable. In her view, she had done nothing to warrant such abuse. Although no law existed granting husbands the right to strike their spouses in the *Siete Partidas* nor in the *Recopilación de Leyes de los Reynos de las Indias*, most people believed that men could punish their wives within reason. State officials investigating cases evidently shared the belief that physical punishment had a legitimate place in a marriage. When making inquiries about the mala vida, they asked what reason the husband had for hitting his wife. Indeed, after Catalina de Valdez's brutal murder, Páez Hurtado had asked witnesses for the "*motivo*" (motive) behind Miguel Luján's attack. Clearly, Páez Hurtado recognized that Miguel Luján's actions were excessive and that he had behaved inhumanely, but he still sought the motivations behind the brutal beating. The justifications men provided helped judges determine whether their behavior was wanton, criminal and negligent, or warranted.

Catholic dogma, for example, explicitly permitted husbands to physically punish their misbehaving wives. Fray Jayme de Corella's confessional manual, published in 1689, relates that husbands could rightfully punish their wives when the women failed to fulfill their wifely duties. In the manual, in a dramatization of dialogue between penitent and confessor, the confessor tells a penitent who had beaten his wife without reason, "When there is a legitimate reason it is lawful for the husband to punish and even to strike his wife, but with moderation and to the end that she mend her ways."[62] Although this manual might not have been found in New Mexico, all friars who came to the northern colony had been educated in New Spain or Spain and might have viewed it there.

Violence within some homes might have occurred frequently. And at some point, maybe, it became excessive and caused severe hardship for wives. But when did husbands cross the line and who decided that a line had been crossed? Juana's actions show that she was unprepared for the onslaught of violence in her marriage and unwilling to accept it. She waited a mere three months after marrying before she fled to seek the governor's aid and protection. In the matter of the broken marriage promise, she had proved more patient, delaying more than five years before pressing her case. Violence had had no place in their courtship, and Juana, most probably, did not expect it once they were married. In the other fourteen cases relating to domestic violence, only two other wives initiated complaints with civil officials. Battered women who sought help might have tried other channels, though. In the case from 1740, María Magdalena Baca, whose husband was an infantryman, sought assistance from her husband's commanding officer.[63]

Because Catalina has no voice in the document, we know little about what her expectations of marriage might have been. Nevertheless, we can discern that as a wife her chief concern was to maintain the honorable place that she and her husband, as a married couple, commanded in society. Upon marrying, men and women assumed a role of honor within the community and entered a Christian moral order.[64] Miguel Luján's unwarranted, extreme violence would have nullified his respectability. So instead of revealing his violent nature and possibly saving herself from more beatings, she chose to conceal his aberrant behavior. When she opted not to share the details of the incident involving the mare with her mother so soon after its occurrence, she might have acted out of fear.

But on another occasion, Catalina made a calculated choice to keep their violent history secret. One witness, an orphan named Tomasa de Manzanares, had lived with the young couple at some point. One day she overheard the couple discussing Catalina's fall from the mare. Catalina said to her husband, "You could have had more heart, [instead of] leaving me full of blood and dirt and with my face all swollen, with me asking you to take me with you even if it was on the back of the horse." He responded, "I put you like that, dark-skinned witch." She answered, "By the most Holy Virgin, I am not making you give false testimony." In front of an onlooker, Catalina urged her husband to dissemble. Although she chose to discuss the incident, she wanted to maintain the semblance of its having been an accident.[65]

In stark contrast to Catalina's protective silence, Juana trumpeted the abuse she suffered. When the governor asked who could corroborate her story of the mala vida, she named two male witnesses. One was the man on the mule who had helped her on the last leg of her journey. When he testified he explained, "I asked her from where she came and what she was doing. She responded that she had come by foot from Albuquerque fleeing the mistreatment that her husband gave her to find shelter under the law (la justicia). Seeing how she could not move from exhaustion and the way she was beaten up by her husband (she showed me the wound on her arm from a blow), I asked her to get on my mule so that I could take her where she wanted to go."[66] Juana Montaño, by revealing her wounds, guaranteed that someone would be able to bear witness and testify for her in her fight against her husband and his family even though doing so compromised family reputation.

Finally, Catalina, in addition to trying to protect her husband from being 'discredited,' may also have remained silent because she loved him. Over the course of courtship, many New Mexicans developed loving relationships and believed this affection was an important part of marriage.[67] Many of the witnesses described Catalina and Miguel as a loving couple. One witness told of a touching scene between the two of them on the day of her murder. She had watched them feed one another a delicacy and called them "very happy."[68]

Tomasa de Manzanares asserted that she had never seen Miguel mistreat his wife and never was Catalina a poor humiliated person (*una pobre humilde*).[69] Between the vicious attacks, Miguel was apparently able to reestablish some kind of relationship between himself and Catalina so that those who knew them and saw them together judged it as caring and affectionate.

The circumstances of María Magdalena Baca, mentioned above for complaining about her husband Juan Márquez's infidelities and seeking help from his superior, also present us with the difficulties a woman faced when trying to survive with a feckless husband who beat her. By going to the authorities, she might risk losing her husband's economic aid as well as their good standing in the community. By not seeking help, however, a woman remained vulnerable. In the case described below, it seems that María Magdalena tried a number of tactics to protect herself.

Don Santiago Roibal ordered the imprisonment of Juan Márquez for committing adultery with Manuela Abeyta. Once in jail, his wife, María Magdalena Baca, tirelessly tried to secure his release. Before the governor, she maintained that Juan lived "peacefully and laudably." She claimed that on the night he supposedly spent with Manuela Abeyta, he had been with her, as he was every night. She actually accused the second lieutenant of complaining about her husband and asked that he, "the accuser and slanderer of her honor," prove his accusations.[70]

The second lieutenant recognized the duplicity of María Magdalena's confusing statements, declaring that determining the truth "was like separating the wheat from the chaff." He provided a number of witnesses who testified that Márquez mistreated his wife. Her sister-in-law related how María Magdalena had attempted to flee to Albuquerque in order to escape from her husband.[71] Yet what motivated María Magdalena to lie when she might have secured some relief? If we interpret her words as truthful, she seemed extremely worried about her honor. She did not want the ecclesiastical judge and other authorities prying into her life, tarnishing the respect that as a married couple she and her husband deserved. More likely, Márquez, from his jail cell, threatened to harm her if she did not help to exonerate him. She used her loud exhortations for respect as a pretense to mislead the investigators and draw attention away from her husband's numerous faults. In the end, her bungled attempts to alter her husband's brutalities proved futile; he most likely murdered her as she lay in bed.

The other main protagonists in the two cases from 1713 and 1714 are Miguel Luján and Nicolás Durán y Chávez. Their actions, of course, are what propelled these cases into public view and finally into the public record. Why did these two men violently attack their wives, the women they were supposed to support, guide, and honor? Men also had expectations about how marriage should be conducted. As heads of their households, they counted on the support of their wives to help maintain their families and homes. In addition, they wanted their wives to be obedient and to respect their authority. Most important, perhaps, they expected sexual fidelity from their wives.

On the matter of sexual fidelity and obedience, Nicolás, who had been reluctant to marry Juana Montaño since he believed that she had had sex with another man, probably felt that she came up short. In Hispanic societies, in order to guard the family lineage, husbands and fathers were expected to control women's sexuality. The inheritance system recognized legitimate children as the necessary, lawful heirs. Laws to punish an adulterous woman included the loss of her dowry, loss of her share of the community property, and imprisonment. And if a husband found his wife and her lover having sex, he could kill them both.[72]

When Nicolás sat in jail, he said that he did not want to marry Juana Montaño because he maintained that one of the two children was not his. He questioned her sexual fidelity. The governor, however, disregarded Nicolás's concern and coerced him into upholding his promise to marry. It is not surprising that the governor ignored Juana's alleged premarital sexual improprieties since New Mexican youth enjoyed some latitude in selecting mates and some chose to engage in sexual relations after they exchanged a marriage promise. Governors and friars believed that young people should be held accountable and honor their vows.[73] Even though the governor found Nicolás's charges inconsequential, one can imagine that Nicolás resented being forced to marry a woman whom he believed had slept with another man.

Men considered adultery an even worse offense than premarital dalliances. An unfaithful wife besmirched a man's honor. The first concern was that a wife might introduce another man's child into his home. A cuckold, moreover, was a man who could not protect his wife from other men's advances and risked public scandal. As husbands, men thought it was their right to remain honorable and respectable. Faithful, honorable wives helped men maintain their reputations.

Yet what of husbands who chose to become involved in an adulterous relationship? Did they enhance their virility and reputation? Throughout Latin America, historians have found that a double standard existed regarding the sexual adventures of men and women.[74] An unfaithful woman tainted her honor, her husband's honor, and the family's honor. A man, on the other hand, might enhance his reputation even as he risked censure from church and state. Was this the case in New Mexico? Scant evidence exists to answer this question confidently.

Once again the available cases suggest that the issue was complex and ambiguous. Take Juan Márquez, the adulterer who murdered his wife, María Magdalena Baca. The documents reveal a picaresque man who convinced people to take considerable risks for his benefit. Did his sexual dalliances increase his reputation, enabling him to take greater and greater chances? Although he was the bane of church and state officials, he seems to have had the ability to woo women and to gain the support of friends. To begin with, the widow, María Magdalena Baca, married the man despite her brother's advice that she should not. After marrying, Márquez persuaded Manuela Abeyta into having an affair with him. Since his wife received little help from him, it is possible that he enticed Manuela Abeyta with promises of material aid, transferring to her what he withheld from his wife.

As a soldier, Márquez apparently formed close ties with his fellow soldiers. Upon receiving the governor's orders to arrest Juan Márquez, soldiers surrounded Manuela Abeyta's house. Márquez escaped, however, eluding arrest. The governor believed that the soldiers had aided Márquez in his escape. These soldiers who risked much to help Márquez ended up paying for their folly when the governor ordered their arrest. Finally, Márquez somehow enmeshed his friend, El Jasque, and possibly others who provided alibis, in his nefarious plot to murder his wife.

Although Márquez might have gained the admiration of a few friends, he by no means had the support of the community at large. Many New Mexicans lived by the teachings of the Catholic Church. The church instructed its flock that any sexual relationship outside of matrimony was sinful. In the Ten Commandments, God commanded that one should not commit adultery. The New Testament of the Bible, I Corinthians, states that both men and women should not engage in adulterous relationships. Recall the objections of New Mexicans to the behavior of Governor Vargas who traveled with his mistress. Even powerful men who engaged in deviant sexual behavior chanced censure by the community at large. In general, though, as was the case with Márquez, it was church and state officials who reprimanded adulterous spouses.

Another reason men might have attacked their wives is simply because they could. Society allowed for a certain amount of violence in marriages. And the husband, as head of the household, was able to judge when punishment was necessary. When husbands punished their wives excessively, however, was there always someone there like Ysavel Chávez, Juana's sister-in-law, to stop the husband? Many times these crimes occurred without witnesses. No one saw Miguel Luján strike the fatal blow against Catalina. An abusive husband in 1751 threatened his wife by saying that neither the governor nor the king could stop him from killing her if he so desired.[75]

Yet when given the opportunity to disclose his misconduct, Miguel Luján opted not to admit that he had given his wife the mala vida. Men knew that the occasional corrective slap and an all-out brutal attack differed substantially. When Páez Hurtado exhorted Miguel to confess that he had beaten his wife and that the mare had not dragged her, Luján responded that Páez Hurtado's account was false. He had never beaten her or mistreated her, and, he said, his wife had never given him any reason to place his hands on her.[76] When he described the event involving the mare, he claimed that they had been so much in love that Catalina was tickling him. Instead of admitting that he might have beaten his wife on occasion, he painted himself as a loving husband. Why did Miguel Luján want to maintain a façade? Evidently, public opinion mattered to New Mexicans.

Another case provides an even clearer idea about how men viewed their roles as husbands and how the community perceived them. In 1719, when Cristóbal Tafoya Altamirano of Santa Cruz complained that Diego de Archuleta had hit his wife while he was away in Mexico City, he expressed outrage that someone would show disrespect toward his wife.[77] He claimed that Archuleta should have recognized that she was the wife of an honorable man, loyal to the governor.[78] Even though her husband had not been present, the woman's status as married should have afforded her protection. The alcalde mayor responded to the husband's righteous anger and placed Archuleta in jail while he investigated. A wife deserved respect from the community. In this case, however, the investigators determined that Tafoya Altamirano's claims were false and had been made out of anger over a land deal the claimant had with Archuleta's mother.

Sometimes a wife's role became uncertain and complicated. Did a wife owe allegiance to a husband who harmed her children? On March 18, 1765, Antonia Martín filed a complaint against her husband, Reymundo Baca.[79] She claimed that he had physically mistreated her. Initially, she said that she had not understood his motives, but she had subsequently discovered the cause, "born in her own house": Baca had demanded sex from her seventeen-year-old daughter, Gertrudis.[80] By instigating the investigation, Antonia Martín saw clearly that as a mother she had to protect her daughters from predators, even if the abuser, as in this case, was her husband, step-father of her children.

Residential Patterns and Familial Involvement

A salient similarity in the two cases is that Juana and Catalina resided with or near their husbands' families. Not all married women did so. As the above evidence suggests, couples accepted land from whomever offered it, setting up households on the more desirable property. Residential patterns played a key part in New Mexican abuse cases, showing that the women, who lived near or with the husbands' families and had no kin living close enough to offer aid, suffered the most abuse at the hands of their husbands and/or in-laws. Women's parents and siblings who lived nearby could help mediate marital problems or offer refuge. They also could give a woman the confidence to act as she saw fit, whether it meant complaining to authorities or fleeing for her life.

Catalina de Valdez lived with her husband's family and no one intervened to prevent her murder. Without any of Catalina's kin watching the couple, she had no one to stem the flood of Miguel Luján's violence. Perhaps Juana Luján tried to moderate his temper while her sister-in-law still lived. What is evident, however, is that once Catalina was dead, Juana hindered the investigation in an effort to protect her brother. Catalina's mother (her only relative mentioned in the document) lived approximately six miles away from Santa Cruz, close to San Ildefonso Pueblo. The distance was too great to allow daily interaction between the mother and the married couple.

In the case of Juana Montaño and her husband, Nicolás, the wife's new living situation proved disastrous. Previously, during their seven-year relationship while they had maintained separate residences, each living with his or her mother, Nicolás had not beaten her. Perhaps Nicolás's temper had never flared. More likely, Juana's family had provided her with a modicum of protection, leaving no opportunity for Nicolás to strike. Something changed dramatically after the wedding; "he beat her since the day they were married." In his own home, with his mother's assistance and encouragement, he let his resentment grow and released his anger on his wife. Only his sister seemed willing to temper his aggression. Even though Juana suffered in her new home, she had recourse to assistance.

In her sister's nearby home, Juana Montaño received temporary shelter. What proved more beneficial than this transitory haven, however, was the encouragement Juana received from her sister and her comadre. They urged her to flee as soon as possible, essentially asking her: What are you waiting for, for him to kill you? Upon her arrival in Santa Fe, Juana once again sought out a sister's aid. Before placing her complaint before the governor, she went to her sister's house. The governor, recognizing that she was safe in her sister's home, deposited her there for the length of the investigation.

Other examples of women's vulnerability living with their husbands' kin exist in the sources. In Santa Cruz de la Cañada, in 1713, María de Tórrez ran to the alcalde mayor telling him that Feliz Luján had killed his wife, Francisca de Tórrez. The alcalde mayor arrested Luján and placed Francisca de Tórrez (who was still alive) in her father's house. After the investigation, Governor don Juan Ignacio Flores Mogollón released Feliz Luján from jail on the condition that he move to Santa Fe and live near his wife's kin. The governor recognized that Francisca's father would watch over her and prevent Luján from mistreating her.[81]

When Antonia de Anaya married, she moved in with her husband, Pascual, and his parents. In 1752, Antonia's sister pleaded with the governor to protect her poor pregnant sister. She claimed that Antonia's in-laws had beaten her sister with such severity that Antonia's two children had been born "dead and broken" (*muertas todas quebradas*). She begged: "For the love of God, order that Pascual remove her from that house and let him care for her in another place where the mother-in-law and father-in-law cannot interfere." The governor helped, ordering that Antonia and Pascual remain with her sister. He commanded that Pascual protect his wife. If people tried to harm her, Pascual should inform them that the governor would punish them. The intervention worked. On November 2, 1752, Fray Manuel Zambrano baptized Juan José, the baby of Pascual Maese and Antonia de Anaya.[82] In the above cases, abuse occurred in the presence of the husbands' kin, and women found refuge among their own families.

When María Magdalena Baca died, smothered in her bed while her young son slept by her side, she was isolated from family and community. It seems likely that her husband, Juan Márquez, and a friend had murdered her.[83] When she and Juan had first married, they had lived in a house among neighbors. For some reason, however, they moved to an unpopulated area, and this isolation contributed to her vulnerability. Moreover, María Magdalena had little aid from her family. In an effort to escape from her abusive husband, she had set out from Santa Fe with her two small sons to walk to her sister's house in Albuquerque. En route, she stopped at her brother's house. Although she told her brother and his wife that her husband did not live with her and beat her, they advised her not to leave him. Her brother, in fact, indicated that he and their other brother would not help. "You married him because you wanted to so you can suffer with him."[84] The only person to defend María Magdalena was an Indian servant. Sadly, her assistance proved ineffective. Juan Márquez expelled the servant from the house for "favoring" his wife.[85]

Kin support proved essential, but the question remains: why did kin not undertake to do more? Antonia de Anaya had lost two babies and suffered twelve years of abuse at the hands of her parents-in-law. Feliz Luján mistreated his wife from the day they married, nine years before her sister ran to the alcalde mayor for aid. Why did María Magdalena's sister-in-law and brothers fail to offer her and her children refuge? After his sister's death, the brother filed a civil suit against Juan Márquez for giving his sister the mala vida, and squandering her inheritance, but the gesture was too little, too late.[86]

Some families might have helped in ways that left no paper trail. Doña María de Cabrera, Catalina de Valdez's mother, for example, tried to assist her daughter, but ultimately had little success because her daughter refused to receive aid. Catalina became angry and rejected her mother's efforts to talk openly about Miguel Luján. Without substantiation from Catalina, an appeal to the governor most likely would have been useless. Doña María resorted to one of the few tools available to her: she spread the word that Miguel Luján had beaten her daughter, hoping that gossip would threaten his reputation and curb his aggression.

When interviewed by Páez Hurtado after Catalina's murder, Captain don Juan de Atienza, revealed that Catalina's mother had told him a few days after the accident with the mare that Miguel Luján had been the aggressor. By informing a state official, doña María acted against her daughter's wishes not to malign Miguel Luján. Perhaps doña María hoped that Miguel Luján would be more reluctant to hurt her daughter if community members knew he was a dangerous bully. And though she did not realize it at the time, by informing people of his brutish ways, doña María helped to establish a history of Miguel Luján's behavior that aided Páez Hurtado's case against Luján.

Although this tactic probably worked with some aggressive men, it proved ineffective in this case because Catalina and her sister-in-law, Juana Luján, actively worked to dispel the rumors and to protect Miguel's reputation. Catalina did so by never discussing the actual events of her fall from the mare. After Catalina's death, Juana Luján further protected Miguel by encouraging the women who were nearby at the time of the murder to lie about Miguel's whereabouts, saying that he had not been around when his wife had fallen.

Children also intervened in adults' disputes and sometimes called for help that led to state officials intervening. Children, of course, did not always have the foresight to recognize how their appeal for aid might ultimately impact their family life. In a case from 1715 in Santa Fe, a little girl ran to the alcalde ordinario, Captain Juan García de las Rivas, seeking assistance.[87] She told him that two men were fighting and one of them was hurting her mother. We can imagine the fear the child felt and her desperate need for aid, yet the alcalde ordinario's involvement did not bode well for the child and her mother. Once the official began investigating, he discovered that one of the men had been involved with the woman for six years without the sacrament of marriage. When the captain banished the man, the woman and child were left without the man's economic help.

In this society, children generally had little power to affect change in the parents' lives. In the sad history above, when two assailants murdered María Magdalena Baca by smothering her in her bed, her son, Nerio Montoya, was asleep beside her. He tried in vain to help, but they held him down, pressing him against his mother's body. Since the son was the only witness, Márquez tried to bribe him with a hat and promised to serve him his whole life, asking him to lie and recant his previous testimony. Although the brave little boy could no longer help his mother, he insisted that his previous statement was true, saying that he had loved his mother, not Juan Márquez. Nevertheless, the investigator, Páez Hurtado, did not have Nerio swear under God to tell the truth due to his young age of twelve years. The governor, when passing judgment, stated that the only witness was the son who was incapable of swearing because he did not understand the gravity of the act due to his young age.[88]

While New Mexicans understood and expected families to provide succor and support to relatives in need, family life, in fact, could prove contentious. The brother who filed the lawsuit against Márquez was persistently unsupportive of his sister while alive and married to Márquez. Having opposed the marriage between his sister and Márquez, he apparently had not forgiven her for ignoring his advice. Other cases show that issues such as inheritance could lead to disagreements between husbands and wives and their respective families.

In 1716, Pedro Vigil came forward after learning that his sister-in-law, Ana María Romero, had filed a complaint about his behavior whereby Vigil, in search of his runaway wife, allegedly had shown up at Ana María's house, verbally assaulting her and hurting her daughter.[89] Vigil proclaimed his innocence, naming his wife as a witness and accusing his sister-in-law of wrongly hiding his wife. Confident in his innocence, he said he would accept punishment if proof of his guilt could be found and that if not, his sister-in-law should be censured.

Ana María Romero countered, proclaiming her innocence and repeating her accusal against him. But she asked that Pedro Vigil not involve her in his problems saying that Vigil's behavior was a result of a disagreement between her father and Vigil. The alcalde ordinario quickly changed the direction of his investigation, and interest ceased in the mistreated women, the fleeing wife, and the angry husband. Instead the root of the problem, a dispute over a dowry, came under scrutiny.

Relatives' reluctance to provide the necessary aid resulted, perhaps, from their beliefs that the husband was the ruler of the family who should have been able to deal justly and affectionately with his family. When husbands failed to live up to this ideal role, kin might have intervened on some level, but did not have the authority to change the men's behavior. Perhaps they turned to the local friar, asking him to talk to the errant husband. The case about the dowry also suggests that a husband's mistreatment might be tied to family disagreements that once resolved might have led to less egregious behavior on the husband's part. Relatives of unwed couples most likely understood that calling the authorities might invite unwanted attention. In the end, there were undoubtedly myriad occasions when adults tried to aid an abused daughter or sister in ways, informal and private, that left no record in the archives.

Governors and Their Officials

Almost all of the cases relating to domestic disagreements, including violence, in the Santa Fe Archives are civil cases. In the instances when women suffered injuries or death, people immediately went to the governor or his officials for aid. In other incidences, however, the path that ultimately led to the state officers might have been more circuitous. There is evidence to suggest that some people first went to the ecclesiastical authorities. Recall that community members beseeched a friar to curb Alejandro Mora's vicious behavior toward his wife and his Indian servant. Perhaps friars successfully resolved many family disagreements. Fray Esteban Aumatell might not have been so unusual when, in 1794, he chose to punish temporally and directly the guilty. He beat Juan Antonio Bernal with his own hands for gravely injuring his wife. Yet because friars could not incarcerate men, they might have turned to the state for aid. Aumatell, after punishing Bernal, requested that the husband be sent to jail.[90] Unfortunately, we do not know how friars typically mediated these situations, and instead we must examine the extant civil investigations.

So how did governors and their officials respond to cases of domestic disturbances? Overall, the governors undertook actions that reveal their concerns for protecting women. They did so by thoroughly investigating cases, incarcerating violent men, and engaging the community in their investigations. Sometimes, however, governors shifted the focus of the investigation, showing that other issues, such as maintaining a moral social order or preserving the peace, took precedence over investigating allegations of family abuse.

Ultimately, what could governors do to curb domestic violence? In this society, the state upheld the sacrament of marriage and tried to reconcile divided couples. After incarcerating men for a period, admonishing them to treat their wives respectfully, and threatening future punishment if violence continued, the governors had few tools left at their disposal. In the murder cases I discuss here, governors chose not to put the guilty men to death, but instead banished them from the communities.

After someone sought assistance, lodged a complaint, or reported a murder, the governors and their officials began investigations to determine the truth of the accusations and often jailed the accused. In seven out of fourteen cases of domestic violence from the eighteenth century in which husbands seriously injured their wives, the governors and their officials, recognizing that the husbands posed a continuing threat to the women that they had already injured, imprisoned the husbands. In three of these murders, the husbands were the prime suspects. In four cases, the governors chose to jail men for reasons of adultery or fighting even though they had physically injured their wives (or in one case, lover). Nicolás Durán y Chávez's fate resulting from the investigation remains uncertain because only a fragment of the case was preserved. And in another case, though the parents-in-law beat their son's wife, the governor did not imprison them nor did he incarcerate the husband. And lastly, although one sister complained that her brother-in-law had mistreated his wife, the governor did not incarcerate the husband because the complaint did not centrally involve spousal abuse.

In addition to locking up the husbands, officials also had the option of placing women in deposit. In some instances, governors selected local citizens to house the wives for the duration of the investigations. Governors opted to jail men first because it achieved much more: firstly, the violent men could no longer harm or intimidate the women during the course of the inquiry; secondly, the imprisonment castigated the men; and finally, the action served as a deterrent to other men.

When governors did deposit women, the reasons seem to have been ones of convenience or expediency. Juana Montaño had already sought shelter at her sister's house when Governor Flores Mogollón formalized the arrangement, taxing the brother-in-law with her protection and ensuring that Juana did not leave the premises without gubernatorial permission. In 1713, when Francisca de Tórrez's sister beseeched the alcalde mayor for his assistance, she believed that her sister Francisca was dead. In all likelihood, the governor then chose to deposit Francisca in her father's house because she needed her family's help and a safe place to recover. In 1765, the alcalde mayor deposited Isabel de Medina because her parents did not live locally, and she needed care while she recovered from her injuries.

Yet, by depositing women, surely the governors also sent a forceful message to the husbands that they had acted dishonorably and forfeited their rights and obligations as husbands and heads of the household. In three of the four cases in which officials deposited wives, the husbands also received jail time, making deposit unnecessary for their protection. In 1795, Governor don Fernando Chacón initiated the investigation into the beating of Juliana Córdova by her husband, Juan Antonio Bernal. Perhaps the friar who had paddled the husband the previous year for beating his wife once again requested state intervention. During the proceedings, the alcalde mayor placed the husband in jail and deposited the wife. Maybe the friar and governor believed that due to the extraordinary age gap between them—Juliana was nearly twenty years older than her twenty-five-year old husband[91]—they needed to reprimand the young husband more pointedly and depositing Juliana accomplished this.

In the extant cases, the governors and their officials set out to determine the guilt or innocence of the husbands and/or in-laws. After the complainants voiced their concerns, the alcalde mayores, in most cases, began interviewing witnesses. The investigators also crucially sought physical evidence that would substantiate the accusations. Once again, the case from 1713 involving the murder of Catalina de Valdez is illustrative. Juan Páez Hurtado's investigation into this murder, the assumptions he made, his thoroughness, and his attempt to sway public opinion regarding Miguel Luján's innocence, reveal a respect for Catalina's life and an intolerance of men who transgressed their patriarchal authority.

From the beginning, the governor took the situation very seriously and showed his desire to find out what had really happened to Catalina. Indeed, after seeing the inconclusive results of the initial investigation carried out by the alcalde mayor of Santa Cruz, Jacinto Sánchez, the governor was dissatisfied. Citing Sánchez's inexperience, the governor instead sent the qualified alcalde ordinario of Santa Fe, Juan Páez Hurtado, to take charge of the investigation. Under Páez Hurtado, the tone of the investigation changed, becoming more professional. In his first interview, he asked questions in order to understand the severity of Catalina's wounds: "Did she have wounds, how many, and on what part of her body? Were they made with a sharp instrument or from a blow by a rock or stick?"[92] The witness, Baltasar Rodarte, responded with a detailed account of the injuries, giving the dimensions and saying that they looked as if an iron instrument, like a hoe, had inflicted them. Páez Hurtado continued asking him about the wounds until every cut and abrasion was listed. Rodarte even speculated that the lesions on her hands might have come from trying to defend herself.

After establishing the extent of the lacerations, Páez Hurtado asked him if Miguel Luján had given Catalina the mala vida. The course of the investigation was set. Páez Hurtado determined from the outset to uncover the physical evidence and to track down the motive. The witness said that when he arrived at Juana Luján's house, he saw the husband who looked sad. Páez Hurtado then went on to interview a child and the four adult women who had helped Juana Luján carry Catalina's body out of the underground storage shed. To each woman, he posed the same question: had she witnessed signs of discord between the wife and husband? They each replied no, that the husband and wife had been happy and loved one another. When the alcalde ordinario then tried to establish whether any sharp instruments were found in the coy, each answered that it had been empty save for the broken shards of pottery.

Upon hearing these testimonies, Páez Hurtado ordered the immediate imprisonment of Miguel Luján. Aside from the seriousness of the wounds and the improbability that she received them from the fall, why did Páez Hurtado order Miguel Luján's arrest? Apparently, Páez Hurtado had information that persuaded him that the most likely suspect was the husband. Perhaps Páez Hurtado had heard talk that Luján had a violent history, but in any case, unfortunately, he did not reveal why he thought Miguel Luján was the culprit.

As Páez Hurtado proceeded with the investigation, he sent a clear message to the witnesses that he would brook no dissembling or obstruction. In his initial testimony, the barber-surgeon, Antonio Durán de Armijo, claimed not to know what had caused the wounds. Páez Hurtado hastily sent this testimony to the governor, pointing out that this was a blatant disregard of the evidence—deep, penetrating lacerations that could only have been caused by a sharp object, inflicted with great force—and constituted a flagrant violation of the barber-surgeon's oath and of his office. The governor ordered Antonio Durán de Armijo's arrest and had him shackled.[93] When Páez Hurtado interviewed the imprisoned barber-surgeon a second time, the barber emphatically stated that Catalina died from severe head wounds that had been inflicted by an iron instrument.[94] The warning had worked. Other witnesses also changed their testimonies. Two witnesses who had claimed that Miguel Luján had gone to get wood, revised their accounts to say that the husband had been present when they moved the body. In her second interview, Tomasa Manzanares admitted that she had lied about Miguel Luján's whereabouts at the time they moved the body, prompting the alcalde ordinario to ask why she had lied. She answered that she was a "poor, unprotected orphan," and that Juana Luján had implored them "for the love of God" not to admit that Miguel Luján was present. Another orphan, Casilda de Herrera, also confessed that she had lied at Juana Luján's urging. Even with the confessions of these two women, Páez Hurtado was unable to persuade Juana Luján to alter her testimony. Firmly loyal to her brother, Juana Luján maintained he was innocent and told the investigator that the couple had loved one another.

With Miguel Luján under lock and key, the alcalde ordinario set out to prove that the husband was indeed the murderer and aimed to shift public opinion against him. Moreover, he wanted those involved in the case to recognize the absurdity of Juana and Miguel Luján's conjecture that Catalina had died from a fall. Páez Hurtado first began to assess the physical evidence. The injuries suggested that the murderer had used a sharp instrument such as a hoe. But the witnesses all said that the coy was empty of any tools and that there were only broken pottery shards on the floor. Witnesses also believed that Catalina had died from the fall. Part of Juan Páez Hurtado's plan in the investigation was to prove that Catalina could not have died from a fall and a few broken pottery shards. He ordered his assistants to measure the ladder, and they found its length to be 2 1/2 varas (one vara = 33 inches) or about six feet. He then asked the seventeen-year-old José Trujillo, nephew of Miguel Luján, "Do you think she could have died from the fall?" He answered that due to the low height of the ladder, he did not think so.

Páez Hurtado then posed questions to doña María, Catalina's mother, "Could your daughter have died from falling off the ladder?" When the mother replied "Yes," he asked her, "Could the fall have caused the eight wounds?" She did not know. Although she claimed that she had no suspicions about who could have killed her daughter, by the end of the interview she no longer believed that it had been an accident. By the time Páez Hurtado interviewed Tomasa de Manzanares on May 6, 1713, his strategy had worked. The witness said that she did not know who had killed Catalina, but that she had heard many people say that Miguel Luján had killed her since it was impossible for her to have died from tumbling off so short a ladder.

In addition, Páez Hurtado discovered that Miguel Luján, on the night of the murder, had traded a pair of white moccasins, stained with blood, for a pair of black shoes. Why did he trade the moccasins? How did they become stained with blood when Luján testified he had not seen his wife's body until the burial? By posing these questions to the men involved in the shoe exchange, he spread the idea that the moccasins belonging to Miguel had been stained with Catalina's blood.

Páez Hurtado's strategy served two purposes. First, by revealing to the community his suspicions about who murdered Catalina and the preponderance of evidence against the suspect, he showed the community the justice of imprisoning Miguel Luján. This type of justification falls under the heading of equidad. When magistrates made their final verdicts in cases, they not only referred to coded law, but also considered how their decisions would affect the community.[95] In convincing the public that a man was guilty, few would question the governor's authority and verdict. In addition, community members obtained a sense of what constituted acceptable behavior. With Miguel Luján sitting in jail, people understood that husbands could not act with impunity. They would face consequences.

In other cases, when women survived an ordeal, their bodies served as evidence. Juana Montaño, while relaying her history to the governor, showed the governor the wound on her right arm and declared that her whole body was similarly covered with injuries. Governor don Juan Ignacio Flores Mogollón immediately called for a midwife to examine Juana's body and "to declare under oath how she finds it." After swearing to tell the truth, the midwife, María Magdalena Moreno, declared that she had examined Juana's entire body and had found it covered with blows and bruises that appeared to be made by whippings.[96]

In the month of June 1765, Isabel de Medina filed a complaint against her husband before the alcalde mayor of Santa Fe, don Francisco Guerrero. Her husband, Bartolomé Garduño, had beat her about the face, and she suffered greatly. Because she had no parents in the town to care for her, the alcalde mayor asked the *alférez* (lieutenant colonel) to take Isabel to his home. The alférez called the barber-surgeon to his home. He came not only to care for her injuries, but also to provide an accounting of her wounds: the blows had injured and twisted her face and broken her nose.[97]

In addition to assessing the physical body, officials asked complainants to name witnesses who could testify. Apparently, accusers knew that their accounts would be questioned because they often came armed with the names of various witnesses. Juana Montaño, while telling the governor of her initial escape and how her mother-in-law had captured her and dragged her by the hair, claimed that Antonio de Silva had been there and could prove the truth of her words.

The governor ordered Antonio de Silva to testify and to describe the chain of events on the day of Juana's first flight from her husband's home. After this interview, he summoned Cristóbal Martín, the man on the mule who had helped Juana on the final leg of her flight to Santa Fe. Because Juana told this stranger of her plight and showed him the wounds her husband had inflicted, the man became a witness who substantiated Juana's story.[98]

In her bid to protect her sister, Juana Anaya called on state officials to interview two midwives who would be able to verify her claims that her sister had been abused and her babies had been born broken.[99] Even though they did not call the midwives as witnesses, Juana Anaya's complaints carried more weight because she had willingly named people who would corroborate her claims.

To establish cases against the men, state officials often went farther afield and asked community members whether the women in question experienced the mala vida. The alcalde mayor pressed Juliana Córdova to prove that she lived the "bad life" with her husband. The wife named six men, five of whom the alcalde mayor called before him. He asked each witness: "How many times has Juan Antonio Bernal given it [beatings] to his wife since they married?"[100] Officials even asked people to judge the severity of the bad life and the beatings inflicted on the women. In 1772, Governor Pedro Fermín de Mendinueta asked witnesses whether María Francisca Peralta's death was a result of a beating her husband gave her or from an illness she had long been suffering.[101]

As in the marital investigations, the community's input proved essential to the outcome of these cases. Yet the contribution could often be imperfect, at best. These crimes frequently took place in the home where few witnessed the beatings. And some of the witnesses chose not to testify against a brother or a son. Even if family members did give evidence, the investigators found their testimony suspect due to their close relations to the accused. Investigators did their best to illicit reliable information from the witnesses.

The domestic violence case from 1765 shows how officials proceeded cautiously, fully recognizing that high emotions between a husband and wife could lead to false accusations. In this situation, they worried that the wife might have acted vindictively and elicited the aid of her daughters to support her complaints. As described earlier, on the eighteenth of March, the fifty-year-old Antonia Martín complained to the alcalde mayor of Santa Cruz that her husband was beating her and that she had discovered the root cause: her husband was making sexual advances towards her adolescent daughter.[102] The alcalde mayor, don Manuel García Pareja, considered this a grave and serious allegation and set out to determine whether her accusation was "right and true." He asked her to "examine her conscience and not be carried by her passion resulting from [her husband's] mistreatment of her."[103]

The alcalde mayor first called for both the husband and wife to appear before him so that he could see whether Antonia would continue to accuse her husband. In Reymundo's presence, she did. This strategy, called a face-to-face (*careo*), was a tool commonly used by investigators. Afterward, the alcalde mayor questioned her two daughters. In the interview, the seventeen-year-old Gertrudis Martín painted a picture of domestic life interrupted by her stepfather's "foolish" requests that soon turned threatening and violent. It commenced one night, when her mother left the house in search of Gertrudis's little brother. As she sat sewing next to the fireplace, Reymundo Baca propositioned her. She replied: "Aren't you married to my mother to want to do something so foolish?" He answered, "You're one thing and your mother another." On the next occasion, while the mother was outside weeding her orchard and Gertrudis was grinding some wheat, he tried to rape her. She ran to her mother for aid. Reymundo denied it, but Gertrudis asked, "Then why was [my] clothing ripped?" In the final incident, her mother sent her to a neighbor's with some squash, and en route she encountered Reymundo hiding in the milpa. He threatened her with punishment if she did not do as he asked. She then ran to her mother and begged her to remove her from the house and place her in an honorable home. The mother concurred and sent her daughter to live with Tomás Mora.[104]

When interviewed, the second daughter, Margarita Martín, twenty years of age, relayed that one night, while her mother was away in Ojo Caliente, she and her stepfather were in their respective beds. He spoke to her saying, "If you grant my desire, I promise to watch over you and affectionately care for you. You won't have to do any of the work you've had to do in the past." Feeling overwhelmed by her onerous workload, she agreed to his proposition. Unfortunately for her, she complained that since they had had sex the demand for her labor had doubled.

The alcalde mayor immediately called on the midwife (*partera*), Petrona Martín, to examine Margarita to determine whether she was "lost or not." The partera, under oath, said that Margarita was indeed a "worldly woman." During the examination, Petrona had asked Margarita whether she was bringing false testimony against Reymundo in order to support her mother. Margarita denied this and said it was her father who had his way with her.

Upon completing the investigation, the alcalde mayor sent the report to Governor don Tomás Vélez Cachupín. Most likely, due to the fact that all of the witnesses were related to Antonia Martín, the governor sought outside verification. He returned the *autos* (the proceedings), noting that Antonia Martín, to protect her daughter, had removed her from her own house and had placed her in the house of Tomás Mora in Ojo Caliente. He wanted the alcalde mayor to call forth Tomás Mora in order to take his declaration. After being sworn in, Tomás Mora reported that when Antonia Martín had come with her daughter, she had asked him to guard the daughter against a visit from her husband, Reymundo Baca, explaining that he was in love with the daughter ("*la andaba enamorado*").[105]

Although officials used public knowledge as a tool, they also recognized that rumormongering could be destructive. They had to determine whether hearsay held truth or was passed on to stir up trouble. On the night of July 13, 1713, María de Tórrez ran to the home of Jacinto Sánchez, alcalde mayor of Santa Cruz de la Cañada, to inform him that Feliz Luján had killed his wife. Immediately, the alcalde mounted his horse and rode to the couple's home to investigate. Fortunately, he found Francisca Tórrez still alive but with welts on her arms. Sánchez questioned the injured wife who told him that her husband had beaten her on a whim. She lived in this manner with her husband beating her because she was charming or because she was not. Three days did not pass without his mistreating her. Her only consolation was that the Royal Justice might take her from this "unconjugal" life, *"vida inmaridable,"* and place her with her parents in Santa Fe.[106]

Governor Flores Mogollón set out to determine the truth of Francisca's assertions. His first witness said it was "well-known public knowledge" that the man gave his wife the mala vida, and in a second interview, the governor discovered that two rumors circulated regarding the husband's motive. One witness remembered hearing that Francisca denied her husband the "marital debt," and he also recalled hearing that the husband's actions were justified.

The governor proceeded to interview eight individuals in order to track down the source of the rumors. He discovered that the husband's former criada, Magdalena Pachane, had spread stories that the wife was having an illicit relationship, *mala amistad*, with her brother-in-law, Juan Luján. She had seen them together in the corral and thought, in her heart, that they had an "attachment."

The governor abhorred Magdalena's behavior, stating that just because she had seen the two people joking around, she had then jeopardized Francisca de Tórrez's reputation as an honest woman, *"el crédito a su honestidad."* The governor ordered the deposit of Magdalena in a home where she would work in servitude for six months. The governor also ordered another witness to take care when listening to rumors that damaged the reputation and good opinion of a married woman. He decided not to punish the man due to his advanced age.

During his many interviews, the governor had discovered that one of the gossipers was the alcalde mayor's wife. The governor did not censure her. Maybe he did not want to chastise the respectable wife of one of his officials. Magdalena, a former servant with little power, apparently had no one to defend her honor. But the most likely reason the governor ferreted out Magdalena's gossip and then punished her is that it was potentially explosive. She maligned not only the honor of a married woman, but also the honor of the two brothers. Could such a rumor incite the two men to harm one another and to divide a family? At a time when the colony depended on all of its men to defend it, the governor did not want divisiveness to fester.

Vital witness contributions allowed governors to determine guilt and empowered them to punish the guilty. In general, however, participation by members of the community mirrors that of kinfolk: they were reluctant to involve themselves in the marital problems of others. At the moment when called forth as witnesses, people became engaged. Only in the exceptional case from 1750 when Alejandro Mora sadistically abused both his wife and servant, did people clamor for state intervention.[107] In most situations, however, community members might have carefully deliberated about whether to share the information they knew since gossiping could be a crime.

A case might involve many issues in addition to violence against women. In these cases, governors and their officials weighed the issues at hand and decided which was the most important problem to address. In a civil case from 1708, the alférez, or second lieutenant, Nícolas Ortiz, filed a complaint with the alcalde ordinario of Santa Fe, Juan García, explaining his complaint thusly: While he and his wife, along with the Sergeant Cristóbal de Góngora, visited a friend, Juan Maese's wife arrived. She had fled from her husband and exclaimed to heaven, "now my husband will kill me."[108] Her husband, Juan Maese, turned up with a stick in hand, saying to her, "Señorita, now you will see what happens when you leave our house." As Ortiz's wife jumped up to defend the woman, Maese hit her on the arm. Later Ortiz explained, "He did not even perceive that I, her husband, was present." The sergeant's effort to pacify the angry husband only enraged him more. Ortiz, who had remained uninvolved in the melee due to an ailment, finally grabbed a stick and hit the "impudent rogue" on his head. Ortiz emphasized that Maese, in addition to committing the crime of hurting his wife, had also failed to pay proper respect to his superior officers.

The alcalde ordinario reminded those involved that he was charged with the duty of looking after the public good and the tranquility of the body politic. In order to ensure that there were no controversies between Ortiz and Maese that could result in grave harm, he ordered that both men remain silent about the past and that they never return to it under threat of a fine of 50 pesos each and a two-year banishment to the Acoma frontier. He also charged them both with the cost of the original complaint.[109]

The alcalde ordinario clearly believed that maintaining the peace between these two men was the most important issue. Discord amongst the soldiers could lead to dangerous ramifications for the community at large while the colony's status remained tenuous. Because Maese's wife did not file a complaint, the alcalde ordinario did not even consider her plight. Maese did what a husband should do if his wife ran away; he fetched her. Although Maese did hurt Ortiz's wife, the alcalde ordinario assumed that the alférez would be there to protect her in the future. Ortiz's complaint also rested on the fact that Maese had not paid due respect to a married woman especially in her husband's presence. Maese had besmirched Ortiz's honor as a husband and as commanding officer. Although the alcalde ordinario placed Maese in jail for a short period, he did not pursue the matter any further.

In the eyes of state officials, another issue that took precedence over violence against wives was adultery. Based on the interest shown in adulterers and the subsequent punishment meted out, it appears that state officials believed that adultery presented a far more pernicious situation than the mala vida. In addition to upholding church beliefs, the lawmen also upheld the laws of the *Siete Partidas*. King Alfonso X made clear that both men and women sinned when committing adultery. He wrote: "All those men who lie with married women are guilty of depravity and great sin, and a sin of this kind is called adultery."[110]

Why else might officials have acted so forcefully against the practice? As suggested above when Governor Flores Mogollón punished the criada Magdalena Pachane, officials feared discord among the community. While violence between husband and wife might draw immediate family members into the tension, adultery spilled over, entangling multiple families. Intent on maintaining public tranquility, officials sought to defuse these situations before they became family feuds.

In June 1765, Isabel de Medina came to the Santa Fe alcalde mayor, don Francisco Guerrero, to complain about her husband, Bartolo Garduño. Her husband had severely beaten her face. When asked what was the "motivo," the wife revealed that the underlying cause was his adulterous relationship with Manuela López, alias La Barranca. Guerrero ordered that Bartolo Garduño be brought before him. He questioned him: "What motivated you to mistreat your poor wife?" Garduño replied that his wife was "very shameless." He would not provide another reason.[111]

The dissatisfied alcalde mayor had Garduño arrested and placed in shackles. This was not the first time that state officials had dealt with Garduño; they had previously exiled him for engaging in an adulterous relationship with La Barranca. His wife revealed that the only reason he had married her was to return from exile. If Garduño was at liberty to marry, the implication is that La Barranca was not.

Bartolo Garduño had four children with La Barranca and wanted to care for them. Yet, upon further questioning, it became clear that Garduño had made little or no effort to put physical distance between himself and La Barranca upon his return; they still lived near each other. Governor Vélez Cachupín decided to banish Garduño again for three years. The governor failed to mention who would provide for the children. Perhaps by not banishing La Barranca, he believed that the mother's nurturing and economic care were sufficient. He also ordered Garduño's wife, Isabel de Medina, to live with her parents in Chimayó.[112]

The above case displays the state officials' continuing keen interest in the adulterous affair of Garduño and La Barranca. Yet, as in previous instances, they did not necessarily seek out adulterers. Instead wives' complaints or serendipity (as in the case in which a child sought help) brought the subject before officials. Did community members complain to officials about these cases? Evidence suggests that they did not. If the affair did not have a negative impact on the greater community, they seemed to understand that it was a private matter between husbands and wives, a part of the mala vida. Take the case in which the alcalde ordinario discovered that a married woman had had a six-year affair with El Jasque. The neighbors did not report the affair nor did El Jasque's *amo* (master) although they had ample time to assess the situation. Did they ponder who was hurt by the affair? Did they worry about the husband who might never return? Did they fret that the two lovers sinned? Neighbors concerned with moral turpitude had some recourse: they could inform the friars. And perhaps they did. The paper trail of this course of action, however, cannot be traced in the New Mexican archives.

In the end, how did the governors punish husbands who murdered their wives? Though Páez Hurtado gathered a wealth of evidence against Miguel Luján during his thorough investigation, the governor seemed reluctant to prosecute without an eyewitness. He ordered that Miguel Luján be sent to New Spain to be tried there. En route, Miguel Luján escaped and never faced prosecution or punishment. But by escaping, he faced a life of self-exile. In 1741, after the investigation into the murder of María Magdalena Baca, the governor banished Juan Márquez and his friend, El Jasque, for four years, threatening to imprison them for two years if they returned to their communities. In another murder case from 1772, Pascual Sedillo sat in jail for eighteen months while the governor tried to determine whether he had indeed murdered his wife or whether she had died from an illness. In the end, the governor banished him to Taos for five years.[113]

To New Mexicans of the eighteenth century, the idea of living without family or friends in a hostile environment must have been seen as a severe hardship. The question arises, however, about whether governors and their officials could enforce the expulsion. Once again, the governors depended on the community to help, this time, with enforcement. One can imagine that María Magdalena Baca's sons and extended family stayed vigilant to ensure that the murderer Juan Márquez did not return, and they probably exacted help from their neighbors to do the same. Husbands, accused of less heinous crimes, however, might have had less difficulty returning to their families and friends. Bartolo Garduño, for example, quickly returned to his wife (or perhaps never left). Perhaps by moving from Santa Fe, Garduño eluded the law. On January 26, 1766, Garduño and his wife Isabel had their daughter, Juana María, baptized in the parish of Santa Cruz de la Cañada.[114]

In cases of domestic violence, governors aimed to temper the husband's behavior and bring more harmony to the conjugal household. They seemed to believe that punishment served as a deterrent that would lead to more amicable relationships in the future. Governors believed that their interference and punishment would moderate a husband's bad conduct. They viewed the incarceration as short-term, because ultimately, the governors aimed to uphold the sanctity of the Catholic Church's sacramental marriage and the conjugal home.

In cases of adultery, on the other hand, governors preferred that the couples live apart. They seemed to believe that removing husbands from the temptation of the mistress, even if it meant a lengthy separation from the lawful wife, was best. In the one case of incest, the governor banished the accused for six years, effectively sundering the man from his wife.

In addition to confining men to jail cells, a couple of officials came up with more creative ways to temper a husband's violent behavior. Governor Flores Mogollón's solution, to require Feliz Luján to live near his wife's family, seems a brilliant move. Juan Páez Hurtado placed an Indian woman in Magdalena's home, one can only suppose, to protect Magdalena from her own husband. After Magdalena's murder, Páez Hurtado asked Antonia, "Why did you leave the house of the dead María Magdalena, having been placed there by my order?" She answered that the soldier Márquez had sent her out of the house under the pretext that she was gossiping to his wife. She claimed that that was not the case; instead, she favored the dead woman when she was able to. According to her testimony, she had saved Magdalena's life by taking a sword away from Márquez who was using it to beat his wife.[115] So on this occasion, Páez Hurtado's strategy of placing an ally in María Magdalena's house had worked. Ultimately it failed, however, because Antonia did not challenge the soldier Márquez's order for her to leave by informing Páez Hurtado. Placing a female servant, considered by society to be weak and powerless, in the home of a male soldier, proved ineffective in protecting the wife.

Finally, the wives participated in the process, appealing to the governors. Initially, in fear or anger, they demanded that the officials end the abuse their husbands inflicted. Once their bruises and welts healed, they came forward and begged for their husbands' release from jail. Living on their own without the economic aid of their husbands proved difficult. Francisca de Tórrez told the governor that she forgave her husband and wanted him released so that he could plant.[116] Even the wife of the vicious Mora implored the governor to release her husband after his imprisonment of fourteen months.[117] In both cases, the respective governors released the men, eliciting promises from them that they would treat their wives with greater respect.

In the end, economic pressures forced many women to remain with violent men. Mora's servant escaped from his clutches, but his wife, with no other options, asked the governor to release her husband from jail. Women, when they appealed to the governor, hoped that he would be able to improve their marital relationships. Perhaps governors' warnings helped the couples reconcile. Before women turned to civil authorities, however, they looked to their kin for aid. Although some relatives stepped in and tried to prevent the situations from deteriorating, in most cases, the evidence suggests that relatives felt reluctant to intervene and only asked for state intervention when lives seemed in imminent danger. Finally, community members played a vital role during the investigation of the cases and might have helped with the enforcement of banishments. They too, however, rarely acted except in the one documented case of extraordinary domestic violence. When the friars read aloud the marriage banns, people had the opportunity to offer information that could prevent a marriage from taking place. In contrast, the public did not have a civil- or ecclesiastical-sponsored forum to pass judgment on people's marriages. Instead, people observed their neighbors, listened to the rumors, and bided their time.

CONCLUSION

When Governor Vargas came north to reconquer New Mexico, he led families that were to be the foundation of the restored colony. There was nothing new in this policy. The Spanish Crown and the Catholic Church believed that strong families led to law-abiding subjects and devout, moral Christians. Most settlers accepted the idea that families formed the basis of their society. Those who had not married already did so before venturing north. Upon arrival to the edge of the empire, confronted with violence and uncertainty, the settlers clung to their families and communities. Catholic rituals, shared with friends and neighbors, grounded them. This study of family and community uncovers some of the unique aspects of life on the frontier.

The church and state worked with the community to uphold the institution of the family. For every ritual and every investigation conducted, the officials relied on community involvement. During marital investigations, for example, the friars needed the neighbors to vouchsafe that the men and women seeking marriage were at liberty to do so. Meanwhile, state officials needed witnesses to corroborate information about dowries and properties so that children could receive their fair inheritances. Although few New Mexicans received a formal education, they understood the institutional rules and regulations governing their lives, from marriage and the joining of possessions to death and the dispersal of accumulated property. The officials' reliance on the community and the willingness of community members to step forward led to the enduring presence of the family in New Mexico.

In addition to the marriage and baptismal books that attest to the persistence of family life, the archives contain civil and ecclesiastical cases in which we see strife, adultery, broken marriage promises, and murder. Recall the history of the grandmother, María Luisa Aragón, who won her appeal to exert influence over her granddaughter's marital plans after complaining to the ecclesiastical court about her son-in-law's interference. This family drama from 1766 provides us with clues about what family formation and life were like in the small villas. We see infidelity, intergenerational conflict, adoption, but what, perhaps, is most telling is the fact that the case appears in the archives at all. The son-in-law spread "sinister accounts" about his mother-in-law and filed a suit before the ecclesiastical court. He did not resort to violence; instead, he used the court of public opinion and the ecclesiastical court to resolve matters. When families could not solve problems that upset family life, such as adultery, many New Mexicans chose to seek out the aid of church and state officials. The officials often crafted solutions that recognized the beliefs and realities of their subjects. Though the son-in-law might have had a legal claim to weigh in on his wife's daughter's wedding, the judge decided in favor of the grandmother. In addition to acknowledging the hard work it took to raise the granddaughter, he also recognized that the witnesses sided with the grandmother.

That a woman, María Luisa Aragón, came forward to argue her case was not unusual in New Mexico. When relationships ended without marriage, women often sought to restore their lost honor by appealing to civil or ecclesiastical officials, asking them to force men to fulfill their promises. Women spoke of their lost virginity as lost honor, but they did not fear overly for their reputations. Because community members had witnessed their courtships, women knew that they could call on them to testify to the seriousness and duration of their liaisons. Instead of judging these women as fallen and disgraced, community members seemed to support them and to condemn the men, to some extent, for violating the community's sense of decency. Indeed, some of the women who lost their honor went on to find husbands.

Civil and ecclesiastical authorities took these cases seriously, recognizing the importance of men honoring their promises. They investigated the women's claims, interviewing numerous witnesses. They willingly imprisoned the men for the duration of the investigations. In most cases, however, the authorities did not press men to marry the women. They seemed to believe that a forced marriage would benefit no one. In addition, some women concluded that marriage with reluctant, angry men might not be worth the restoration of their honor so instead asked for monetary compensation.

In the isolated communities of New Mexico, a small number of cousins, unable to find other mates, opted to marry one another. To marry, they needed to apply to the church for a dispensation. These records show that families did not have an overarching strategy to unite family wealth and to maintain family honor and blood purity. Instead, many men explained that they wanted to marry their cousins so that they could rescue them from poverty. Others married for love and friendship. Fewer than 30 percent of the cousins responded that they wished to marry their cousins because of their quality. Yet these respondents all defined quality uniquely, revealing that New Mexicans' ideas about social status differed from the thoughts of those living in more central regions like Mexico City.

In the face of this isolation, it is understandable that New Mexicans needed to have some flexibility when forming families. What is remarkable though is that in such small communities, year after year, men and women looked for spouses with whom they did not share ties of consanguinity or affinity. Often times, brothers and sisters lived near each other and raised their children in close proximity. Cousins played and worked together yet did not see one another as potential mates because their parents made clear that these first cousins would not be acceptable marriage partners.

Family formation began in adolescence. In many cases, parents gave their children latitude in choosing a spouse by allowing them an opportunity to engage in flirtations and courtships. Other parents tried to influence their children's selection of a spouse. For example, parents who were able bestowed property (in the form of dowries and patrimonies) on their children as a means to manipulate the selection process. In most cases, however, they did not favor one child over another and tried to grant an equal portion of property to all of their offspring. By evenly distributing their property, parents had little leverage with which to control their children. Other parents tried to use gossip to maneuver young men into marrying their daughters. The cases available suggest that gossip proved an ineffectual tool. Overall, parents who tried to force unwilling children to marry failed to achieve their goals.

Once married, couples, in many cases, established their own homes, living apart from their parents. Over the course of their lives, they maintained nuclear households, and only widows or widowers, on occasion, moved in with adult children. Many parents granted land to their male and female children when they married. A consequence is that the children built their new homes on adjoining plots. Apparently, couples chose to live on the best land they received, regardless of whether they obtained it from the men's or women's parents.

Proximity to relatives affected the lives of young married couples. On a practical level, families shared tasks and economic endeavors. Yet residential patterns also had a profound impact on the lives of women married to violent men. Parents watched over their daughters and gave them the confidence to deal with abusive husbands. Knowing that their wives' fathers and brothers lived nearby, probably gave men pause. Women, isolated from their kin, fared the worst. When battered women did need help, they turned to their sisters, who, if the situation was desperate, appealed to civil authorities.

In many respects, families lived their lives without much intervention from civil and ecclesiastical authorities. Friars did not stay long in their posts and probably did not know all of their parishioners. Governors, concerned with the constant raiding, gave citizens relative autonomy. With this independence some citizens found it possible to live together without the benefit of marriage or to deliver children out of wedlock. When the grandmother's daughter committed adultery, the authorities had not become involved. Nor did they intervene when she adopted the baby and raised her as a daughter. Even so, the community developed standards and expected members to abide by them. María Luisa Aragón had adhered to the codes of conduct by providing for her granddaughter's physical needs and raising her with Christian morals. That the baby was born of an adulterous relationship mattered little over time. Yet when individuals transgressed these principles, community members demanded civil and ecclesiastical intervention. The community's dependence on the authorities in these situations belies the idea that Hispanics settled their own problems with force and that frontier institutions were weak, ineffectual, and meaningless. In the end, communities developed standards that allowed for flexibility and proved less stringent than Spanish laws and strict codes of honor. Forgiveness of minor transgressions led to neighborly and familial cooperation, an effective strategy in the vast Kingdom of New Mexico.

APPENDIX

TABLE 1. Proportion of Interracial Marriages, 1694–1800

		Interracial	
Race	Total[¥]	Number	Percentage
Español	390	17	4.3
Española	405	32	7.9
Indio	51	25	49
India	38	12	32
Coyote	32	19	59
Coyota	35	22	63
Mestizo	24	12	50
Mestiza	29	17	59
Mulato	12	9	75
Mulata	8	5	63
Genízaro	9	3	33
Genízara	7	1	14
Castizo	1	0	0
Castiza	1	0	0
Color quebrado	2	2	100
Color quebrada	1	1	100
Negro	2	2	100
Negra	0	0	—

Source: Diligencias matrimoniales, 1694–1800. AASF, rolls 59–66.
Note: Total includes only those cases for which race data were listed for both spouses.

TABLE 2. Pattern of Interracial Marriages, 1694–1800

	Española	India	Coyota	Mestiza	Mulata	Genízara	Color quebrada	Negra
Español		4	3	9	1	—	—	—
Indio	6		13	3	1	1	1	—
Coyote	14	2		2	1	—	—	—
Mestizo	8	2	1		1	—	—	—
Mulato	2	3	3	1		—	—	—
Genízaro	0	1	1	1	—		—	—
Color quebrado	2	—	—	—	—	—		—
Negro	—	—	1	1	—	—	—	
Other	—	—	—	—	1	—	—	—

Source: Diligencias matrimoniales, 1694–1800. AASF, rolls 59–66.

TABLE 3. Honor Negotiated: A Summary of the Cases

	Year	Case	Civil or ecclesiastical?	Filed by whom?	Reason	Woman pregnant, children?	Woman deposited?	Man imprisoned?	Couple married?	Fine levied to pay woman?	Man punished?	Woman married?	Man married?
1	1702	Juana Luján v. Ventura de Esquibel	Ecclesiastical	Impediment filed by Juana Luján	Broken marriage promise	Yes	Yes	No	No	Yes, 200 pesos	No	Yes	Yes
2	1705	Juana Rodríguez v. Sebastián Luján	Ecclesiastical	Impediment filed by Juana Rodríguez	Marriage promise and deflowering	No	Yes	No	No	No	No	Yes	Yes
3	1705	Juana de Guadalupe v. Antonio Velázquez	Ecclesiastical	Impediment filed by Juana de Guadalupe	Broken marriage promise	No	No	No	No	No	No	No evidence	Yes
4	1714	Juana Montaño v. Nicolás Durán y Chávez	Civil	Civil and criminal suit filed by Juana Montaño	Marriage promise and deflowering	Yes	No	Yes	Yes	No	No	Yes	Yes
5	1716	Juan de León Brito v. Antonio de Abeita	Civil	Civil and criminal complaint filed by the father	Marriage promise and deflowering	Yes	No	Yes	Pages missing	Pages missing	Pages missing	No evidence	No evidence
6	1725	Manuela de Armijo v. Juan Lovato	Ecclesiastical	Complaint filed by Manuela de Armijo	Marriage promise and deflowering	No	Yes	Yes, 5 weeks	No	Yes, 200 pesos	No	Yes	No evidence
7	1736	Inés Griega v. Marcial Martínez	Ecclesiastical	Complaint filed by Inés Griega	Marriage promise and deflowering	Yes	No	Yes	No	Yes, 35 pesos	No	No evidence	No evidence
8	1750	Rape of Margarita García by Juan Lobato	Civil	Bernabé Montaño, lieutenant	Montaño caught the couple sleeping together.	No	Yes	Yes, 2 months	No	No	Threatened with punishment	Yes	No evidence

#	Year	Parties	Venue	Complaint	Issue							
9	1763	Gertrudis de Armijo v. Blas López	Civil	Civil and criminal complaint filed by the mother	Blas climbed into mother's house, bothering daughter.	No	Yes, 3 months	No	Yes, 50 pesos	Banished	No evidence	Yes
10	1766	Miguel Chávez v. José Antonio Salazar	Ecclesiastical	Complaint filed by father	Father claimed Salazar raped and impregnated daughter.	Yes	Pages missing	No	Pages missing	Pages missing	No evidence	No evidence
11	1767	María Manuela de la Luz Romero v. Mariano Baca	Civil	Civil and criminal complaint filed by María Manuela	Defamation of character	No	Yes, 9 months	No	No	Banished	Yes	Yes
12	1775	Gregorio Martín v. Salvador García	Civil	Civil and criminal complaint filed by father	Deflowering of daughter	Not known	No	No	Yes, 150 pesos	No	No evidence	No evidence
13	1777	Petrona Martín v. José Vigil	Ecclesiastical	Complaint filed by Petrona Martín	Broken marriage promise, deflowering, pregnancy	Yes	No	No	Pages missing	Pages missing	No evidence	No evidence
14	1777	Juana Padilla v. Gregorio, Alias El Satebo	Ecclesiastical	Complaint filed by Juana Padilla	Broken marriage promise	Yes	No	No	Yes, two black shawls	No	No evidence	No evidence

Sources: Impediment filed by Juana Luján, 1702, ASSF, roll 60, frame 266. Diligencia matrimonial of Sebastián Luján and Juana Teresa Trujillo, February 1705, AASF, roll 60, frames 374–390. Impediment filed by Juana de Guadalupe against Antonio Velázquez, 30 June 1705, AASF, roll 60, frames 428, 365–368. Civil complaint filed by Juana Montaño against Nicolás Durán y Chávez for a broken marriage promise, 1714, SANM II, roll 4, frames 1056–1068. Civil complaint filed by Juan de León Brito against Antonio de Abeita, 11 August 1716, Santa Fe, SANM II, roll 5, frames 602–622. Complaint filed by Manuela de Armijo against Juan Lobato, 24 February 1725, Loose Documents 1680–1743, AASF, roll 51, frames 952–964. Pre-marital dispute filed by Inés Griega against Marcial Martínez, 13 January 1736, AASF, roll 62, frame 187. Criminal case against Juan Lobato for the rape of Margarita García Jurado filed by Bernabé Montaño, May–June 1750, Bernalillo, SANM II, roll 8, frames 963–977. Civil and criminal complaint against Blas López filed by Gertrudis de Armijo, 30 December 1762, Santa Fe, SANM II, roll 9, frames 468–491. Complaint against José Antonio Salazar filed by Miguel Chávez, January 1766, Albuquerque, AASF, roll 62, frames 510–516. Civil and criminal case filed by María de la Luz Romero against Mariano Baca, April 1767, SANM II, roll 10, frames 4–25. Civil complaint filed by Gregorio Martín against Salvador García, 1775, Santa Cruz de la Cañada, SANM II, roll 10, frames 868–871. Complaint filed by Petrona Martín, 1777, AASF, roll 63, frames 663–665. Pre-marital dispute filed by Juana Padilla against El Satebo, 17 January 1777, AASF, roll 63, frames 609–611.

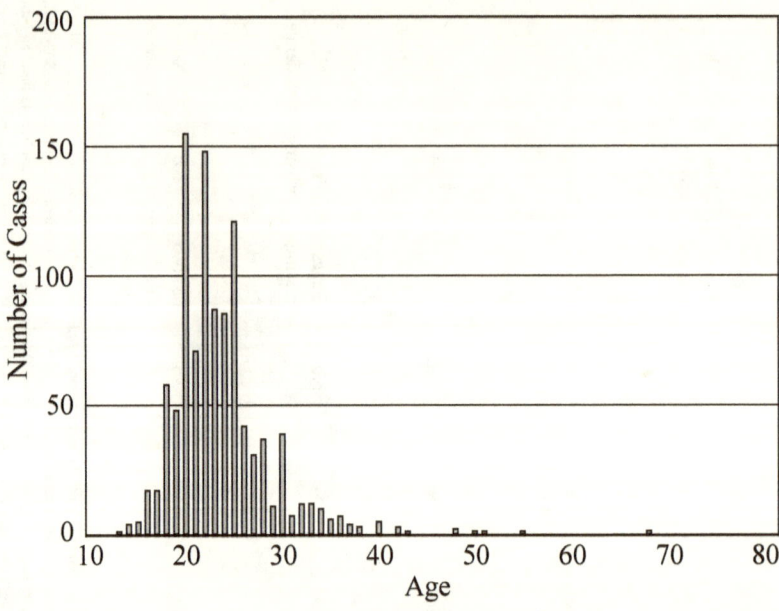

Figure 3. Distribution of Ages for First Marriages among Males, 1694–1800. Mean age was 23.5 for a population of 1,312. Source: Diligencias matrimoniales, AASF, rolls 59–66.

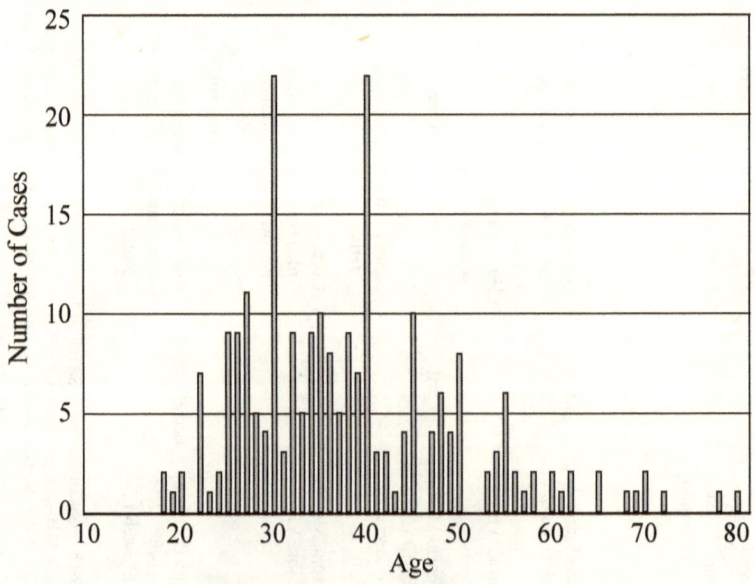

Figure 4. Distribution of Ages for Non-First Marriages among Males, 1694–1800. Mean age was 38 for a population of 235. Source: Diligencias matrimoniales, AASF, rolls 59–66.

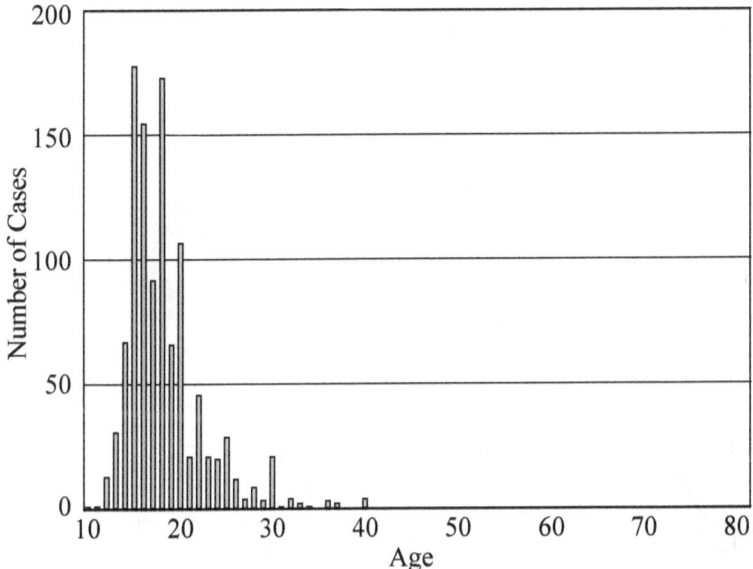

Figure 5. Distribution of Ages for First Marriages among Females, 1694–1800. Mean age was 18.3 for a population of 1,240. Source: Diligencias matrimoniales, AASF, rolls 59–66.

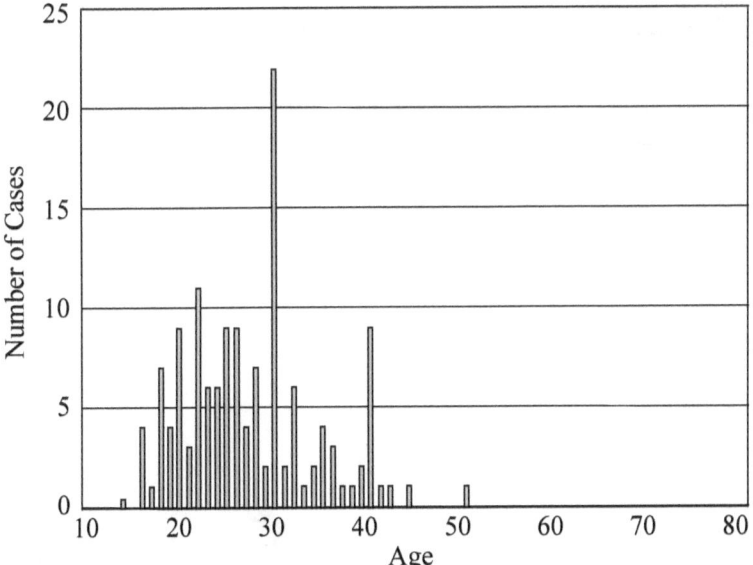

Figure 6. Distribution of Ages for Non-First Marriages among Females, 1694–1800. Mean age was 27 for a population of 141. Source: Diligencias matrimoniales, AASF, rolls 59–66.

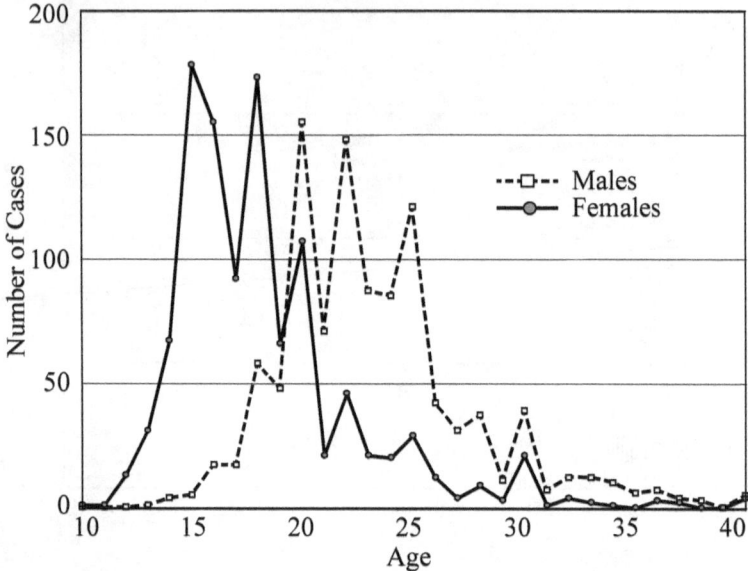

Figure 7. Age of First Marriages, 1694–1800. Distribution of ages for first marriages (1694–1800) showing females typically married about five years earlier than males. Mean age for males was 23.5, whereas mean age for females was 18.3. Population of males with age listed was 1,312; population of females with age listed was 1,240. Source: Diligencias matrimoniales, AASF, rolls 59–66.

APPENDIX

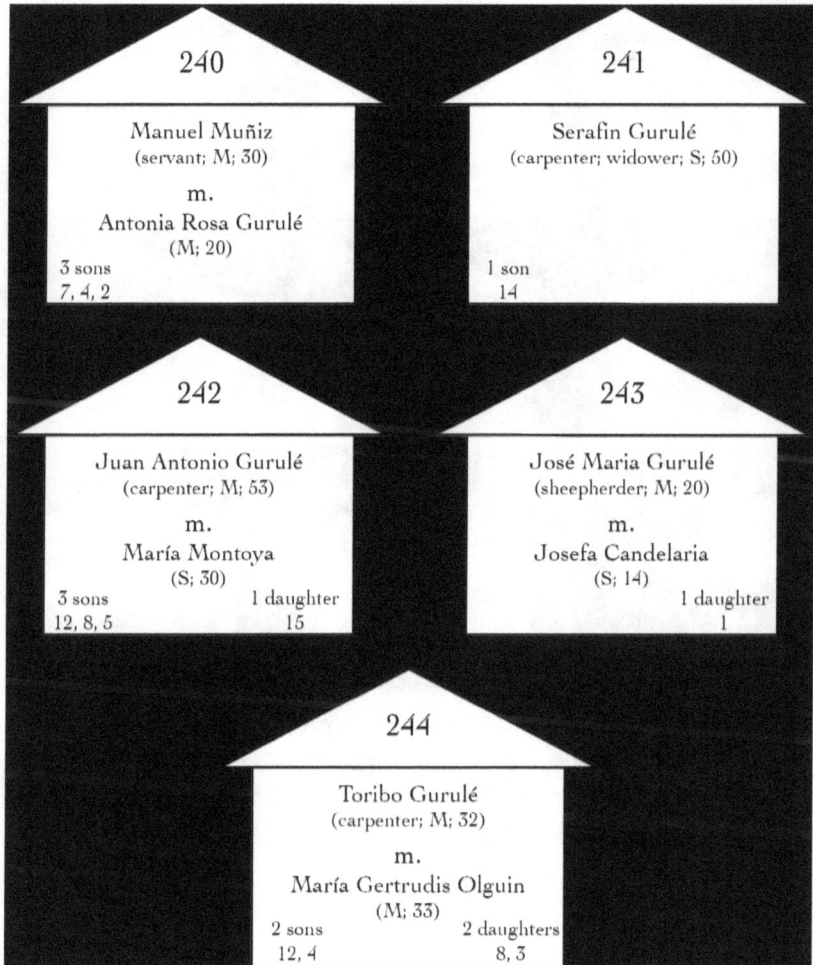

Figure 8. Surname Clusters for Albuquerque. Source: Data extracted from Virginia Langham Olmsted, compiler, *Spanish and Mexican Censuses of New Mexico, 1750–1830* (Albuquerque: Genealogical Society, Inc., 1981), 1–14. CQ = Color Quebrado/Broken Color, M = Mulato, S = Spaniard.

APPENDIX

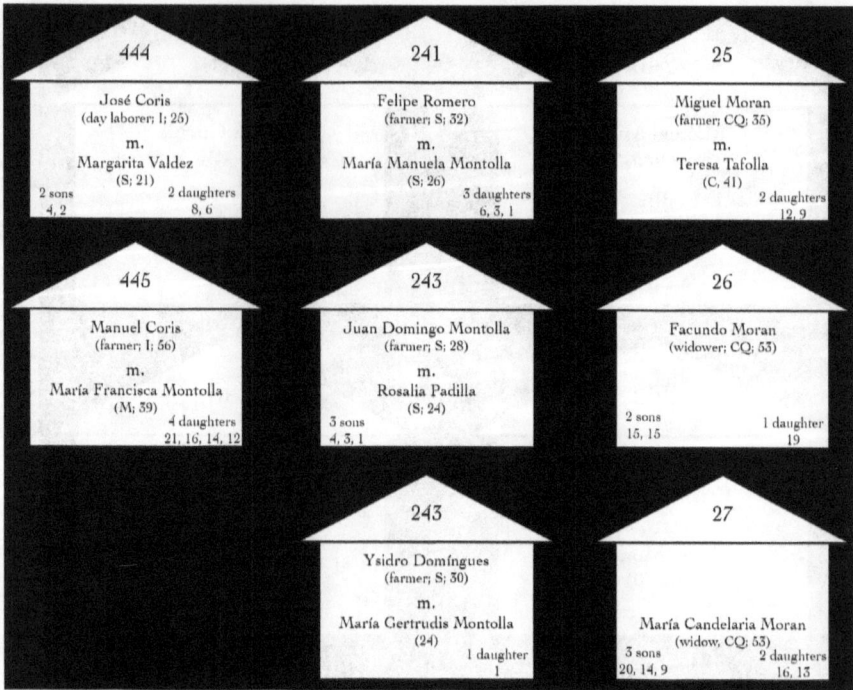

Figure 9. Surname Clusters for Santa Fe. Source: Data extracted from Virginia Langham Olmsted, compiler, *Spanish and Mexican Censuses of New Mexico, 1750–1830* (Albuquerque: Genealogical Society, Inc., 1981), 51–78.

APPENDIX

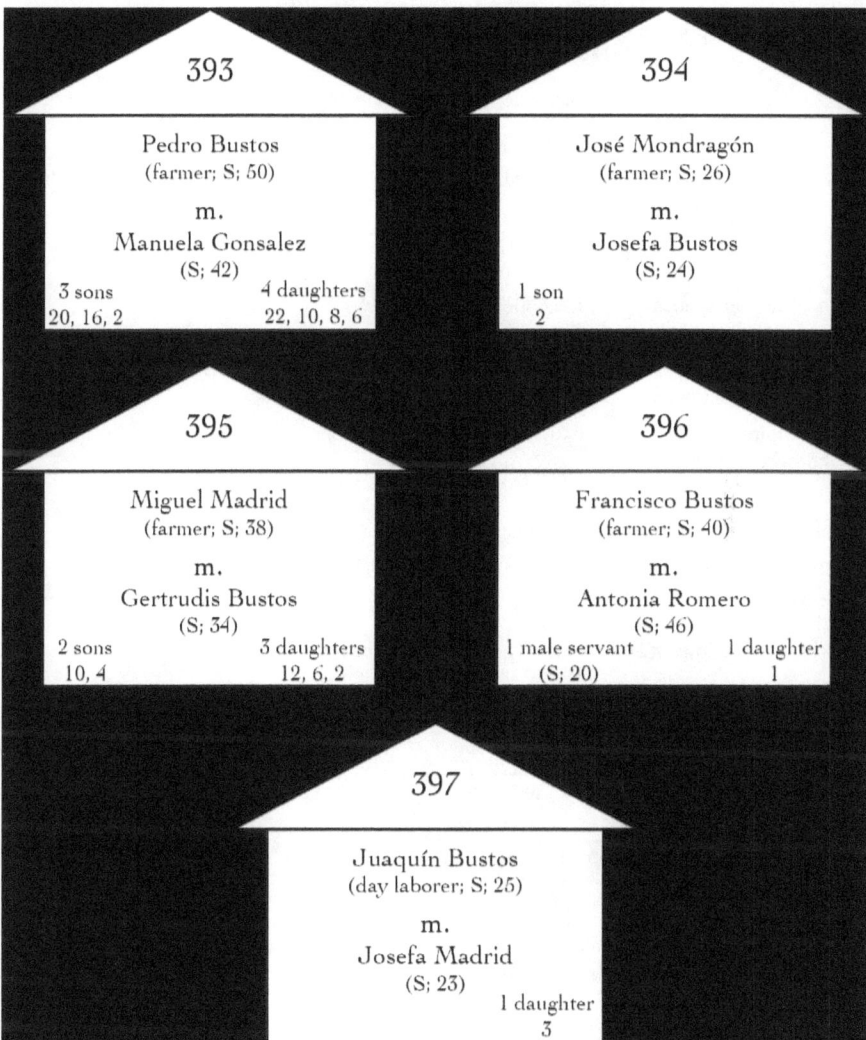

Figure 10. Surname Clusters for Santa Cruz de la Cañada. Source: Data extracted from Virginia Langham Olmsted, compiler, *Spanish and Mexican Censuses of New Mexico, 1750–1830* (Albuquerque: Genealogical Society, Inc., 1981), 82–105.

TABLE 4. Proportion of Different Types of Households, 1790

	Albuquerque	Santa Fe	Santa Cruz
Total households	248	561	497
Dual-headed households	203 (81.9%)	433 (77.2%)	394 (79.3%)
Widow-headed households	30 (12.1%)	87 (15.5%)	86 (17.3%)
Widower-headed households	14 (5.6%)	19 (3.4%)	15 (3.0%)
Single-headed households (male)	0 (0%)	7 (1.2%)	2 (0.4%)
Single-headed households (female)	0 (0%)	5 (0.9%)	0 (0%)

Source: Virginia Langham Olmsted, compiler, *Spanish and Mexican Censuses of New Mexico, 1750–1830* (Albuquerque: Genealogical Society, Inc., 1981), 1–14, 51–78, 82–105.

TABLE 5. Distributions of Household Types for Male-Headed Households in Albuquerque, 1790

Age group of head	Single	Wife only	Wife + children only	Wife + siblings	Complex families	
					Wife + parents +/− siblings	Wife + other
<20	0	1	0	0	0	0
	0%	100%	0%	0%	0%	0%
20–29	4	20	42	3	2	12
	4.8%	24.1%	50.6%	3.6%	2.4%	14.5%
30–39	0	2	54	3	1	3
	0%	3.2%	85.7%	4.8%	1.6%	3.6%
40–49	1	4	24	0	1	6
	2.8%	11.1%	66.7%	0%	2.8%	7.2%
50–59	6	0	12	0	0	4
	27.3%	0%	54.5%	0%	0%	4.8%
>59	4	1	6	0	1	1
	30.8%	7.7%	46.2%	0%	7.7%	1.2%

Source: Data extracted from Virginia Langham Olmsted, compiler, *Spanish and Mexican Censuses of New Mexico, 1750–1830* (Albuquerque: Genealogical Society, Inc., 1981), 1–14.

TABLE 6. Distributions of Household Types for Male-Headed Households in Santa Fe, 1790

Age group of head	Single	Wife only	Wife + children only	Complex families			
				Wife + siblings	Wife + parents +/- siblings	Wife + other
<20	0	4	5	0	0	0
	0%	44.4%	55.6%	0%	0%	0%
20–29	3	44	85	3	1	3
	2.2%	31.7%	61.2%	2.2%	0.7%	2.2%
30–39	5	10	97	2	1	8
	4.1%	8.1%	78.9%	1.6%	0.8%	5.8%
40–49	4	4	64	0	0	0
	5.6%	5.6%	88.9%	0%	0%	0%
50–59	5	6	41	1	1	4
	8.6%	10.3%	70.7%	1.7%	1.7%	2.9%
>59	12	9	23	0	0	10
	22.2%	16.7%	42.6%	0%	0%	7.2%

Source: Data extracted from Virginia Langham Olmsted, compiler, *Spanish and Mexican Censuses of New Mexico, 1750–1830* (Albuquerque: Genealogical Society, Inc., 1981), 51–78.

TABLE 7. Distributions of Household Types for Male-Headed Households in Santa Cruz, 1790

					Complex families	
Age group of head	Single	Wife only	Wife + children only	Wife + siblings	Wife + parents +/− siblings	Wife + other
<20	0	0	0	0	0	0
	0%	0%	0%	0%	0%	0%
20–29	7	41	60	5	0	0
	6.2%	36.3%	53.1%	4.4%	0%	0%
30–39	3	8	110	7	0	1
	2.3%	6.2%	85.3%	5.4%	0%	0.9%
40–49	3	9	84	2	0	5
	2.9%	8.7%	81.6%	1.9%	0%	4.4%
50–59	1	3	40	0	0	6
	2.0%	6.0%	80.0%	0%	0%	5.3%
>59	3	0	11	1	0	1
	18.8%	0%	68.8%	6.3%	0%	0.9%

Source: Data extracted from Virginia Langham Olmsted, compiler, *Spanish and Mexican Censuses of New Mexico, 1750–1830* (Albuquerque: Genealogical Society, Inc., 1981), 51–105.

NOTES ON SOURCES

In this study, I employ both ecclesiastical and civil records dating from 1692 to 1800. The ecclesiastical records include marital investigations (diligencias matrimoniales), dispensation appeals, premarital disputes, baptismal records, marriage records, and one divorce petition. The diligencias matrimoniales date from 1640 to 1800. There is a large thirty-year gap in marital investigations missing from the archives, however, dating from 1730 to 1760. Also, investigations of presidial soldiers have not been uncovered if they still exist. I also did not include investigations from the El Paso region. In general, the marital investigations are formulaic, but rich nonetheless. They list facts about the marrying couples—legitimacy, place of birth, race, age, and the names of witnesses. Some of the investigations lack information on race or legitimacy, as the friars were not always consistent. In addition to the friars' errors, applicants provided false information. Some called themselves children of unknown parents, when in fact, they knew who their parents were. The friars focused on the applicants and their witnesses and did not interview any family members, leaving little evidence about how family members involved themselves in the process. On occasion an impediment arose, and friars investigated. These marital investigations yield more information about courtship, family involvement, and the applicants' feelings. The marriage books from Santa Fe, Albuquerque, and Santa Cruz de la Cañada do not contain as much information. Friars listed the date and names of the bridegroom, bride, witnesses, padrinos, and the friar. They also listed whether the brides and bridegrooms had been previously married. Occasionally, a friar marked down the race, especially if the people marrying were Indians. I used microfilm of the Archives of the Archdioceses of Santa Fe (AASF) found in the New Mexico State Record Center and Archives in Santa Fe, New Mexico. Many of the dispensation cases are from the Archdioceses of Durango, Mexico. Historian Rick Hendricks transcribed and translated the cases pertaining to New Mexico. The State Archives also contains a number of transcriptions by various genealogists from the New Mexico Genealogical Society. Due to the poor quality of some of the microfilm, having the chance to get a "second opinion" on a name, date, or word proves helpful. The books I turned to were by the following genealogists: Ella Louise May, Margaret Leonard Windham, Evelyn Lujan Baca, Marie J. Roybal, Lila Armijo Pfeufer, Henrietta Christmas, and Patricia Sanchez Rau.

The civil cases revolve around family issues such as broken engagements and domestic violence. In most cases local officials investigated, bringing their findings to the governors. At times, I noted officials failed to ask pertinent questions. As members of the communities they governed, they may have had certain biases. On the other hand, they may have declined to ask piercing questions because they understood and observed more than they wrote down. Little research exists about the personal biases of the governors. More research on governors' judgments over the course of their careers (gleaned from previous and subsequent posts) might shed light on how they interpreted the cases in New Mexico.

Most civil cases revolve around an extraordinary act (murder) or deviant behavior (abuse). The reactions of the officials and the witnesses expose how people viewed the events, how they reacted, and the state's response. Even if the cases shocked community members, they had an oral history which informed them about past lawbreakers. These civil case records are housed in the New Mexico State Record Center and Archives and are known as the Spanish Archives of New Mexico, Series I and II (SANMI, SANMII). Series I is also known as Land Records of New Mexico. Further, I examined 105 randomly chosen wills and inventories. All in all, approximately 245 wills and settlements exist for the period under study.

I also rely heavily on the census of 1790 to help understand household composition. I examined data about Santa Fe, Santa Cruz de la Cañada, and Albuquerque from Virginia Langham Olmsted's transcription and translation of the 1790 census.[1] In the past, family historians have pointed out the dangers of employing census data.[2] States often called for censuses for tax purposes. Errors undoubtedly affect the record, and inconsistencies are evident in the New Mexican census. In identifying a person's race, the enumerator for Santa Fe used the phrase "color quebrado," (mixed race), but the enumerators for Albuquerque and Santa Cruz de la Cañada did not. Census data also marks a particular moment in time. After the enumerators left, household composition might have shifted dramatically. The census would also be sensitive to historical changes. The 1790 census took place a decade after the smallpox epidemic ravaged New Mexico. This might account for higher levels of orphans or nieces and nephews in households than would have been present a decade later.

The census data are rich, nonetheless, and provide the best clues available to household composition. I group men in age categories and try to find who resided in their households. At the time of the census, younger men had less complex households than did older men. I decipher changes in the patterns of household composition and try to discern how shifts occurred as people matured from young spouses to old parents.

The records left by the friars and civil authorities are rife with inconsistencies. It is not surprising that the individuals who took notes over a hundred-year period brought their own ideas about what was important to write down and how to spell it. Variation between the documents is the rule. Even though the church expected friars to record the same information in its baptism books, for example, the books show remarkable differences. Some friars noted that parents were legitimately married, others noted that the children were legitimate, and still others forgot to write down whether the parents were married. When compiling the data for the charts, I had to make certain assumptions and interpretations. Sometimes it is evident that it was an oversight when a friar or the scribe deviated from proper form. In the end, although I tried to minimize my own errors, some undoubtedly occurred.

I used the following archival resources:

Archives of the Archdiocese of Santa Fe, Book of Baptisms, Santa Fe, New Mexico.

Archives of the Archdiocese of Santa Fe, Diligencias Matrimoniales, Santa Fe, New Mexico.

Archives of the Archdiocese of Santa Fe, Loose Documents, Mission, Santa Fe, New Mexico.

Archives of the Archdiocese of Santa Fe, Marriage Books, Santa Fe, New Mexico.

Spanish Archives of New Mexico, series I, New Mexico State Records Center and Archives, Santa Fe, New Mexico.

Spanish Archives of New Mexico, series II, New Mexico State Records Center and Archives, Santa Fe, New Mexico.

NOTES

Introduction

1. Complaint filed by María Luisa de Aragón against Pedro Yturrieta, 9 April 1766, Albuquerque, Archives of the Archdiocese of Santa Fe (AASF), roll 62, frames 619–23 (hereafter cited as Aragón against Yturrieta).
2. Aragón against Yturrieta, frame 619.
3. Ibid., frames 619–23. See frame 620.
4. Ibid. See frame 619.
5. Kessell, *Pueblos, Spaniards, and the Kingdom of New Mexico*, 152–54.
6. Guy and Sheridan, *Contested Ground*, 10.
7. Weber, *The Spanish Frontier in North America*, 10.
8. Johnson and Lipsett-Rivera, *The Faces of Honor*, 2.
9. Lavrin, "Introduction," 10.
10. Johnson and Lipsett-Rivera, *The Faces of Honor*, 5.
11. Alonso, *Thread of Blood*, 54.
12. Brooks, *Captives and Cousins*, 132–33.
13. Gutiérrez, *When Jesus Came*, 214.
14. Alonso, *Thread of Blood*, 86.
15. Erickson, "Violence and Manhood," 196.
16. Gutiérrez, *When Jesus Came*, 214.
17. See both authors: Martinez-Alier, *Marriage, Class and Colour*; Seed, *To Love, Honor, and Obey*.
18. Gutiérrez, *When Jesus Came*, xix.
19. Ann Twinam, "The Negotiation of Honor," 84.
20. Gutiérrez, *When Jesus Came*, 230.
21. Ibid., 244.

22. Cavallo and Cerutti, "Female Honor and Social Control," 86.
23. See Rock, "'Pido y Suplico,'" 145–59.

Chapter 1

1. Gerhard, *The North Frontier of New Spain*, 313.
2. Kessell and Hendricks, *By Force of Arms*, 5.
3. Ibid., 3–5.
4. Frank, *From Settler to Citizen*, 3.
5. Bustamante, "'The Matter Was Never Resolved,'" 146.
6. Tjarks, "Demographic, Ethnic and Occupational Structure," 58–59.
7. Brugge, *Navajos in the Catholic Church Records*, 1–2.
8. The origins of the genízaros included Apache, Jumano, Pawnee, Crow, Kiowa, Comanche, Ute, and Navajo. See Brooks, *Captives and Cousins*, 146.
9. Ibid., 124–33.
10. Bustamante, "'The Matter Was Never Resolved,'" 157.
11. Ibid.
12. Cutter, *The Protector de Indios*, 77.
13. Adams and Chavez, *The Missions of New Mexico, 1776*, 84.
14. Hendricks, *New Mexico in 1801*, 71.
15. Quoted in Bustamante, "'The Matter Was Never Resolved,'" 159. Mendinueta's bando against damages to crops from livestock, Santa Fe, 12 March 1768, roll 10, frames 401–4. The Spanish for "mixed race" is *color quebrado*.
16. See chapter 5.
17. Tjarks, "Demographic, Ethnic and Occupational Structure," 50. Tjarks mentions venereal diseases and the use of contraceptive herbs and abortions. I found evidence to suggest that women did use abortifacients.
18. Ibid., 60–61.
19. Frank, *From Settler to Citizen*, 47.
20. Ibid., 56–57.
21. Cutter, *The Protector de Indios*, 23.
22. Jones, *Los Paisanos*, 114.
23. Tjarks, "Demographic, Ethnic and Occupational Structure," 86.
24. Hendricks, *New Mexico in 1801*, 5.
25. Ibid., 70.
26. Ibid., 78. *Gente de razón* means "non-Indians."
27. Ibid., 106.
28. Ibid., 79.
29. Ibid., 73.
30. Baxter, *Las Carneradas*, 20. The churro was a hardy sheep that could drink morning dew and eat succulent plants without needing a drinking hole. They were able to withstand drought better than cattle.

31. Ibid., 21.
32. Hendricks, *New Mexico in 1801*, 74.
33. Baxter, *Las Carneradas*, 22.
34. Ibid., 28.
35. Hendricks, *New Mexico in 1801*, 106.
36. Baxter, *Las Carneradas*, 29, 31.
37. Hendricks, *New Mexico in 1801*, 80. The manta was a standard-size cloth used mostly for exchange, and the *rebozo* a shawl for women.
38. Quoted in Frank, *From Settler to Citizen*, 14. Informe del estado de la Nuevo México a su majestad según su cédula de 1748, written by ex-custodio Fray Andrés Varo, Mexico, 29 January 1749, AFBN 28:553.1,1773, 5R.
39. Brooks, *Captives and Cousins*, 120.
40. Frank, *From Settler to Citizen*, 20.
41. Hendricks, *New Mexico in 1801*, 80.
42. Frank, *From Settler to Citizen*, 37.
43. Ibid.
44. Ibid., 50.
45. Brooks, *Captives and Cousins*, 35.
46. Frank, *From Settler to Citizen*, 71.
47. Ibid., 70.
48. Ibid., 132.
49. Ibid., 137.
50. Ibid., 83.
51. Ibid., 108.
52. Baxter, *Las Carneradas*, 42.
53. Frank, *From Settler to Citizen*, 55.
54. Ibid., 156.
55. Jones, *Los Paisanos*, 164.
56. Baxter, *Las Carneradas*, 21.
57. Will of Cristóbal Baca, 1739, Santa Fe, SANM I, roll 1, frames 637–80.
58. Van Young, *Hacienda and Market*, 114–26.
59. Weber, *The Spanish Frontier in North America*, 320. Also see Simmons, "Settlement Patterns," 100.
60. Adams and Chavez, *The Missions of New Mexico*, 40.
61. Simmons, "Settlement Patterns," 105.
62. Ibid., 99. "By royal concession, private individuals or groups of persons might apply for lands, and after fulfilling certain legal requirements, receive a grant called a *gracia* or *merced real*."
63. Snow, "Rural Hispanic Community Organization," 47.
64. Ibid., 47. For more details on the merced, see Adams and Chavez, *The Missions of New Mexico*, 182.
65. Quoted in Simmons, "Settlement Patterns," 109.
66. Ibid., 106.

67. Bunting, *Taos Adobes*, 3.
68. Frank, *From Settler to Citizen*, 43. Today Carnué is known as Carnuel.
69. Morfi, *Account of Disorders in New Mexico*, 14. People probably did not run around without any clothes. Clothes protected people from the burning sun and the frigid nights and winters. Historian Françoise Barret-Ducrocq, who writes about nineteenth-century London, may offer a clue about what Morfi meant when he stated that people ran around naked. She notes that upper-class observers noted that the lower classes showed their nakedness. By this they meant that the women did not use appropriate underwear (corsets) and exposed more shoulders and legs than the observers thought proper. Barret-Ducrocq, *Love in the time of Victoria*, 20–21.
70. Brooks, "'Lest We Go in Search of Relief,'" 168–69.
71. See ibid., 169. "Manuel de Armijo y José Miguel de la Peña," 2 June 1780, Document 5, Sender Collection, roll 1, frames 27–38, New Mexico State Records Center.
72. Brooks, "Lest We Go in Search of Relief," 169.
73. Iowa, *Ageless Adobe*, 24.
74. Bunting, *Taos Adobes*, 6.
75. Bunting, *Early Architecture in New Mexico*, 63.
76. Will of Diego Márquez, 1729, SANM I, roll 3, frame 743.
77. Bunting, *Early Architecture*, 69.
78. Ibid., 63.
79. Ibid., 65.
80. Ibid., 67.
81. Ibid., 59.
82. Bunting, *Taos Adobes*, 6.
83. Simmons, "Hygiene", 219–20.
84. Pierce and Snow, "'A Harp for Playing,'" 73.
85. Will of Juan Manuel Gabaldón, 1745, SANM I, roll 2, frame 805.
86. Boyd, *Popular Arts of Colonial New Mexico*, 11.
87. Bakker, "New Mexican Spanish Colonial Furniture," 124.
88. Will of Diego Márquez, 20 April 1729, SANM I, roll 3, frames 742–43.
89. Will of Juana Anaya Almazán, 10 November 1736, SANM I, roll 6, frames 757–60.
90. Simmons, "Hygiene," 209.
91. Bakker, "New Mexican Spanish Colonial Furniture," 126.
92. Inventory of Tomasa Benavides, SANM I, roll 1, frames 776–82.
93. Boyd, *Popular Arts of Colonial New Mexico*, 11.
94. Veyna, "'It Is My Last Wish That . . . ,'" 97.
95. Will of Juan Ruis Cordero, 1723, SANM I, roll 6, frames 658–61. Will of Luis López, 1728, SANM I, roll 3, frames 288–290.
96. Will and Inventory of Manuel Holguín, SANM I, roll 4, frames 296–314. See frame 302.

97. Ibid., roll 3, frames 327-57. See frame 343.
98. Bakker, "New Mexican Spanish Colonial Furniture," 120, 123.
99. Will of Dimas Jirón de Tejeda, 1733, SANM I, roll 6, frames 748-51.
100. Ahlborn, "Frontier Possessions," 40.
101. Ibid., 40-41.
102. Grizzard, *Spanish Colonial Art and Architecture*, 75.
103. Demos, *A Little Commonwealth*, 38.
104. Ahlborn, "Frontier Possessions," 43. Ahlborn, "The Will of a New Mexico Woman," 349.
105. Ahlborn, "Frontier Possession," 36.
106. Pierce and Snow, "'A Harp for Playing,'" 77.
107. Will of doña Francisca de Mizquía, 1714, SANM I, roll 3, frames 660-65.
108. Will of Manuel Holguín, SANM I, roll 4, frame 296.
109. Van Young, "Material Life," 68.
110. Cunningham and Miller, "Trade Fairs in Taos," 95.
111. Will of Juan Manuel de Herrera, SANM I, roll 3, frames 96-98. See frame 97.
112. Hendricks, *New Mexico in 1801*, 75.
113. Pierce and Snow, "'A Harp for Playing,'" 81.
114. Will of Juana Domínguez, 1717, SANM I, roll 2, frames 238-41.
115. Will of Captain don Juan José Moreno, 1756, SANM I, roll 3, frames 1042-56. See frame 1052.
116. Simmons, *Coronado's Land*, 32.
117. Pierce and Snow, "'A Harp for Playing,'" 83.

Chapter 2

1. Lockhart and Schwartz, *Early Latin America*, 8.
2. Morse, "The Heritage of Latin America," 156.
3. Quotation from Arrom, *The Women of Mexico City*, 77.
4. Ibid., 77.
5. Ibid., 81.
6. Angel, "Spanish Women in the New World," 68.
7. Burns, *Las Siete Partidas*, vol. 4, *Family, Commerce and the Sea*, partida IV, title II (hereafter cited with first the number of the partida, the title, and the law). See also Brooks, *Captives and Cousins*, 24.
8. Dillard, *Daughters of the Reconquest*, 214.
9. Lockhart and Schwartz, *Early Latin America*, 29.
10. An encomendero was the holder of an encomienda—a grant of administrative authority over a number of Indians who in turn provided tribute (taxes) in the form of labor or goods or a combination thereof.
11. Konetzke, "R. C. Para Que Los Encomenderos Sean Obligados A Casarse," 193.
12. Lockhart, *Spanish Peru*, 157.

13. Kessell and Hendricks, *By Force of Arms*, 11–12.
14. Kessell, Hendricks, and Dodge, *To the Royal Crown Restored*, 99.
15. Kessell and Hendricks, *By Force of Arms*, 15.
16. Diego de Vargas, Census of the El Paso district, El Paso, 22 December–2 January 1693, in Kessell and Hendricks, *To the Royal Crown Restored*, 45–46.
17. Ibid., 51. See also the interviews on pages 52–54 where each head of household agreed to go contingent upon being given aid.
18. Ibid., 63.
19. Ibid., 40.
20. Ibid., 41. See other examples on pages 42 and 51.
21. Ibid., 56.
22. Esquibel and Colligan, *The Spanish Recolonization*, 7.
23. Hernández, "The U.S. Southwest," 94.
24. Fray Francisco Farfán to the Conde de Galve, Mexico City, September 1693, in Kessell and Hendricks, *To the Royal Crown Restored*, 253.
25. Esquibel and Colligan, *The Spanish Recolonization*, 14.
26. Colligan, *The Juan Páez Hurtado Expedition*, 13.
27. Ibid., 17.
28. Diego de Vargas to the Conde de Galve, Zacatecas, 1 May 1693, in Kessell and Hendricks, *To the Royal Crown Restored*, 146–47.
29. Hall, *Social Change in the Southwest*, 92.
30. General Junta, Mexico City, 16 June 1693, in Kessell and Hendricks, *To the Royal Crown Restored*, 236.
31. Hernández, "The U.S. Southwest," 100.
32. Colligan, *The Juan Páez Hurtado Expedition*, 18.
33. Ibid., 72.
34. Ibid., 48–54.
35. Hernández, "The U.S. Southwest," 83–84.
36. General Junta, Mexico City, 16 June 1693, in Kessell and Hendricks, *To the Royal Crown Restored*, 234.
37. Colligan, *The Juan Páez Hurtado Expedition*, 18.
38. Kessell et al., introduction to *That the Disturbances Cease*, 3–15.
39. Governors appointed between 1700 and 1719 paid for their positions by way of donation. After this date, the crown appointed governors who received salaries. Cutter, *The Legal Culture of Northern New Spain*, 81.
40. Ibid., 71.
41. Quotation from ibid., 75.
42. Ibid., 79.
43. Ibid., 81.
44. Ibid.
45. Ibid., 82.
46. Civil Suit filed by Julián Rael de Aguilar and others against Melchora de

Sandoval and Antonio de Ulibarrí, 1750, Santa Fe, SANM I, roll 8, frames 118–235. See frame 156.
47. Petition filed by Manuela de Chávez and the settlement of Pedro de Chávez's estate, 1736, Albuquerque, SANM I, roll 8, frames 364–457. See frames 364–65.
48. The Cabildo of Santa Fe to Lázaro de Mizquía, Power of attorney, 2 January 1697, Santa Fe, in Kessell et al., introduction to *That the Disturbances Cease*, 35–36.
49. Kessell et al., introduction to *A Settling of Accounts*, 3.
50. The residents registered their complaints after the residencia was complete. For more information, see page 7 in Kessell et al., introduction to *That Disturbances Cease*.
51. Ibid., 8.
52. Ibid.
53. Brooks, "Lest We go in Search of Relief," 174.
54. Cutter, *The Legal Culture of Northern New Spain*, 34–35.
55. Ibid., 37.
56. Arrom, *The Women of Mexico City*, 55.
57. O'Callaghan, "Alfonso X and the *Partidas*," xxxii.
58. Burns, *Las Siete Partidas*, 4.1: 2, 877.
59. Ibid.
60. Ibid., 1.23: 12.
61. Ibid., 4.1: 2 and 4.1: 4.
62. See chapter 3.
63. Rape of Margarita García Jurado, 1750. SANM II, roll 8, frames 963–77.
64. Norris, "The Breakdown of Franciscan Hegemony," 85.
65. Gubernatorial decree by don Juan Ignacio Flores Mogollón, 30 April 1714, SANM II, roll 4, frames 1014–1016. For the quote see frame 1014.
66. Gubernatorial decree by don Juan Ignacio Flores Mogollón, 30 April 1714, SANM II, roll 4, frames 1014–1016. For the quote see frame 1014.
67. Petition of Ana Bernal before the ecclesiastical court, 11 February 1704, San Ildefonso Pueblo, Diligencias matrimoniales, 1697–710, AASF, roll 60, frames 340–345 (hereafter cited as DM).
68. Petition of Ana Bernal before the ecclesiastical court, 11 February 1704, San Ildefonso Pueblo, DM, 1697–1710, AASF, roll 60, frame 343.
69. Petition of Ana Bernal before the ecclesiastical court, 11 February 1704, San Ildefonso Pueblo, DM, 1697–710, AASF, roll 60, frame 344.
70. Saether, "Bourbon Absolutism," 487.
71. Seed, *To Love, Honor, and Obey*, 204.
72. Saether, "Bourbon Absolutism," 490.
73. Ibid., 506.
74. Copy of royal decree regarding marriage regulations, 26 May 1783, SANM II, roll 11, frames 582–86.

75. Burns, *Las Siete Partidas*, 4.11:7.
76. Ibid., 4.11:7.
77. Ibid.
78. Ibid., 4.11:8.
79. *Las Leyes de Toro*.
80. Civil complaint filed by Francisco de Silva against Nicolás Durán y Chávez, December 1732, SANM I, roll 4, frames 1451–77.
81. Petition of Carlos Fernández to the governor and the Inventory of Margarita Martín's Estate, Santa Cruz de la Cañada, 8 August 1744, SANM I, roll 3, frames 859–81.
82. Children became adults at the age of twenty-five. See Arrom, *The Women of Mexico City*, 57. Also see Ley 47 of the *Leyes de Toro*.
83. *Las Leyes de Toro*, Leyes 14 and 15.
84. Petition of Carlos Fernández to the governor and the Inventory of Margarita Martín's Estate, 8 August 1744, Santa Cruz de la Cañada, SANM I, roll 3, frames 867–68.
85. Ibid., frames 870–71.
86. The property remained intact so that he could raise his children. If he remarried, the dotal property would return to his children when they reached their majority.
87. Tamarón quoted in Simmons, *Spanish Government in New Mexico*, 173.
88. Settlement of estate of José Durán y Chávez, 10 March 1783, San Francisco de Bernalillo, roll 2, frames 316–53.
89. Leyva, "'A Poor Widow Burdened with Children,'" 88.
90. Simmons, *Spanish Government in New Mexico*, 174.
91. Petition of Carlos Fernández to the governor, and the Inventory of Margarita Martín's Estate, 8 August 1744, Santa Cruz de la Cañada, SANM I, roll 3, frame 873.
92. Civil Complaint filed by Francisco de Silva against Nicolás Durán y Chávez, December 1732, SANM I, roll 4, frame 1466.
93. Cutter, *The Legal Culture*, 88, 101.
94. I was unable to track down this author since he only referred to the author as Villalobos. It may refer to fray Enrique de Villalobos, *Manual de Confesores*, Salamanca, 1628, Valladolid, 1628, and later editions. See Adams, "Two Colonial New Mexico Libraries, 1704, 1776," 162.
95. Petition filed by Juana Ortega asking for her maternal inheritance, 1744, Santa Fe, SANM I, roll 8, frames 920–93.
96. Quoted in Leyva, "'A Poor Widow Burdened with Children,'" 88. See also original, Complaint of Teodora Ortiz, 1781, SANM II, roll 11, frame 354.
97. Banishment of Juan Galván and investigation of Juana Hurtado, Zia Pueblo, 22 August, 1727, SANM II, roll 6, frames 524–541. Also see James Brooks's account of Juana Hurtado in *Captives and Cousins*, 101–2.

98. Criminal Investigation against Alejandro Mora, resident of Bernalillo, 23 September 1751, SANM II, roll 8, frames 1032–48.
99. Ibid., frame 1033.
100. Ibid., frame 1035.
101. Ibid., frame 1045.
102. Ibid., frame 1043.

Chapter 3

1. DM of Cristóbal Durán and Rosa Navarro, 1719, Archives of the Archdiocese of Santa Fe, roll 61, frames 517–520 (hereafter cited as AASF).
2. DM of don Salvador Martínez and doña Simona Valdez, 1761, AASF, roll 62, frames 311–14.
3. DM, AASF, rolls 59–66.
4. Kinnaird and Kinnaird, "Secularization of Four New Mexican Missions," 35.
5. Wright, "How Many Are 'A Few'?" Wright notes that by 1803, the secular priests had left New Mexico and that Franciscans manned the posts once again.
6. Kessell and Hendricks, *By Force of Arms*, 7–8.
7. Norris, *"The Year Eighty,"* 23.
8. Ibid., 162.
9. Adams, "Bishop Tamraón's Visitation," 231–32.
10. Adams and Chavez, *The Missions of New Mexico*, 244.
11. Ibid., 30.
12. Norris, *"The Year Eighty,"* 150.
13. Adams and Chavez, *The Missions of New Mexico*, 245.
14. A fanega is a unit of dry measure equal in Spain to 1.58 US bushels. *The Random House Dictionary of the English Language* (1966), s.v. "fanega."
15. Adams and Chavez, *The Missions of New Mexico*, 245.
16. Adams, "Bishop Tamarón's Visitation," 305–6
17. *The Doctrinal Decrees and Canons of the Council of Trent*, 87.
18. Entries regarding "libertad y soltura" of Gaspar and Thomas Ortiz, Santa Fe Marriages, AASF, roll 31, frame 103.
19. DM of Ramón García Jurado and doña Antonia de la Heras, 10 February 1697, AASF, roll 60, frame 10.
20. Ibid.
21. Some New Mexicans formed relationships and families that fell outside the scope of the Catholic Church, but I do not address them in this work.
22. DM of Juan Márquez and Josefa de Apodaca, AASF, roll 60, frames 548–50.
23. Salvador Vigil and Gertrudis Martín, Abiquiú, 11 November 1777–9 January 1781, Archivos Históricos del Arzobispado de Durango (AHAD)-27, f. 468–80.

For the transcription and translation see Hendricks, *New Mexico Prenuptial Investigations*, 30–31.

24. Hendricks, *New Mexico Prenuptial Investigations*, 30–31.
25. Serra, *Manual de Administrar los Santos Sacramentos*, 51–64.
26. *Manual de párrocos*, 458.
27. Marriage between Joseph Miguel de la Peña and doña María Francisca Rael de Aguilar, 23 April 1737, Santa Fe Marriages, AASF, roll 31, frame 27.
28. Adams and Chavez, *Missions of New Mexico*, 351.
29. Marriage between Estevan de Estrada and Juana Mata de Espinosa, 5 October 1734, Santa Fe Marriages, AASF, roll 31, frame 21.
30. DM of Miguel Martín and María Archuleta, AASF, roll 60, frames 302–5.
31. Boyer, *Lives of the Bigamists*, 31.
32. Greenleaf, "The Inquisition," 35.
33. DM of Santiago Grolet and doña Elena Gallegos, 1699, AASF, roll 60, frames 168–69. This French name became the Hispanicized *Gurulé*.
34. DM of Pedro Fresqui and Clara Granillo, 1719, AASF, roll 61, frames 514–16.
35. DM of Juan de Arichibeque and Antonia Gutiérrez, 1697, AASF, roll 60, frames 49–54.
36. Seed, *To Love, Honor, and Obey*, 68.
37. Ibid.
38. DM of Antonio Sambrano and Lorenza García, 1705, AASF, roll 60, frame 398.
39. *New Catholic Encyclopedia*, vol. 4, 192–93.
40. Ibid.
41. Ibid.
42. *New Catholic Encyclopedia*, vol. 1, 167.
43. *New Catholic Encyclopedia*, vol. 4, 195.
44. *New Catholic Encyclopedia*, vol. 1, 169.
45. Rípodas, *El Matrimonio en Indias*, 169.
46. Margadant, "La Familia en Derecho Novohispano," 39.
47. Decree from Bishop Francisco Gabriel de Olivares, 1798, AASF, roll 65, frames 579–80.
48. DM of Ramón de Medina and Balentina de Montes de Oca, 1718, AASF, roll 61, frame 388.
49. Mateo García de Noriega and Catalina de Aranda Tafoya, Santa Cruz de la Cañada, 6 November 1787–26 January 1788, AHAD-92, f. 280–88. Hendricks, *New Mexico Prenuptial Investigations*, 93–96.
50. DM of Juan Antonio Montaño and Antonia Rita Chávez, 1767, AASF, roll 62, frames 702–6.
51. DM of Melchor de Herrera and Catalina Griego, 1707, AASF, roll 60, frame 485.
52. DM of Juan Antonio Baca and doña María Gallegos, 1716, AASF, roll 61, frame 252.
53. DM of Manuel Sánchez Bañares Tagle and Antonia González, 1766, AASF, roll

62, frames 586–590, and DM of Cristóbal Montoya and Margarita Lucero, 1766, AASF, roll 62, frames 594–99.
54. DM and dispensation of Isidro Antonio González and Tomás López, 1781, AASF, roll 64, frames 288–91. See also frames 197–98, 369, 382, 503–4.
55. DM of Luis García and Josefa Javier, 1704, AASF, roll 60, frame 329–31.
56. DM of Francisco Durán y Chávez and doña Juana Baca, 1713, AASF, roll 61, frame 85–89.
57. José Pascual García de la Mora and Saturnina Rosalía García de Noriega, Santa Fe, 12 April–22 June 1795, AHAD-171, f. 780–93, incomplete. Hendricks, *New Mexico Prenuptial Investigations*, 119–20.
58. Hendricks, *New Mexico Prenuptial Investigations*, 119–20.
59. López de Ayala, 401.
60. *New Catholic Encyclopedia*, 1967 ed., s.v. "feast days."
61. Adams and Chavez, *The Missions of New Mexico*, 21.
62. DM of Miguel Antonio Gutiérrez and María Simona Griego, 1798, AASF, roll 66, frame 30. For another example of a friar reading the banns on consecutive days, see AASF roll 58, frame 107.
63. DM of Marián Tórrez and María Isabel Armijo, 1794, AASF, roll 65, frame 485–89.
64. DM of Antonio María Montoya and Gertrudis Peña, 1795, AASF, roll 65, frames 498–500.
65. Impediment filed by Juana Luján, 1702, ASSF, roll 60, frame 266.
66. Seed, *To Love, Honor, and Obey*, 78.
67. Norris, "The Breakdown of Franciscan Hegemony," 86.
68. Seed, *To Love, Honor, and Obey*, 269.
69. DM of Nicolás de Espinosa and Josefa de la Cruz, 1697, AASF, roll 60, frame 68.
70. Petition filed by Inés Griega against Marcial Martínez, 1736, Santa Cruz de la Cañada, AASF, roll 62, frames 183–90.
71. Seed, *To Love, Honor, and Obey*, 78.
72. Petition filed by Inés Griega against Marcial Martínez, 1736, Santa Cruz de la Cañada, AASF, roll 62, frames 183–90. For quote see frame 188.
73. Petition filed by Inés Griega against Marcial Martínez, 1736, Santa Cruz de la Cañada, AASF, roll 62, frames 183–90. For quote see frame 188.

Chapter 4

1. Civil and criminal complaint against Blas López filed by Gertrudis de Armijo, 30 December 1762, Santa Fe, SANM II, roll 9, frames 468–491.
2. Gutiérrez, *When Jesus Came*, 209, 213.
3. Johnson and Lipsett-Rivera, introduction to *The Faces of Honor*, 15.
4. Gutiérrez, *When Jesus Came*, 215.

5. Weeks, *Sex, Politics and Society*, 2.
6. Ibid., 11.
7. See, for example, Salisbury, "The Latin Doctors of the Church," 279–89.
8. Lavrin, "Sexuality in Colonial Mexico, 49.
9. Knight, *Catholic Encyclopedia*, vol. 14.
10. Knight, *Catholic Encyclopedia*, vol. 11.
11. Foucault, *The History of Sexuality*, 19.
12. Ibid., 21.
13. Adams, "Two Colonial New Mexico Libraries, 152–63. When Domínguez came to New Mexico in 1776, he inspected the custody's library kept at the convent of Santo Domingo. It contained 256 items including duplicates. The author who appeared most frequently was Fray Clemente de Ledesma.
14. Ledesma, *Despertador de Noticias*, 225.
15. Ibid., 225–33.
16. The friar is quoted in Gutiérrez, *When Jesus Came*, 211. Unfortunately, there is no date provided, and I was unable to track down the original, which is housed in the Archivo General de la Nación in Mexico City. From the context of the paragraph, I assumed that it was an eighteenth-century source.
17. Dispensation request filed by Cristóbal de Gamboa, El Paso, AASF, roll 59, frames 554–57. Cristóbal de Gamboa was from Santa Fe.
18. Criminal case filed against Antonio Linba and Acencio Povia, 25 June 1731, Santa Fe, SANM II, roll 6, frames 836–837.
19. Lavrin, "Sexuality in Colonial Mexico," 79–80.
20. See next chapter.
21. DM of Antonio Martín and Gertrudis Sánchez de Otón, 7 February, AASF, roll 61, frame 357.
22. In chapter 2, I outline the state's family policy.
23. *Las Siete Partidas*, 4.1: 7–8.
24. Norris, "The Breakdown of Franciscan Hegemony," 63.
25. Wall, *Fierce Communion*, 62.
26. Ibid., 65.
27. Ibid.
28. *Las Siete Partidas*, 4.19: 5.
29. Civil complaint of broken marriage promise and resulting pregnancy, 24 November 1805, SANM II, roll 15, frame 1038. Civil complaint of broken marriage promise and resulting pregnancy, 9 October 1805, SANM II, roll 15, frame 945.
30. Criminal case against Manuel Martín, 8 February 1766, Santa Cruz de la Cañada, SANM II, roll 9, frames 922–49.
31. Colligan, *The Juan Páez Hurtado*, 18.
32. Brooks, "'This Evil Extends Especially to the Feminine Sex,'" 99.
33. Ibid., 110.

34. Baptismal records 1732–1800, AASF, roll 13, frames 1–854. In this case, "infidel" refers to Indians who did not live in Hispanic, Christian communities.
35. *Párvulo* means "infant" or "small child." The term did not have a precise meaning.
36. Baptismal record of María Rosa de la Trinidad, 8 April 1798, Santa Cruz de la Cañada, AASF, roll 13, frame 795.
37. Zavala, *Los esclavos en Nueva España*, 359–60.
38. Ibid., 255–56.
39. Ibid., 255. "'Ahora puedes tomarla, ahora es buena.'"
40. Atondo Rodríguez, "De la perversión de la práctica a la perversión de discurso," 148–49.
41. Hurtado, *Intimate Frontiers*, 13–16.
42. Stern, *The Secret History of Gender*, 164.
43. Brooks, "This Evil Extends Especially to the Feminine Sex," 112–14.
44. Ibid.
45. There were seven types of illegitimacy with different degrees of offensiveness. Natural children were born to parents who were single. Other types of illegitimacy included those born of adulterous, incestuous, or sacrilegious unions. See Margadant, "La Familia en el Derecho Novohispano," 48.
46. Santa Cruz baptisms, 1732–1800, AASF, roll 13, frames 1–854.
47. Albuquerque baptisms, 1706–1783, AASF, roll 1, frames 255–884.
48. Gutiérrez, *When Jesus Came*, 221. "For males, seduction, aside from fulfilling sexual urges, was an opportunity to exhibit their virility."
49. Complaint filed by Juana Montaño against Nicolás Durán y Chávez for a broken marriage promise, 1714, SANM II, frames 1056–68. For quote, see frame 1063.
50. Complaint filed by Manuela de Armijo against Juan Lobato, 24 febrero 1725, loose documents, 1680–1743, AASF, roll 51, frames 952–64. For the quote see frame 955. For an example in central Mexico, see Boyer, "Honor Among Plebians," 173–75.
51. *Las Siete Partidas*, 4.2: 8.
52. Lavrin, introduction to *Sexuality and Marriage in Colonial Latin America*, 10.
53. Johnson and Lipsett-Rivera, introduction to *The Faces of Honor*, 4.
54. Ibid., 2.
55. Ibid.
56. Criminal complaint against Catalina de Villalpando filed by José Domínguez, 17 May 1719, Santa Fe, SANM II, roll 5, frames 827–34.
57. Complaint against José Antonio Salazar filed by Miguel Chávez, January 1766, Albuquerque, AASF, roll 62, frame 512.
58. Criminal case against Juan Lobato for the rape of Margarita García Jurado filed by Bernabé Montaño, May–June 1750, Bernalillo, SANM II, roll 8, frames 963–77.

59. DM of Nicolás de Espinosa and Josefa de la Cruz, 1697, AASF, roll 60, frame 68.
60. *Las Siete Partidas*, 4.1: 4.
61. Civil and criminal complaint against Blas López filed by Gertrudis de Armijo, 30 December 1762, Santa Fe, SANM II, roll 9, frames 468–91.
62. Complaint against José Antonio Salazar filed by Miguel Chávez, January 1766, Albuquerque, AASF, roll 62, frames 510–16 (hereafter cited as Complaint against José Antonio Salazar). See quote on frame 515.
63. Complaint against José Antonio Salazar, frame 514.
64. Ibid., frame 515b.
65. Ibid., frame 516.
66. Premarital dispute filed by Juana Padilla against Satebo, 17 January 1777, AASF, roll 63, frames 609–11.
67. Impediment to the marriage of Sebastián Luján, 14 February 1705, AASF, roll 60, frame 377.
68. Impediment to the marriage of Ventura de Esquibel, 7 April 1702, AASF, roll 60, frame 276.
69. Premarital dispute filed by Miguel Chávez against José Antonio Salazar, 11 January 1766, AASF, roll 62, frame 516.
70. Civil and criminal complaint against Blas López filed by Gertrudis de Armijo, 30 December 1762, Santa Fe, SANM II, roll 9, frame 473.
71. Civil and criminal complaint against Blas López filed by Gertrudis de Armijo, 30 December 1762, Santa Fe, SANM II, roll 9, frame 480.
72. Santa Cruz de la Cañada baptisms, 1732–1800, AASF, roll 13, frames 1–854.
73. Santa Fe baptisms, 1747–1800, AASF, roll 15, frames 3–841.
74. Albuquerque baptisms, 1706–1783, AASF, roll 1, frames 255–884.
75. Ann Twinam, who studies the honor of elite women and men, has found evidence in baptismal books that shows the priests returning to a baptismal entry of a natural child and writing that the parents had since married. Twinam, "The Negotiation of Honor," 83.
76. Santa Cruz de la Cañada baptisms, 1732–1800, AASF, roll 13, frames 1–854.
77. Santa Fe baptisms, 1747–1800, AASF, roll 15, frames 3–841.
78. Albuquerque baptisms, 1706–1783, AASF, roll 1, frames 255–884.
79. Santa Cruz de la Cañada baptismal records for the daughter and two sons of Sebastiana Martín, roll 13, frames 517, 584, and 724. Diligencia matrimonial of Juan Pedro Mascareñas and Sebastiana Martín, 1785, Santa Cruz de la Cañada, roll 64, frames 669–671.
80. D'Emilio and Freedman, *Intimate Matters*, 26. Van de Walle, "Motivations and Technology," 150–51.
81. Premarital dispute filed by Inés Griega against Marcial Martínez, 13 January 1736, AASF, roll 62, frame 187.
82. Noonan, *Contraception*, 364–65.

83. Van de Walle, "Motivations and Technology," 145–46. Van de Walle notes that at least 10 percent of all conceptions end in spontaneous abortions.
84. Gutiérrez, *When Jesus Came*, 216.
85. Impediment filed by Juana Luján, 17 April 1702, AASF, roll 60, frames 265–82. See especially frames 266–267.
86. Complaint filed by Manuela de Armijo against Juan Lobato, 24 February 1725, loose documents 1680–1743, AASF, roll 51, frames 952–64. For the quote see frame 957.
87. Impediment filed by Juana Luján, 17 April 1702, AASF, roll 60, frame 275.
88. Lipsett-Rivera, "A Slap in the Face of Honor," 180.
89. Ibid., 193. Twinam also finds evidence of elite women concealing their pregnancies, which was far easier for them since they had more resources than poor women. Twinam, "The Negotiation of Honor," 84.
90. Impediment filed by Juana Luján, 17 April 1702, AASF, roll 60, frame 276.
91. Civil and criminal case filed by María de la Luz Romero against Mariano Baca, April 1767, SANM II, roll 10, frames 4–25. See in particular frame 5.
92. Complaint filed by Juana Padilla against Satebo, 16 January 1777, AASF, roll 63, frames 609–11.
93. Complaint of Miguel Chávez, January 1766, AASF, roll 62, frame 515.
94. Impediment filed by Juana Luján, 17 April 1702, AASF, roll 60, frame 280.
95. Ibid.
96. Boyer, "Honor Among Plebians," 153.
97. DM of Sebastián Luján and Juana Teresa Trujillo, February 1705, AASF, roll 60, frames 374–90. For the quote see frame 375.
98. Juana Rodíguez's mother, Juana de Valencia, also filed a civil suit against Sebastián Luján. After hearing her petition, the alguacil passed the case over to the ecclesiastical court.
99. DM of Sebastián Luján and Juana Teresa Trujillo, February 1705, AASF, roll 60, frame 385.
100. Ibid., frame 380.
101. See Gutiérrez, *When Jesus Came*, 220. Gutiérrez also uses this case when discussing honor and virtue. "Luján presented enough evidence to impugn Juana Rodríguez's sexual purity. Luján was allowed to marry Juana Trujillo, leaving Juana Rodríguez destitute and dishonored."
102. Impediment filed by Juana de Guadalupe against Antonio Belasques, 30 June 1705, AASF, roll 60, frames 428, 365–68.
103. Will of María de la Candelaria González, 1750, Santa Fe, SANM I, roll 2, frames 890–93.
104. Ahlborn, "The Will of a New Mexico Woman in 1762," 326, 330. Also see Chávez, *Origins of New Mexico Families*, 187. In his article, Ahlborn questions whether Chavez's contention that Juana Luján had three children prior to 1693 is correct. I contend that Juana Luján had her first illegitimate child with

Ventura de Esquibel. If she were sixteen in 1702 when she filed the impediment, she would have been seventy-six when she dictated her will. I wrote Richard Ahlborn with the evidence from 1702, and he agrees that both women were more than likely one and the same.
105. Ahlborn, "The Will of a New Mexico Woman in 1762," 323.
106. Complaint filed by Juana Montaño against Nicolás Durán y Chávez for a broken marriage promise, 1714, SANM II, roll 4, frames 1056–1068. For quote see frame 1067.
107. Criminal case against Juan Lobato for the rape of Margarita García Jurado filed by Bernabé Montaño, May–June 1750, Bernalillo, SANM II, roll 8, frames 963–77.
108. Complaint filed by Manuela de Armijo against Juan Lobato, 24 February 1725, loose documents 1680–1743, AASF, roll 51, frames 952–64.
109. DM of Bernardo Vallejos and Francisca de Silva, 1725, AASF, roll 61, frame 754. DM of Cayetano de Moya and Manuela de Armijo, 1727, AASF, roll 62, frame 35.

Chapter 5

1. Seed, *To Love, Honor and Obey*, 123–35. Gutiérrez, "From Honor to Love," 237–60.
2. Arrom, "Perspectivas sobre Historia de la Familia en México," 396–99.
3. Boyer, "Honor among Plebians," 162–63.
4. DM, 1694–1800, AASF, rolls 59–66.
5. Twinam, *Public Lives, Private Secrets*, 218–20.
6. Ibid.. The issue became even more complicated if the child was considered a bastard.
7. *Las Siete Partidas*, 4.13: 2.
8. Twinam, *Public Lives, Private Secrets*, 47.
9. Baptisms, Santa Cruz de la Cañada, 1786–1787, AASF, roll 13, frames 597–98.
10. Will of Vicente de Armijo, 1743, SANM I, roll 1, frames 246–50.
11. See chapter 6.
12. Esquibel and Colligan, 396–402. Using the genealogies in this book, Rob Martinez and I compiled and examined the marriages of settlers and their children to determine how many married into New Mexican families. Out of eighty-five marriages, sixty-three children married New Mexicans. In the thirteen cases of adult settlers marrying, ten married into New Mexican families.
13. See for example, Socolow, "Acceptable Partners," 209–51. Martinez-Alier, *Marriage, Class and Colour*.
14. Thanks to Richard Greenleaf for identifying the term *hábito de miserocordia*.
15. DM of Gerónimo de Ortega and Sebastiana de Jesús, 1715, AASF, roll 61, frames 209–13.
16. DM of Miguel de Martín and María de Archuleta, 1703, Santa Cruz de la Cañada, AASF, roll 60, frame 302.

17. DM of Antonio Martín and Josefa Domínguez, 1696, Santa Fe, AASF, roll 59, frame 632.
18. DM of Sebastián González and María del Río, 1714, ASSF, roll 61, frame 94.
19. Complaint of José de Armijo, June 1710, Santa Fe, AASF, roll 60, frames 680–88.
20. DM of Ventura de Esquibel and Bernardina Rosa Lucero, 1702, Santa Fe, AASF, roll 60, frame 272.
21. DM of Alonso García and María de la Rosa Manzanares, Albuquerque, 1707, AASF, roll 60, frames 488–93.
22. Metcalf, *Family and Frontier in Colonial Brazil*, 100–102.
23. Settlement of the estate of don José Durán y Chávez, Bernalillo, 1783, SANM I, roll 2, frames 316–353. See frame 326: "Dise que traxo a poder de su marido dos bacas preñadas."
24. Will of Miguel de Archibeque, SANM I, roll 1, frames 183–88.
25. Will of Ramón García, 1768, SANM I, roll 2, frames 1016–20.
26. Conveyance of Land from Lorenzo Griego to Teresa de Ansures, San Felipe de Albuquerque, 4 December 1733, SANM I, roll 1, frames 190–92. See also SANM I Translations, Twitchell 18.
27. Petition of Carlos Fernández to the governor and the inventory of Margarita Martín's estate, Santa Cruz de la Cañada, 8 August 1744, SANM I, roll 3, frames 859–81.
28. Lavrin and Couturier, "Dowries and Wills," 282–83.
29. Will of Nicolás Ortiz, 17 September 1742, SANM I, roll 4, frames 250–54.
30. Will of José Antonio Griego, Santa Fe, 1785, SANM I, roll 2, frames 1051–66. See in particular frames 1064–65.
31. Civil complaint filed by Francisco de Silva against Nicolás Durán y Chávez, Albuquerque, 1733, SANM I, roll 4, frame 1452.
32. Arrom, *The Women of Mexico City*, 62.
33. Inventory of the estate of don Pedro Chávez, San Felipe de Albuquerque, 1736, SANM I, roll 8, frames 363–457. See also SANM I Translations, Twitchell 177. For complaint filed by Jacinto Sánchez see frames 366–67.
34. Inventory of the estate of don Pedro Chávez, San Felipe de Albuquerque, 1736, SANM I, roll 8, frame 377.
35. Ibid., frame 433.
36. Civil complaint filed by Francisco de Silva against Nicolás Durán y Chávez, Albuquerque, 1733, SANM I, roll 4, frames 1468–69.
37. Gutiérrez, *When Jesus Came*, 230.
38. Dotal letter for Ana Valdez, Villa Nueva de Santa Cruz, 1712, SANM I, roll 1, frame 1152.
39. Settlement of the estate of don José Durán y Chávez, Bernalillo, 1783, SANM I, roll 2, frames 316–53. See frame 326.
40. Will of Andrés Montoya, La Cieneguilla, 1740, SANM I, roll 3, frames 841–44.
41. Ibid. See in particular frame 843.
42. Settlement of the estate of Juana Luján, Santa Cruz de la Cañada, 15 July–22 August

1761, SANM II, roll 9, frames 352–385. See Ahlborn, "The Will of a New Mexico Woman," 331.
43. Will of don José Maldonado, 1785, SANM I, roll 3, frames 1296–356.
44. Will of Nicolás Durán y Chávez, 1768, SANM I, roll 1, frames 1399–401.
45. For more details on this case, see chapter 3.
46. Settlement of the estate of don Jose Durán y Chávez, Bernalillo, 1783, SANM I, roll 2, frames 321–24 (hereafter cited as Settlement of Durán y Chávez). Also see SANM I Translations, Twitchell 250.
47. Settlement of Durán y Chávez, frame 327.
48. Ibid., frame 343.
49. Ibid., frame 338. See SANM I Translations, Twitchell 250, p. 14.
50. Settlement of Durán y Chávez, frame 330.
51. Ibid., frame 345.
52. Ibid., frame 349.
53. Lavrin and Couturier, "Dowries and Wills," 284.
54. See Gutiérrez, *When Jesus Came*, 263.
55. Complaint of Inés Griega, Santa Cruz de la Cañada, January 1736, AASF, roll 62, frames 183–90.
56. DM of Sebastián Luján and Juana Teresa Trujillo and Impediment filed by Juana Rodríguez, Santa Fe, 1705, AASF, roll 60, frames 374–390. See frames 381–82.
57. Ibid., frame 385.
58. Ibid., frame 383.
59. Ibid., frame 384.
60. Ibid., frame 376.
61. DM of José Antonio Rodríguez and María Gerónima Montaño, 1729 and 1730, roll 62, frames 123–25 and 161–63.
62. Mateo García de Noriega and Catalina Aranda Tafoya, Santa Cruz de la Cañada, 6 November 1787–26 January 1788, Archivos Históricos del Arzobispado de Durango (AHAD)-92, f. 280–288. See Hendricks, *New Mexico Prenuptial Investigations*, 93–96.
63. See Gutiérrez, *When Jesus Came*, 244.
64. See chapter 3 for more information on the role of friars in the dispensation process.
65. DM of Antonio Sambrano and Lorenza García, 1705, AASF, roll 60, frame 398.
66. José Manuel Silva and María Josefa Silveria Sánchez, Isleta, 14 April 1778–13 March 1779, AHAD-30, f. 56–71. See Hendricks, *New Mexico Prenuptial Investigations*, 38–41.
67. José de Jesús Montoya and Rosa Archuleta, Santa Cruz de la Cañada, 8 August–14 September 1796, AHAD-98, f. 572–75. See Hendricks, *New Mexico Prenuptial Investigations*, 122–23.
68. DM of Urgencio de Jesús Savedra and Juana María García Jurado, 1762, AASF, roll 62, frame 375.

69. Vicente Romero and Tomasa Trujillo, San Ildefonso, 6 November 1792–17 January 1793, AHAD-97, f. 369–79. See Hendricks, *New Mexico Prenuptial Investigations*, 111–113.
70. DM of Luis de Chávez and Leonor Montaño, 1707, AASF, roll 60, frame 466.
71. Domingo Sánchez and María Guadalupe Baca, Nuestra Señora de Belén, 19 November 1796–3 January 1797, AHAD-99, f. 375–80. See Hendricks, *New Mexico Prenuptial Investigations*, 125–26.
72. José Manuel Silva and María Josefa Silveria Sánchez, Isleta, 14 April 1778–13 March 1779, AHAD-30, f. 56–71. See Hendricks, *New Mexico Prenuptial Investigations*, 40.
73. Miguel Hermenegildo Baca and María de los Reyes Padilla, Isleta, 11 February–13 March 1779, AHAD-30, f. 51–55. See Hendricks, *New Mexico Prenuptial Investigations*, 45–46.
74. DM of Salvador García and doña Margarita Durán y Chávez, Albuquerque, 1761, AASF, roll 62, frame 272.
75. Antonio José Romero and María Baca, Presidio of Santa Fe, 16 February–12 March 1779, AHAD-30, f. 46–49. See Hendricks, *New Mexico Prenuptial Investigations*, 46.
76. DM of Juan Antonio Baca and doña María Gallegos, Bernalillo, 1716, AASF, roll 61, frame 252. "Y ser solo mi animo amparar a esta virtuosa doncella."
77. DM of Juan Antonio Baca and doña Bárbara Montoya, Albuquerque, 1770, AASF, roll 63, frames 8–11.
78. In the other three cases in which men mentioned both "igualdad" and poverty, they did not use titles.
79. Petition for a dispensation filed by Ignacio Chávez, Atrisco, 1768, AASF, roll 63, frames 3–5, and 12–13.
80. Petition filed by María del Rosario, Pueblo de San Juan de los Caballeros, June 1785, AASF, roll 64, frame 618. Dispensation granted by Fray Juan Bermejo, 15 June 1785, AASF, roll 64, frames 620–21.

Chapter 6

1. Complaint of Ana Bernal, February 1704, Santa Fe, AASF, roll 60, frames 340–45.
2. Ibid., frame 343.
3. Gutiérrez, *When Jesus Came*, 231. He writes: "Daughters seldom received land rights at marriage because parents fully expected the husband's family to meet this need."
4. Herrero, "Evolución Demográfica y Estructura Familiar," 345.
5. Tjarks, "Demographic, Ethnic and Occupational Structure," 77. Tjarks calculates the percentage of broad family groups at 18.89 in Albuquerque, 20.67 in Santa Fe, and 15.69 in Santa Cruz de la Cañada.

6. Complaint of José Domínguez against Catalina Villalpando, 1719, Santa Fe, SANM II, roll 5, frames 827–34. See in particular frame 831.
7. Tjarks, "Demographic, Ethnic and Occupational Structure," 46.
8. It is highly likely that some of the men and women who lived with partners and claimed to the enumerators that they were married, in fact, were not. It is difficult to assess the proportion, however.
9. Hareven, "The Family as Process," 323.
10. See for example: Will of Miguel de Archibeque, 14 August 1727, SANM I, roll 1, frames 183–88. He stated that he and his "dear" sister jointly owned the house and the surrounding lands where he resided. See also Inventory of Juanotilla, 1747, San Buenaventura de Cochiti, SANM I, roll 1, frames 1332–38. One emancipated daughter offered to sell her share of her mother's house to the heirs who still resided there.
11. Olmsted, *Spanish and Mexican Censuses*, 1–14, 51–78, 82–105.
12. Because siblings shared the same surnames, it is quite evident that parents often asked siblings. They might have been asking cousins, as well.
13. Olmsted, *Spanish and Mexican Censuses*, 5.
14. Teresa C. Vergara, "Growing Up Indian," 92. For instances in colonial New England, see Wall, *Fierce Communion*, 100.
15. Olmsted, *Spanish and Mexican Censuses*, 53.
16. Don José de Reaño's appeal to raise Juan de Mascareñas, 1732, Santa Fe, SANM II, roll 6, frames 1170–1226. Also see inventory of documents for the governorship of Gervasio Cruzat y Gongora, 1736, SANM I, roll 6, frame 403.
17. Will of Luis Jaramillo, 1764, SANM I, roll 3, frames 201–4.
18. Will of Juan José Moreno, 1756, roll 3, frames 1042–1056.
19. Olmsted, *Spanish and Mexican Censuses*, 94.
20. Criminal Case against Manuel Martín, 8 February 1766, Santa Cruz de la Cañada, SANM II, roll 9, frames 922–49.
21. Petition of don Tomás de Herrera Sandoval to Governor Vargas, 14 February 1704, SANM II, roll 3, frame 97.
22. Will of Nicolás Ortiz, 17 September 1742, SANM I, roll 4, frames 250–54.
23. Will of Andrés Montoya, 1740, La Cieneguilla, SANM I, roll 3, frames 841–44.
24. This represents an undercount. I only included households listed consecutively in the census, that is, as immediate neighbors to one another. Often, however, people with the same surnames lived nearby—one house away or across from the other household clusters.
25. Olmsted, *Spanish and Mexican Censuses*, 1–14, 51–78, 82–105.
26. Ibid., 97–98.
27. Ibid., 77.
28. Ibid., 73.
29. See governor's decree regarding conjugal household for Indians. Friars strongly believed that Hispanics needed to set up conjugal households in order to set a

Gallegos, Bernardo P. *Literacy, Education, and Society in New Mexico, 1693–1821.* Albuquerque: University of New Mexico Press, 1992.

Gauderman, Kimberly. *Women's Lives in Colonial Quito: Gender, Law, and Economy in Spanish America.* Austin: University of Texas Press, 2003.

Gerhard, Peter. *The North Frontier of New Spain.* Princeton, NJ: Princeton University Press, 1982.

González, Ondina E., and Bianca Premo, eds. *Raising an Empire: Children in Early Modern Iberia and Colonial Latin America.* Albuquerque: University of New Mexico Press, 2007.

Goody, Jack. *The Development of the Family and Marriage in Europe.* Cambridge: Cambridge University Press, 1983.

Gotkowitz, Laura. "Trading Insults: Honor, Violence, and the Gendered Culture of Commerce in Cochabamba, Bolivia, 1870s–1950s." *Hispanic American Historical Review* 83, no. 1 (2003): 83–118.

Graham, Sandra Lauderdale. "Honor Among Slaves." In *The Faces of Honor*, edited by Lyman L. Johnson and Sonya Lipsett-Rivera. Albuquerque: University of New Mexico Press, 1998.

———. *House and Street: The Domestic World of Servants and Masters in Nineteenth-Century Rio de Janeiro.* Austin: University of Texas Press, 1992.

Greenleaf, Richard. "The Inquisition in Eighteenth-Century New Mexico." *New Mexico Historical Review* 60 (April 1985): 29–60.

Griswold, Robert L. "Anglo Women and Domestic Ideology in the American West in the Nineteenth and Early Twentieth Centuries." In *Western Women: Their Land, Their Lives*, edited by Lillian Schlissel, Vicki L. Ruiz, and Janice Monk, 15–33. Albuquerque: University of New Mexico Press, 1988.

Grizzard, Mary. *Spanish Colonial Art and Architecture of Mexico and the Southwest.* Lanham, MD: University Press of America, 1986.

Gutiérrez, Ramón A. "From Honor to Love: Transformations of the Meaning of Sexuality in Colonial New Mexico." In *Kinship Ideology and Practice in Latin America*, edited by Raymond T. Smith, 237–63. Chapel Hill: University of North Carolina Press, 1984.

———. *When Jesus Came, the Corn Mothers Went Away: Marriage, Sexuality, and Power in New Mexico, 1500–1846.* Stanford, CA: Stanford University Press, 1991.

Guy, Donna J., and Thomas E. Sheridan, eds. *Contested Ground: Comparative Frontiers on the Northern and Southern Edges of the Spanish Empire.* Tucson: The University of Arizona Press, 1998.

Guzzi-Heeb. "Sex, Politics, and Social Change in the Eighteenth and Nineteenth Centuries: Evidence from the Swiss Alps." *Journal of Family History* 36, no. 4 (October 2011): 367–86. Accessed May 8, 2014. http://jfh.sagepub.com.proxy.alumni.jhu.edu/content/36/4/367.full.pdf+html.

Hall, Thomas D. *Social Change in the Southwest, 1350–1880.* Lawrence: University Press of Kansas, 1989.

good example for the Indians. See, for example, Complaint of Inés de Aspitia, before the vice-custody, Juan de Tagle, 4 June 1705, Santa Fe, AASF, roll 60, frames 369–74.
30. Arrom, *The Women of Mexico City*, 65.
31. Complaint of Inés de Aspitia, before the vice-custodian, Juan de Tagle, 4 June 1705, Santa Fe, AASF, roll 60, frames 369–74. See frame 369.
32. Arrom, *The Women of Mexico City*, 67.
33. *The Canons and Decrees of the Council of Trent*, 182. "If anyone says that the Church errs when she declares that for many reasons a separation may take place between husband and wife with regard to bed and with regard to cohabitation for a determinate or indeterminate period, let him be anathema." See also Rípodas, *El Matrimonio en*, 388, and Arrom, *The Women of Mexico City*, 208–9.
34. Noonan, *Contraception*, 42. Noonan quotes Paul and notes that Corinthians 7:3–6 became the heart of the Catholic doctrine on marital intercourse. Paul wrote: "Let the husband render to his wife what is due her, and likewise the wife to her husband. A wife has not authority over her body, but her husband; the husband likewise has not authority over his body, but his wife. You must not refuse each other, except perhaps by consent, for a time, that you may give yourselves to prayer, and return together again lest Satan tempt you because you lack self-control. But this I say by way of concession, not commandment."
35. Petition for divorce by Inés Martín, 22 March 1695, Santa Fe, AASF, roll 59, frames 548–50.
36. Ibid. See frames 548–49a.
37. Arrom, *The Women of Mexico City*, 69–70.
38. Don Jose de Reaño's appeal to raise Juan de Mascareñas, 1732, Santa Fe, SANM II, roll 6, frames 1170–226.
39. The boy's father, Juan de Archibeque, died intestate. The alcalde mayor gave the bulk of the estate to the legitimate children. Out of the fifth, he gave money to Juan's mother, María de Mascareñas, recognizing that Archibeque had taken her virginity and had left her with a child. María de Mascareñas met her death in 1726, and her son inherited her property. The boy, therefore, had some sheep that helped his guardians pay for his sustenance.
40. Gallegos, *Literacy, Education, and Society*, 66.
41. Cutter, *The Legal Culture*, 87–88.
42. Will of Luis López, SANM I, reel 3, frame 288–90.
43. Quotation in Boyer, "La Mala Vida," 257. Boyer discusses de Corella's work and Alonso de Herrera's *Espejo de la perfecta casada*. There is no evidence that New Mexican friars had access to these works, but it is not unlikely. Domínguez listed Fray Jaime de Corella's *Suma de la Theología moral*, Barcelona 1690, in the Custody of St. Paul's library in 1776. See Adams, "Two Colonial New Mexico Libraries," 158.

44. Civil complaint filed by Juana Montaño against Nicolás Durán y Chávez, her husband, 14 October 1714, Albuquerque, SANM II, roll 4, frames 1106–11 (hereafter cited as Montaño against Durán y Chávez).
45. Ibid., frame 1106.
46. Ibid., frame 1107.
47. Ibid.
48. Criminal case against Miguel Luján, 20 April 1713, SANM II, roll 4, frame 757 (hereafter cited as Miguel Luján).
49. Ibid., frame 758.
50. Ibid., frame 790.
51. Ibid., frame 775.
52. Arrom, *The Women of Mexico City*, 65.
53. Gubernatorial decree by don Juan Ignacio Flores Mogollón, 30 April 1714, SANM II, roll 4, frames 1014–16. For the quote see frame 1014.
54. Boyer, "*La Mala Vida*," 261. See *Las Siete Partidas*, 4.9: 7.
55. Steve J. Stern, *The Secret History of Gender*, 80–83.
56. Order for the arrest of Juan Márquez for committing adultery, 1740, Santa Fe, SANM II, roll 7, frames 1064–1106 (hereafter cited as Arrest of Juan Márquez). See frame 1101.
57. Complaint made by Isabel de Medina against Bartolomé Garduño, 1765, SANM II, roll 9, frames 821–45 (hereafter cited as Medina against Garduño). See frames 822–23.
58. *Las Siete Partidas*, 1.23: 11.
59. Arrom, *The Women of Mexico City*, 65.
60. *Las Siete Partidas*, 4.2: 7.
61. Montaño against Durán y Chávez, frame 1106.
62. Boyer, "*La Mala Vida*," 256.
63. Arrest of Márquez, see frame 10.
64. Richard Boyer, "Honor among Plebians," 162–63.
65. Miguel Luján, frame 778.
66. Montaño against Durán y Chávez, frame 1111.
67. Hendricks, *New Mexico Prenuptial*, 111–13.
68. Miguel Luján, frames 753–54.
69. Ibid., frame 777.
70. Arrest of Juan Márquez, frame 1068.
71. Ibid., frames 1090, 1101–2.
72. Arrom, *The Women of Mexico City*, 64–65, 71.
73. See pages 154–55.
74. Graham, "Honor Among Slaves." Socolow, *The Women of Colonial Latin America*, 66.
75. Criminal investigation against Alejandro Mora, 23 September 1751, SANM II, roll 8, frame 1032–48. See frame 1045.

76. Miguel Luján, frame 791.
77. Complaint filed by Cristóbal Tafoya Altamirano, 12 May 1719, SANM II, roll 5, frames 835–60.
78. Ibid., frame 835.
79. Complaint filed by Antonia Martín, 18 March 1765, SANM II, roll 9, frames 731–50.
80. Ibid., frame 748.
81. Criminal case against Feliz Luján for the bad life he gives Francisca de Tórrez, July 1713, SANM II, roll 4, frames 924–53 (hereafter cited as Luján against Tórrez).
82. Complaint made by Juana de Anaya before the governor regarding the mistreatment of Antonia de Anaya, 2 October 1752, Santa Fe, SANM II, roll 8, frames 1124–26. See frame 1125.
83. Murder investigation of Juan Márquez and El Jasque, 1741, Santa Fe, SANM II, roll 8, frames 1–37 (hereafter cited as Murder investigation of Márquez and El Jasque).
84. Arrest of Juan Márquez, frames 1064–1106. See frame 1102.
85. Murder investigation of Márquez and El Jasque, frame 9.
86. Ibid., frame 23.
87. Complaint against Juan López and Francisco de Rosas, 14 August 1715, SANM II, roll 5, frames 214–19.
88. Murder investigation of Márquez and El Jasque, frame 33.
89. Complaint filed by Pedro Vigil and the subsequent investigation, 1716, SANM II, roll 5, frames 592–601.
90. Investigation into Juan Antonio Bernal and Juliana Córdova ordered by Governor don Fernando Chacón, 1795, SANM II, roll 13, frames 714–28.
91. Ibid.
92. Miguel Luján, frame 751.
93. Ibid., frames 760–61.
94. Ibid., frame 763.
95. Cutter, *The Legal Culture of Northern New Spain*, 34–35.
96. Montaño against Durán y Chávez, frames 1106–11.
97. Medina against Garduño, frame 824.
98. Montaño against Durán y Chávez, frames 1106–11.
99. Complaint made by Juana de Anaya before the governor regarding the mistreatment of Antonia de Anaya, 2 October 1752, Santa Fe, SANM II, roll 8, frames 1124–26.
100. Civil suit against Juan Antonio Bernal, 1795, SANM II, roll 13, frames 714–28.
101. Criminal case against Pascual Sedillo for the death of his wife María Francisca Peralta, 1772, SANM II, roll 13, frames 743–46.
102. Civil complaint filed by Antonia Martín against Reymundo Baca, her husband, 18 March 1765, Santa Cruz de la Cañada, SANM II, roll 9, frames 731–50.

103. Ibid., frames 732–33.
104. Ibid., frames 733–34.
105. Ibid., frames 747–48.
106. Luján against Tórrez, frames 925–53.
107. Criminal investigation against Alejandro Mora, Bernalillo, 23 September 1751, SANM II, roll 8, frames 1032–48.
108. Complaint filed by Nicolás Ortiz, 1708, SANM II, roll 4, frames 142–148.
109. Ibid., frame 146.
110. *Las Siete Partidas*, 4.2: 19.
111. Medina against Garduño, frame 822.
112. Ibid., frame 844.
113. Criminal case against Pasqual Sedillo for the death of his wife María Francisca Peralta, 1772, SANM II, roll 13, frames 743–46.
114. Baptism of Juana María, 26 January 1766, AASF, roll 13, frame 252.
115. Murder investigation of Márquez and El Jasque, frame 8.
116. Luján against Tórrez, July 1713, SANM II, roll 4, frame 950.
117. Criminal case against Alejandro Mora, resident of Bernalillo, 23 September 1751, SANM II, roll 8, frames 1032–48.

Notes On Sources

1. Olmsted, *Spanish and Mexican Censuses of New Mexico*, 1–14, 51–78, 82–105.
2. See Anderson, *Approaches to the History of the Western Family*, 26–38.

BIBLIOGRAPHY

Adams, Eleanor B. "Bishop Tamarón's Visitation of New Mexico, 1760." *New Mexico Historical Review* 28 (April 1953): 192–233.

———. "Two Colonial New Mexico Libraries, 1704, 1776." *New Mexico Historical Review* 19 (1944): 327–41.

Adams, Eleanor B., and Fray Angelico Chavez, eds. *The Missions of New Mexico, 1776: A Description by Fray Atanasio Dominguez with Other Contemporary Documents*. Albuquerque: University of New Mexico Press, 1956.

Adams, Eleanor B., and Keith W. Algier. "A Frontier Book List—1800." *New Mexico Historical Review* 43 (1968): 49–59.

Ahlborn, Richard E. "Frontier Possessions: The Evidence from Colonial Documents." In *Colonial Frontiers*, ed. Christine Mather, 35–57. Santa Fe, NM: Ancient City Press, 1983.

———. "The Will of a New Mexico Woman in 1762." *New Mexico Historical Review* 65 (July 1990): 319–55.

Alonso, Ana María. *Thread of Blood: Colonialism, Revolution, and Gender on Mexico's Northern Frontier*. Tucson: University of Arizona Press, 1995.

Anderson, Michael. *Approaches to the History of the Western Family, 1500–1914*. London: The Macmillan Press LTD, 1980.

Angel, Amanda Patricia. "Spanish Women in the New World: The Transmission of a Model Polity to New Spain, 1521–1570." PhD diss., University of California, Davis, 1997.

Arrom, Silvia Marina. "Perspectivas sobre Historia de la Familia en México." In *Familias Novohispanas: Siglos XVI al XIX*, edited by Pilar Gonzalbo Aizpuru, 389–399. Mexico City: El Colegio de México, 1991.

———. *The Women of Mexico City, 1790–1857*. Stanford, CA: Stanford University Press, 1985.

Athearn, Frederic James. "Life and Society in Eighteenth-Century New Mexico, 1692–1776." PhD diss., University of Texas at Austin, 1974.

Atondo Rodríguez, Ana María. "De la perversión de la práctica a la perversión de discurso: la fornicación." In *De la Santidad a la Perversión: o de porqué no se cumplía la ley de Dios en la sociedad novohispana*, edited by Sergio Ortega. Mexico: Grijalbo, 1986.

Bakker, Keith. "New Mexican Spanish Colonial Furniture." In *El Camino Real de Tierra Adentro*. Vol. 2, edited by June-el Piper, 117–132. Santa Fe, NM: Bureau of Land Management, 1999.

Balderston, Daniel, and Donna J. Guy, eds. *Sex and Sexuality in Latin America*. New York: New York University Press, 1997.

Bancroft, Hubert Howe. *History of Arizona and New Mexico, 1530–1888*. Albuquerque: Horn and Wallace, Publishers, 1962.

Barr, Juliana. "From Captives to Slaves: Commodifying Indian Women in the Borderlands." *The Journal of American History* 92, no. 1 (June 2005): 19–46. Accessed July 18, 2013. http://www.jstor.org/stable/3660524.

Barret-Ducrocq, Françoise. *Love in the Time of Victoria: Sexuality and Desire among Working-Class Men and Women in Nineteenth-Century London*. New York: Penguin Books USA Inc., 1992.

Bauer, Arnold J. *Goods, Power, History: Latin America's Material Culture*. Cambridge, England: Cambridge University Press, 2001.

Baxter, John O. *Las Carneradas: Sheep Trade in New Mexico, 1700–1860*. Albuquerque: University of New Mexico Press, 1987.

Berkner, Lutz K. "The Use and Misuse of Census Data for the Historical Analysis of Family Structure." *Journal of Interdisciplinary History* 4 (Spring 1975): 721–38.

Bolton, Herbert Eugene. "The Mission as a Frontier Institution in the Spanish American Colonies." In *New Spain's Far Northern Frontier: Essays on Spain in the American West, 1540–1821*, edited by David J. Weber, 49–65. Dallas, TX: Southern Methodist University Press, 1979.

Boswell, John. *The Kindness of Strangers: The Abandonment of Children in Western Europe from Late Antiquity to the Renaissance*. New York: Pantheon Books, 1988.

Bouvier, Virginia Marie. *Women and the Conquest of California, 1542–1840: Codes of Silence*. Tucson: The University of Arizona Press, 2001.

Boyd, E. *Popular Arts of Colonial New Mexico*. Santa Fe, NM: Museum of International Folk Art, 1959.

———. *Popular Arts of Spanish New Mexico*. Santa Fe, NM: Museum of New Mexico Press, 1974.

Boyer, Richard. "Honor among Plebians: *Mala Sangre* and Social Reputation." In *The Faces of Honor: Sex, Shame, and Violence in Colonial Latin America*, edited by Lyman L. Johnson and Sonya Lipsett-Rivera, 152–178. Albuquerque: University of New Mexico Press, 1998.

———. *Lives of the Bigamists: Marriage, Family, and Community in Colonial Mexico.* Albuquerque: University of New Mexico Press, 1995.

———. "Women, *La Mala Vida* and the Politics of Marriage." In *Sexuality and Marriage in Colonial Latin America*, edited by Asunción Lavrin, 252–86. Lincoln: University of Nebraska Press, 1989.

Brooks, James. *Captives and Cousins: Slavery, Kinship, and Community in the Southwest Borderlands.* Chapel Hill: University of North Carolina Press, 2002.

———. "'Lest We Go in Search of Relief to Our Lands and Our Nation': Customary Justice and Colonial Law in the New Mexico Borderlands, 1680–1821." In *The Many Legalities of Early America*, edited by Christopher L. Tomlins and Bruce H. Mann, 150–80. Chapel Hill: University of North Carolina Press, 2001.

———. "'This Evil Extends Especially to the Feminine Sex': Captivity and Identity in New Mexico, 1700–1846." In *Writing the Range: Race, Class, and Culture in the Women's West*, edited by Elizabeth Jameson and Susan Armitage, 97–121. Norman: University of Oklahoma Press, 1997.

Brown, Judith C. *Immodest Acts: The Life of a Lesbian Nun in Renaissance Italy.* New York: Oxford University Press, 1986.

Brucker, Gene. *Giovanni and Lusanna: Love and Marriage in Renaissance Florence.* Berkeley: University of California Press, 1986.

Brugge, David M. "Captives and Slaves on the Camino Real." In *El Camino Real de Tierra Adentro*. Vol. 2, edited by June-el Piper, 103–10. Santa Fe, NM: Bureau of Land Management, 1999.

———. *Navajos in the Catholic Church Records of New Mexico 1694–1875.* Tsaile, AZ: Navajo Community College Press, 1985.

Bunting, Bainbridge. *Early Architecture in New Mexico.* Albuquerque: University of New Mexico Press, 1976.

———. *Taos Adobes: Spanish Colonial and Territorial Architecture of the Taos Valley.* Santa Fe, NM: Fort Burgwin Research Center and Museum of New Mexico Press, 1964.

Burguiere, André. "The Formation of the Couple." *Journal of Family History* 12 (1987): 39–53.

Burns, Robert I., S.J., ed. *Las Siete Partidas.* Translated by Samuel Parsons Scott. Philadelphia: University of Pennsylvania Press, 2001.

Bustamante, Adrian. "'The Matter Was Never Resolved': The Casta System in Colonial New Mexico, 1693–1823." *New Mexico Historical Review* 66, no. 2 (April 1991): 143–63.

Calvo, Thomas. "Matrimonio, Iglesia y sociedad en el occidente de México: Zamora (siglos XVII a XIX)." In *Familias Novohispanas Siglos XVI al XIX*, edited by Pilar Gonzalbo Aizpuru, 101–108. Mexico City: El Colegio de México, 1991.

The Canons and Decrees of the Council of Trent. Translated and edited by Rev. H. J. Schroeder, O.P., 182. Rockford, Ill.: Tan Books and Publishers, 1978.

Castañeda, Antonia I. "Engendering the History of Alta California, 1769–1848:

Gender, Sexuality, and the Family." *California History* 76 (Summer/Fall, 1997): 230–59.

———. "Presidarias y Pobladoras: Spanish-Mexican Women in Frontier Monterey, Alta California, 1770–1821." PhD diss., Stanford University Press, 1990.

Castañeda, Carmen. "La Formación de la Pareja y el Martimonio." In *Familias Novohispanas Siglos XVI al XIX*, edited by Pilar Gonzalbo Aizpuru, 73–90. Mexico City: El Colegio de México, 1991.

Cavallo, Sandra, and Simona Cerutti. "Female Honor and the Social Control of Reproduction in Piedmont between 1600 and 1800." In *Sex and Gender in Historical Perspective*, edited by Edward Muir and Guido Ruggiero, 73–109. Baltimore, MD: Johns Hopkins University Press, 1990.

Chambers, Sarah C. "'To the Company of a Man Like My Husband, No Law Can Compel Me': The Limits of Sanctions against Wife Beating in Arequipa, Peru, 1780–1850." *Journal of Women's History* (Spring 1999): 31–52.

Chávez, Fray Angélico. *Origins of New Mexico Families: A Genealogy of the Spanish Colonial Period*. Santa Fe, NM: Museum of New Mexico Press, 1992.

Cohen, Elizabeth S. "Court Testimony from the Past: Self and Culture in the Making of Text." In *Essays on Life Writing: From Genre to Critical Practice*, edited by Marlene Kadar, 83–93. Toronto: University of Toronto Press, 1992.

Collier, Jane, Michelle A. Rosaldo, and Sylvia Yanagisako. "Is There a Family? New Anthropological Views." In *Rethinking the Family: Some Feminist Questions*, edited by Barrie Thorne and Marilyn Yalom, 31–48. Boston: Northeastern University Press, 1992.

Colligan, John B. *The Juan Páez Hurtado Expedition of 1695: Fraud in Recruiting Colonists for New Mexico*. Albuquerque: University of New Mexico Press, 1995.

Cope, R. Douglas. *The Limits of Racial Domination: Plebeian Society in Colonial Mexico City, 1660–1720*. Madison: The University of Wisconsin Press, 1994.

Couturier, Edith. "Women and the Family in Eighteenth-Century Mexico: Law and Practice." *Journal of Family History* (Fall 1985): 294–304.

Cunningham, Elizabeth, and Skip Miller. "Trade Fairs in Taos." In *El Camino Real de Tierra Adentro*. Vol. 2, edited by June-el Piper, 87–102. Santa Fe, NM: Bureau of Land Management, 1999.

Cutter, Charles R. "Community and the Law in Northern New Spain." *The Americas* 50, no. 4 (April 1994): 467–80. Accessed October 16, 2013. http://www.jstor.org/stable/1007892.

———. *The Legal Culture of Northern New Spain, 1700–1810*. Albuquerque: University of New Mexico Press, 1995.

Cruz, Jesus. "Building Liberal Identities in 19th Century Madrid: The Role of Middle Class Material Culture." *The Americas* (January 2004): 391–410.

Darrow, Margaret H. "Popular Concepts of Marital Choice in Eighteenth-Century France." *Journal of Social History* (Winter 1985): 261–72.

de Corella, Jaime. *Práctica de el confessionario y explicación de las 65 Proposiciones*

condenandas por la santidad de N. S. P. Inocencio XI: Su materia los casos más selectos de la theología moral: Su forma un diálogo entre el confesor y penitente, 66. Valencia: Imprenta de Iaume de Bordazar, 1689.
Deeds, Susan. "Land Tenure Patterns in Northern New Spain," *The Americas* (April 1985): 446–61.
D'Emilio, John, and Estelle B. Freedman. *Intimate Matters: A History of Sexuality in America*, 26. New York: Harper and Row, 1988.
Demos, John. *A Little Commonwealth: Family Life in Plymouth Colony.* Oxford: Oxford University Press, 2000.
Dillard, Heath. *Daughters of the Reconquest: Women in Castilian Town Society, 1100–1300.* Cambridge, England: Cambridge University Press, 1984.
The Doctrinal Decrees and Canons of the Council of Trent. New York: American and Foreign Christian Union, 1857.
Duby, Georges. *The Knight, the Lady and the Priest: The Making of Modern Marriage in Medieval France.* New York: Pantheon Books, 1983.
Earle, Rebbeca. "Letters and Love in Colonial Spanish America." *The Americas* (July 2005): 17–46.
Ebright, Malcolm, and Rick Hendricks. *The Witches of Abiquiu: The Governor, the Priest, the Genízaro Indians, and the Devil.* Albuquerque: University of New Mexico Press, 2006.
Erickson, Bruce A. "Violence and Manhood: Military Culture on the Northern Frontier of Colonial New Spain." PhD diss., University of New Mexico, 2001.
Esquibel, José Antonio. "Mexico City to Santa Fe." In *El Camino Real de Tierra Adentro.* Vol. 2, edited by June-el Piper, 55–70. Santa Fe, NM: Bureau of Land Management, 1999.
Esquibel, José Antonio, and John B. Colligan. *The Spanish Recolonization of New Mexico: An Account of the Families Recruited at Mexico City in 1693.* Albuquerque, NM: Hispanic Genealogical Research Center of New Mexico, 1999.
Espinosa, Carmen. *Shawls, Crinolines, Filigree.* El Paso: Texas Western Press, 1970.
Foote, Cheryl J., and Sandra K. Schackel. "Indian Women of New Mexico, 1535–1680." In *New Mexico Women: Intercultural Perspectives*, edited by Joan M. Jensen and Darlis A. Miller, 17–40. Albuquerque: University of New Mexico Press, 1986.
Foucault, Michel. *The History of Sexuality: Volume 1: An Introduction.* New York: Vintage Books, 1990.
Frank, Ross Harold. "From Settler to Citizen: Economic Development and Cultural Change in Late Colonial New Mexico, 1750–1820." PhD diss., University of California Berkeley, 1992.
———. *From Settler to Citizen: New Mexican Economic Development and the Creation of Vecino Society, 1750–1820.* Berkeley: University of California Press, 2000.
Frederick, Jake. "Without Impediment: Crossing Racial Boundaries in Colonial Mexico." *The Americas* 67, no. 4 (April, 2011): 495–515. Accessed July 20, 2014. http://muse.jhu.edu/journals/tam/summary/v067/67.4.frederick.html.

Hanna, Edward. *The Catholic Encyclopedia*. Vol. 11., s.v. "The Sacrament of Penance." New York: Robert Appleton Company, 1911.

Harevan, Tamara K. "The Family as Process: The Historical Study of the Family Cycle." *Journal of Social History* 7 (Spring 1974): 322–29.

———. "Family History at the Crossroads." *Journal of Family History* 12 (1987): ix–xxiii.

Hendricks, Rick. *New Mexico in 1801: The Priests Report*. Los Ranchos de Albuquerque, New Mexico: Rio Grande Books, 2008.

———, ed. *New Mexico Prenuptial Investigations from the Archivos Históricos del Arzobispado de Durango*. Las Cruces: Rio Grande Historical Collection New Mexico State University Library, 1996.

Hernández, Salomé. "Nueva Mexicanas as Refugees and Reconquest Settlers, 1680–1696." In *New Mexico Women: Intercultural Perspectives*, edited by Joan M. Jensen and Darlis A. Miller, 41–69. Albuquerque: University of New Mexico Press, 1986.

———. "The U.S. Southwest: Female Participation in Official Spanish Settlement Expeditions: Specific Case Studies in the Sixteenth, Seventeenth, and Eighteenth Centuries." PhD diss., University of New Mexico, 1987.

Herrero, Pedro Pérez. "Evolución Demográfica y Estructura Familiar en México (1730–1850)." In *Familias novohispanas Siglos XVI al XIX*, edited by Pilar Gonzalbo Aizpuru, 345–371. Mexico City: El Colegio de México, 1989.

Hunefeldt, Christine. *Liberalism in the Bedroom: Quarreling Spouses in Nineteenth-Century Lima*. University Park: The Pennsylvania State University Press, 2000.

Hurl-Eamon, Jennine. "Domestic Violence Prosecuted: Women Binding over their Husbands for Assault at Westminster Quarter Sessions, 1685–1720." *Journal of Family History*, 4, no. 26 (October 2001): 435–54.

Hurtado, Albert L. *Intimate Frontiers: Sex, Gender, and Culture in Old California, Histories of the American Frontier*. Albuquerque: University of New Mexico Press, 1999.

Iowa, Jerome. *Ageless Adobe: History and Preservation in Southwestern Architecture*. Santa Fe, NM: Sunstone Press, 1985.

Jaffary, Nora E. "Reconceiving Motherhood: Infanticide and Abortion in Colonial Mexico." *Journal of Family History*, 37, no. 1 (2012): 3–22. Accessed June 5, 2014. jfh.sagepub.com at Johns Hopkins University.

Jameson, Elizabeth. "Women as Workers, Women as Civilizers: True Womanhood in the American West." In *The Women's West*, edited by Susan Armitage and Elizabeth Jameson, 145–64. Norman and London: University of Oklahoma Press, 1978.

Jenkins, Mary Ellen. "Some Eighteenth-Century New Mexico Women of Property." In *Hispanic Arts and Ethnohistory in the Southwest*, edited by Marta Weigle, 335–45. Santa Fe, NM: Ancient City Press, 1983.

Jensen, Joan M., and Darlis A. Miller, eds. *New Mexico Women: Intercultural Perspectives*. Albuquerque: University of New Mexico Press, 1986.
Johnson, Lyman L., and Sonya Lipsett-Rivera, eds. *The Faces of Honor: Sex, Shame, and Violence in Colonial Latin America*. Albuquerque: University of New Mexico Press, 1998.
Jones, Oakah, Jr. *Los Paisanos: Spanish Settlers on the Northern Frontier of New Spain*. Norman: University of Oklahoma Press, 1979.
Kelly, Henry W. "Franciscan Missions of New Mexico, 1740–1760." *New Mexico Historical Review*, 15 (1940), 349–59.
Kessell, John L. *Pueblos, Spaniards, and the Kingdom of New Mexico*. Norman: University of Oklahoma Press, 2008.
———, ed. *Remote Beyond Compare: Letters of don Diego de Vargas to His Family from New Spain and New Mexico, 1675–1706*. Albuquerque: University of New Mexico, 1989.
Kessell, John L., and Rick Hendricks, eds. Introduction to *By Force of Arms: The Journals of Don Diego de Vargas, 1691–1693*. Albuquerque: University of New Mexico Press, 1993.
Kessell, John L., Rick Hendricks, and Meredith D. Dodge, eds. *To the Royal Crown Restored: The Journals of Don Diego de Vargas, 1691–1693*. Albuquerque: University of New Mexico Press, 1995.
Kessell, John L, Rick Hendricks, Meredith D. Dodge, and Larry D. Miller, eds. *That Disturbances Cease: The Journals of Don Diego de Vargas, New Mexico, 1697–1700*. Albuquerque: University of New Mexico Press, 2000.
———. *A Settling of Accounts: The Journals of Don Diego de Vargas, New Mexico, 1700–1704*. Albuquerque: University of New Mexico Press, 2002.
Kinnaird, Lawrence, and Lucia Kinnaird. "Secularization of Four New Mexican Missions." *New Mexico Historical Review* 54 (January 1979): 35–41.
Konetzke, Richard. "R. C. Para Que Los Encomenderos Sean Obligados A Casarse dentro de Tres Años, Madrid, 8 de noviembre de 1539." In *Coleción de Documentos para la Historia de la Formación Social de Hispanoamérica, 1493–1810*. Madrid, Spain: Consejo Superior de Investigaciones Cientificas, 1953.
Kuznesof, Elizabeth Anne. "Raza, Clase y Matrimonio en la Nueva España: Estado Actual del Debate." In *Familias Novohispanas: Siglos XVI al XIX*, edited by Pilar Gonzalbo Aizpuru, 373–88. Mexico City: El Colegio de México, 1991.
Latasa, Pilar. "'If they remained as mere words': Trent, Marriage, and Freedom in the Viceroyalty of Peru, Sixteenth to Eighteenth Centuries." *The Americas* 73, no. 1 (January 2016): 13–38. Accessed May 17, 2016. https://muse.jhu.edu/article/614113.
Lavrin, Asunción. "Introduction: The Scenario, the Actors, and the Issues." In *Sexuality and Marriage in Colonial Latin America*, edited by Asunción Lavrin, 47–92. Lincoln: University of Nebraska Press, 1989.
———. "Sexuality in Colonial Mexico: A Church Dilemma." In *Sexuality and*

Marriage in Colonial Latin America, edited by Asunción Lavrin, 49. Lincoln: University of Nebraska Press, 1989.
Lavrin, Asunción, and Edith Couturier. "Dowries and Wills: A View of Women's Socioeconomic Role in Colonial Guadalajara and Puebla, 1640–1790." *Hispanic American Historical Review* 59 (1979): 280–304.
Ledesma, Fr. Clemente de. *Despertador de Noticias de los Santos Sacramentos.* Mexico City: Doña Maria de Benavides, viuda de Juan de Ribera, 1695.
Las Leyes de Toro. Madrid: Servicio de Publicaciones de Ministerio de Educación y Ciencia Imprime, n.d.
Leyes de Toro. Madrid: Imprime: Gaez, S. A.
Leyva, Yolanda Chávez. "'A Poor Widow Burdened with Children': Widows and Land in Colonial New Mexico." In *Writing the Range: Race, Class, and Culture in the Women's West*, edited by Elizabeth Jameson and Susan Armitage, 85–96. Norman: University of Oklahoma Press, 1997.
Lipsett-Rivera, Sonya. "A Slap in the Face of Honor." In *The Faces of Honor: Sex, Shame, and Violence in Colonial Latin America*, edited by Lyman L. Johnson and Sonya Lipsett-Rivera, 180. Albuquerque: University of New Mexico Press, 1998.
Lockhart, James. *Spanish Peru: 1532–1560: A Colonial Society.* Madison: University of Wisconsin Press, 1968.
Lockhart, James, and Stuart B. Schwartz. *Early Latin America: A History of Colonial Spanish America and Brazil.* Cambridge, England: Cambridge University Press, 1983.
López de Ayala, Ignacio, tr. *El sacrosanto y ecuménico Concilio de Trento.* Madrid: Imprenta Real, 1785.
Manual de los Sacramentos. Puebla de los Angeles: Imprenta de D. Pedro de la Rosa, 1810.
Manual de párrocos para la administración de los sacramentos. Puebla de Los Ángeles: Imprenta de D. Pedro de la Rosa, Mexico, 1810.
Margadant, Guillermo F. "La Familia en el Derecho NovoHispano." In *Familias Novohispanas: Siglos XVI al XIX*, edited by Pilar Gonzalbo Aizpuru, 27–56. Mexico City: El Colegio de México, 1991.
Martin, Cheryl English. *Governance and Society in Colonial Mexico: Chihuahua in the Eighteenth Century.* Stanford, CA: Stanford University Press, 1996.
Martín, Luis. *Daughters of the Conquistadores: Women of the Viceroyalty of Peru.* Dallas, TX: Southern Methodist University Press, 1983.
Martinez-Alier, Verena. *Marriage, Class and Colour in Nineteenth-Century Cuba: A Study of Racial Attitudes and Sexual Values in a Slave Society.* Ann Arbor: University of Michigan Press, 1989.
McDonald, Dedra Shawn. "Negotiated Conquests: Domestic Servants and Gender in the Spanish and Mexican Borderlands, 1598–1860." PhD diss., University of New Mexico, 2000.

Megged, Amos. "The Social Significance of Benevolent and Malevolent Gifts among Single Caste Women in Mid-Seventeenth-Century New Spain." *Journal of Family History* 24, no. 4 (October 1999): 420–40.

Meschke, Amy. "Women's Lives Through Women's Wills in the Spanish and Mexican Borderlands, 1750–1846." PhD diss., Southern Methodist University, 2004.

Metcalf, Alida C. *Family and Frontier in Colonial Brazil: Santana de Parnaíba, 1580–1822.* Berkley: University of California Press, 1992.

Morfí, Fray Juan Agustín de. *Account of Disorders in New Mexico, 1778.* Edited and translated by Marc Simmons. Isleta Pueblo: Historical Society of New Mexico, 1977.

Morse, Richard M. "The Heritage of Latin America." In *The Founding of New Societies*, edited by Louis Hartz, 123–77. New York: Harcourt, Brace & World, Inc., 1964.

Muir, Edward, and Guido Ruggiero. "Afterword." In *History from Crime*, edited by Edward Muir and Guido Ruggiero, 226–36. Baltimore, MD: The Johns Hopkins University Press, 1994.

Nazzari, Muriel. *Disappearance of the Dowry: Women, Families, and Social Change in São Paulo, Brazil (1600–1900).* Stanford, CA: Stanford University Press, 1991.

New Catholic Encyclopedia. New York: McGraw-Hill Book Company, 1967.

Noonan, John T., Jr. *Contraception: A History of Its Treatment by the Catholic Theologians and Canonists.* Cambridge, MA: Harvard University Press, 1965.

Norris, Jim. *After "The Year Eighty": The Demise of Franciscan Power in Spanish New Mexico.* Albuquerque: University of New Mexico Press, 2000.

Norris, Jimmy D. "The Breakdown of Franciscan Hegemony in the Kingdom of New Mexico, 1692–1752." PhD diss., Tulane University, 1992.

O'Callaghan, Joseph F. "Alfonso X and the *Partidas*." In *Las Siete Partidas.* Vol. 1, *The Medieval Church: The World of Clerics and Laymen*, Title XXIII, Law XII, xxxii, edited by Robert I. Burns, S. J. Philadelphia: University of Pennsylvania Press, 2001.

O'Neil, Arthur Charles. *The Catholic Encyclopedia.* Vol. 14., s.v. "Sin." New York: Robert Appleton Company, 1912.

Olmsted, Virginia Langham, comp. *Spanish and Mexican Censuses of New Mexico, 1750–1830.* Albuquerque: New Mexico Genealogical Society, Inc., 1981.

Ortner, Sherry B. "The Virgin and the State." *Feminist Studies* 4 (October 1978): 19–35.

Perry, Mary Elizabeth. *Gender and Disorder in Early Modern Seville.* Princeton, NJ: Princeton University Press, 1990.

Penyak, Lee M., and Veronica Vallejo. "Expectations of Love in Troubled Mexican Marriages during the Late Colonial and Early National Periods." *The Historian* 65 no. 3 (Spring 2003): 563–87.

Pierce, Donna, and Cordelia Snow. "'A Harp for Playing.'" In *El Camino Real de*

Tierra Adentro. Vol. 2, edited by June-el Piper, 71–86. Santa Fe, NM: Bureau of Land Management, 1999.

Piper, June-el, ed. *El Camino Real de Tierra Adentro.* Vol. 2. Santa Fe, NM: Bureau of Land Management, 1999.

Pollock, Linda A. "Rethinking Patriarchy and the Family in Seventeenth-Century England." *Journal of Family History* 23, no. 1 (January 1998): 3–27.

Porter, Amy M. *Their Lives, Their Wills: Women in the Borderlands, 1750–1846.* Lubbock: Texas Tech University Press, 2015.

Rapp, Rayna, Ellen Ross, and Renate Bridenthal. "Examining Family History." In *Sex and Class in Women's History*, edited by Judith L. Newton, Mary P. Ryan, and Judith R. Walkowitz, 232–58. London: Routledge & Kegan Paul, 1985.

Rípodas, Daisy Ardanaz. *El Matrimonio en Indias: Realidad Social y Regulación Jurídica.* Buenos Aires: Fundación para la Educación, la Ciencia y la Cultura, 1977.

Rock, Rosalind Z. "*Mujeres de Substancia*–Case Studies of Women of Property in Northern New Spain." *Colonial Latin American Historical Review* 2 (Fall 1993): 425–40.

———. "Pido y Suplico: Women and the Law in Spanish New Mexico: 1697–1763." *New Mexico Historical Review* 65, no. 2 (April 1990): 145–59.

Rubin, Gayle. "Thinking Sex: Notes for a Radical Theory of the Politics of Sexuality." In *Pleasure and Danger: Exploring Female Sexuality*, edited by Carole S. Vance, 267–319. Boston: Routledge and Kegan Paul, 1985.

Saether, Steinar A. "Bourbon Absolutism and Marriage Reform in Late Colonial Spanish America." *The Americas* 59, no. 4 (April 2003): 475–509. Accessed December 5, 2010. http://muse.jhu.edu.

Salisbury, Joyce E. "The Latin Doctors of the Church on Sexuality." *Journal of Medieval History*, 12 (1986): 279–89.

Scott, Joan. *Gender and the Politics of History.* New York: Columbia University Press, 1999.

Seed, Patricia. *To Love, Honor, and Obey in Colonial Mexico: Conflicts over Marriage Choice, 1574–1821.* Stanford, CA: Stanford University Press, 1988.

Segalen, Martine, and Philippe Richard. "Marrying Kinsmen in Pays Bigouden Sud, Brittany." *Journal of Family History* 11, no. 2 (June 1986): 109–130. Accessed May 8, 2014. http://jfh.sagepub.com.proxy.alumni.jhu.edu/content/11/2/109.full.pdf+html.

Serra, Angel. *Manual de Administrar los Santos Sacramentos a los españoles y naturales de esta provincial de Michuacan, conforme a la reforma de Paulo V y Urbano VIII.* Mexico: Impressor del Real y Apostólico Tribunal de la Santa Cruzada, 1731. Accessed November 10, 2015. http://catalog.hathitrust.org/Record/009349141.

Simmons, Marc. "Hygiene, Sanitation, and Public Health in New Mexico." *New Mexico Historical Review* 67, no. 3 (July 1992): 145–59.

———. "Settlement Patterns and Village Plans in Colonial New Mexico." In *New Spain's Far Northern Frontier: Essays on Spain in the American West, 1540–1821*, edited by David J. Weber, 97–115. Dallas, TX: Southern Methodist University Press, 1979.

———. *Spanish Government in New Mexico*. Albuquerque: University of New Mexico Press, 1968.

Snow, David H. "Rural Hispanic Community Organization in Northern New Mexico: An Historical Perspective." In *The Survival of Spanish American Villages*, edited by Paul Kutsche, 45–52. Colorado Springs, CO: The Research Committee, 1979.

Socolow, Susan M. "Acceptable Partners: Marriage Choice in Colonial Argentina, 1778–1810." In *Sexuality and Marriage in Colonial Latin America*, edited by Asunción Lavrin, 209–51. Lincoln: University of Nebraska Press, 1989.

———. *The Women of Colonial Latin America*. Cambridge, England: Cambridge University Press, 2000.

Stern, Steve J. *The Secret History of Gender: Women, Men, and Power in Late Colonial Mexico*. Chapel Hill: The University of North Carolina Press, 1995.

Thompson, E. P. "Anthropology and the Discipline of Historical Context," *Midland History* 1, no. 3 (Spring 1972): 41–55.

Tilly, Charles. "Family History, Social History, and Social Change." *Journal of Family History* 12 (1987): 319–30.

Tjarks, Alicia V. "Demographic, Ethnic and Occupational Structure of New Mexico, 1790." *The Americas* 35 (July 1978): 45–88.

Twinam, Ann. "Honor, Sexuality, and Illegitimacy in Colonial Spanish America." In *Sexuality and Marriage in Colonial Latin America*, edited by Asunción Lavrin, 118–55. Lincoln: University of Nebraska Press, 1989.

———. "The Negotiation of Honor." In *The Faces of Honor: Sex, Shame, and Violence in Colonial Latin America*, edited by Lyman L. Johnson and Sonya Lipsett-Rivera. Albuquerque: University of New Mexico Press, 1998.

———. *Public Lives, Private Secrets: Gender, Honor, Sexuality, and Illegitimacy in Colonial Spanish America*. Stanford, CA: Stanford University Press, 1999.

van Deusen, Nancy E. "Determining the Boundaries of Virtue: The Discourse of *Recogimiento* Among Women in Seventeenth-Century Lima." *Journal of Family History* 22 (October 1997): 373–89.

van de Walle, Etienne. "Motivations and Technology in the Decline of French Fertility." In *Family and Sexuality in French History*, edited by Robert Wheaton and Tamara K. Hareven, 135–78. Philadelphia: University of Pennsylvania Press, 1980.

Van Young, Eric. *Hacienda and Market in Eighteenth-Century Mexico: The Rural Economy of the Guadalajara Region, 1675–1820*. Berkeley: University of California Press, 1981.

Vergara, Teresa C. "Growing Up Indian: Migration, Labor, and Life in Lima

(1570–1640)." In *Raising an Empire: Children in Early Modern Iberia and Colonial Latin America*, edited by Ondina E. González and Bianca Premo, 75–106. Albuquerque: University of New Mexico Press, 2007.

Veyna, Angelina F. "'It Is My Last Wish That . . .': A Look at Colonial Nuevo Mexicanas through Their Testaments." In *Building With Our Hands: New Directions in Chicana Studies*, edited by Adela de la Torre and Beatríz M. Pesquera, 91–108. Berkeley: University of California Press, 1993.

Wall, Helena M. *Fierce Communion: Family and Community in Early America*. Cambridge, MA: Harvard University Press, 1990.

Walsh, Margaret. "Women's Place on the American Frontier." *Journal of American Studies* 29, no. 2 (August 1995): 241–55.

Weber, David J. *The Spanish Frontier in North America*. New Haven, CT: Yale University Press, 1992.

Weeks, Jeffrey. *Sex, Politics and Society: The Regulation of Sexuality since 1800*. London: Longman Group Limited, 1981.

Wiarda, Howard J. "Toward a Framework for the Study of Political Change in the Iberic-Latin Tradition: The Corporative Model." *World Politics* 25, no. 2 (January 1973): 206–35.

Will, Martina Elaine. "God Gives and God Takes Away: Death and Dying in New Mexico, 1760–1850." PhD diss., University of New Mexico, 2000.

Will de Chaparro, Martina. *Death and Dying in New Mexico*. Albuquerque: University of New Mexico Press, 2007.

Wright, Robert E. "How Many Are 'A Few'? Catholic Clergy in Central and Northern New Mexico, 1780–1851." In *Seeds of Struggle/Harvest of Faith: The Papers of the Archdiocese of Santa Fe Catholic Cuatro Centennial Conference: The History of the Catholic Church in New Mexico*, edited by Thomas J. Steele, S.M., Paul Rhetts, and Barbe Awalt, 219–62. Albuquerque: LPD Press, 1997.

Zavala, Silvio. *Los Esclavos Indios en Nueva España*. Mexico: El Colegio Nacional, 1967.

INDEX

Abeyta, Manuela, 151, 153
adultery, 147, 171–72
affinity, 64–65, 81
Aguilar, Julián Rael de, 35–36
Aguilar, María Francisca Rael de, 58
alcaldes mayores, 15, 35, 38, 43, 45–46
Anaya, Antonia de, 156–57
angustia loci (restricted place), 126
Anza, Juan Bautista de (governor), 19, 45
Apodaca, Josefa de, 57
Aragón, María Luisa de, 1–3, 180
Archibeque, Juan de, 26
Archibeque, Miguel de, 117
Archuleta, Diego, 154
Archuleta, María, 60
Archuleta, Micaela de, 61
Armijo, Gertrudis de, 77, 90, 94
Armijo, José de, 113–14
Armijo, Manuela de, 98
Armijo, Vicente de, 110
arras, 54, 59, 122
Arrom, Silvia, 27–28, 107–8
Aspitia, Inés de, 140
Atiensa, Lazaro de, 56

Baca, Antonia, 131

Baca, Juana, 67, 131
Baca, Juan Antonio, 66, 129–30
Baca, María, 129
Baca, María Guadalupe, 127–28
Baca, María Magdalena, 151, 157
Baca, Mariano, 104–5
Baca, Miguel Hermenegildo, 128
banns, 55, 68–69, 71
baptisms, 65, 96, 110, 136
Benavides, Tomasa, 22
Bernal, Ana, 40, 133, 142
bigamy, 61, 63
Blásquez, María, 113–14
Boyer, Richard, 108
Bustamante y Tagle, Bernardo Antonio (lieutenant governor), 46, 91

Cabrera, Maria de, 119, 157–59, 164–65
Camargo, fray Antonio, 57
Catholic Church: dogma on sexuality, 79–81; ensoulment, 97; power to punish, 74
census of 1790, 134–35; household types, 189–90, 192–93; surname clusters, 188–89, 191
Chávez, Antonia Rita, 65

237

Chávez, Antonio de, 131
Chávez, Domingo, 86
Chávez, Ignacio, 130
Chávez, Isabel, 86
Chávez, Luis de, 127
Chávez, Manuela de, 36
Chávez, María, 1–3
Chávez, María Rosa, 95, 101
Chávez, Miguel, 90, 93–94, 101
Chávez, Pedro, 118
Codallos y Rabal, Joaquín, 43
communities: configuration of, 17–18; defense of, 18–19; establishment of, 17–19
community property (*bienes gananciales*), 43
Concha, Fernando de la (governor), 38
conjugal debt, 140, 219n34
conjugal household, 29, 40, 133, 147–48
conjugal life, 40, 139
consanguinity: defined 63–64; examples of, 65–66; genealogical chart, 66; tree of, 63
contraceptives, 96–97
Córdova, Juliana, 166
Council of Trent, 41, 51–52, 55, 60, 64–65, 113
courtship: community involvement, 7–8, 99–100, 123–24; men in, 92–94, 104–6; parental involvement, 94, 100–101; peer involvement, 7–8, 94–95; women in, 92–99
Cuervo y Valdés, Francisco (governor), 17

De la Cruz, Josefa, 72
deposit (*depósito*), 70, 98
derecho indiano, 38
diligencias matrimoniales (marital investigations), 52, 55–56, 62, 65, 113, 181–87
dispensations, 7, 57, 65–68, 82, 124–32

divorce, 140
domestic violence: abuse of wives, 48–49; Catholic dogma regarding, 149; cruelty to servants, 48–49; *mala vida* (hard life), 143, 147, 148, 157, 163, 166, 169, 172; sexual abuse of servants, 85–89; state laws, 148
Domínguez, fray Francisco Atanasio, 11, 17, 54
Domínguez, Josefa, 113
Domínguez, Juana, 26
dowry: as settlement, 102–3; as strategy to control marriages, 115–24; conflicts about, 42; defined, 42; examples of, 44, 119–20
Durán, Cristóbal, 51
Durán de Armijo, Antonio, 163–64
Durán y Chávez, Francisca, 131
Durán y Chávez, Francisco, 67
Durán y Chávez, José, 45
Durán y Chávez, Margarita, 128–29
Durán y Chávez, María Rosa, 93
Durán y Chávez, Nicolás, 42, 46, 101, 118, 121, 126, 144–45, 152, 161

education, 141–42
elopement, 70–71
El Satebo, 93–94
endogamy, 111
Espinosa, Juana Mata de, 60
Espinosa, Nicolás de, 72, 91
Esquibel, Ventura de, 71–72, 94–95, 99, 101–2, 114–15
Estrada, Esteban de, 60
exogamy, 111

Fajardo, Cayetano, 103
farming, 12–14
fathers, 27, 141–42
feast days, 68–69
Fermín de Mendinueta, Pedro (governor), 166

Fernández, Carlos, 43
Flores Mogollón, Juan Ignacio (governor), 40, 145, 147, 161, 165, 169
Foucault, Michel, 80–81
Franciscans: Custody of the Conversion of St. Paul, 52; the *custos*, 53; obventions, 54–55; ínodos (stipends), 54
free will, 60, 70–71, 113
Fresqui, Pedro, 61

Gallegos, María, 129
Gallegos, Tomás, 91
Galván, Juan, 47
Gamboa, Cristóbal de, 81
García, Alonso, 115
García, Margarita, 105
García, Salvador, 128–29
García de la Mora, José Pascual, 67–68
García de Noriega, Mateo, 124
García de Noriega, Rosalía Saturnina, 67–68
García Jurado, Juana María, 127
García Pareja, Manuel (alcalde mayor), 167
Garduño, Bartolomé, 166
Genízaros: 5, 10–11, 19, 85
godparents, 136
Góngora, Cristóbal de, 140
González, Baltasar, 95
González, María de la Candelaria, 104
González, Sebastián, 30, 113
gossip, 91, 122–23
governors, 34–35, 37–38
grandparents, 137–38
Griega, Inés, 73–74, 99
Griego, José Antonio, 116–17
Griego, Juana, 26
Grolet, Santiago, 61
Guerrero, Francisco (alcalde mayor), 166, 171
Gurulé, Elena, 121
Gutiérrez, Antonia, 61

Gutiérrez, Ramón, 97–98, 107–8, 119, 213n101, 217n3

Herrera, Juan Manuel de, 26
Herrera, Matilda, 92
Herrera, Melchor de, 66
Hispanics, 10–12, 15, 17, 32, 34
honor: bestowed upon legitimate children, 109; binary approach, 78; chart, 184–85; definition of, 5; men's, 5, 91; women's, 5–6, 97–9; women's defense of 98–99; women's loss of, 102–4
households, 134, 189–90, 192–93
Hurtado, Juana, 47
husbands, 27, 58, 139–40, 143–44, 147–48

igualdad (equality), 124–25, 129–31
illegitimacy: children born to Indian servants (*criadas*), 87–88; rates of, 95; role of state, 83; support of illegitimate children, 83; types of, 211n45
impediments, 7, 55–58, 60, 62, 64–66, 81, 102–5, 123–25, 127
incest, 81, 84, 141, 167–68, 173, 211n45
inheritance: community property (*bienes gananciales*), 43; example of division of property, 43–45; for illegitimate children, 104; for legitimate children, 109; New Mexicans knowledge of laws regarding, 46–47; role of *alcaldes mayores* in, 45–48

Jaramillo, Casilda, 116
Jiménez, Vicente, 139
Jirón de Tejeda, Dimas (barber-surgeon), 23
Jurado, Ramón García, 47, 56

Lavrin, Asunción, 82
legitimacy, 4, 43, 55, 109

Lobato, Juan, 105–6
López, Antonia, 81
López, Blas, 77, 90–92, 95
López, Luis, 133, 142
Lucero, Antonio, 71–72
Lucero, María, 88
Lucero, Miguel, 88
Luján, Ana, 71
Luján, Juana, 70–72, 94–95, 98–99, 101–2, 104, 119–20, 145, 164, 213n104
Luján, Miguel, 146, 172
Luján, Sebastián, 94, 102–3
lust, 81

Madrid, Lorenzo, 113
Madrid, Pedro, 81
Madril, Antonio, 95
Maese, Alonso, 62
Maldonado, José, 120
Manzanares, María de la Rosa, 115
Marquéz, Diego, 20
Marquéz, Juan, 57, 151, 153
marriage: ages of men at, 91, 183, 186–87; ages of women at, 91, 186–87; benefits of, 108–10; broken promises, 70–75, 92–93; ceremony, 58–60; the conjugal home, 40; consummation, 91–92; control of, 6–7; cousin, 7, 124–32; fees, 53–54; the fourth *partida*, 39; impediments to, 60–65; interracial, 181–82; parental involvement in, 112–13; peer influence on, 7; promise, 39, 91; sacrament of, 55
Martín, Antonio, 82, 113
Martín, Francisco, 104
Martín, Gertrudis, 56
Martín, Juan, 82
Martín, Juan Tomás, 73
Martín, Manuel, 84, 88, 104, 137–38
Martín, Margarita, 43–46
Martín, María del Rosario, 131
Martín, Melchora, 84, 88

Martín, Miguel, 60
Martínez, Marcial, 73–74, 99
Martínez, Salvador, 51
Mascareñas, Francisco de, 137, 141–42
material culture. *See* possessions
Medina, Isabel de, 147, 165
Medina, Josefa de, 97
Medina, Ramón de, 65
Mendinueta, Pedro Fermín de (governor), 11, 15
midwife (*partera*), 97, 100, 165, 168
Miranda, Juana, 48–49
Montaño, Juana, 101, 144–47, 150, 155–56, 161, 165
Montaño, Juan Antonio, 65
Montaño, Leonor, 127
Montaño, María Gerónima, 124
Montaño, Nicolás, 65
Montoya, Andrés, 119
Montoya, Antonio, 73
Montoya, Bárbara, 129–30
Montoya, Juana, 118
Montoya, María, 111
Montoya, Nerio, 45
Mora, Alejandro, 48–49
Moreno, Juan José, 26, 137
mothers, 141–42
Moya, Lucas, 77

natural children, 96, 109, 141, 211n45, 212n75
Navarro, Rosa, 51
nuclear family, 134–35

Ortega, Gerónimo, 112–13
Ortiz, Francisco, 43–44, 46
Ortiz, Lucía, 112
Ortiz, Nicolás, 116, 138

Padilla, Juana, 44, 93–94
Padilla, María de los Reyes, 128
padres no conocidos (unknown parents), 96

Páez Hurtado, Juan (lieutenant governor), 32–34, 40–41, 61, 154, 158–59, 162–65
patrimony, 119
Peña, Miguel de la, 58
Peralta, María Francisca, 166
population, 12
possessions: as barter, 26; as investment, 24; clothing, 24–25; furniture, 22–23; houses, 20–22; kitchens, 23–24; outbuildings, 21; religious, 24; tools of the trade, 23–24
Pragmática (*Pragmática sanción de matrimonios*): implementation, 41; issued on and by, 41; parental consent, 41
prenda, 91, 93–94, 99
prenuptial relationships, 67, 70, 90–106
promise to marry, 60, 70–75, 92–93
Pueblo people, 4–5, 9–13, 15, 21, 29, 33, 40, 84, 87
punishment: for adultery, 173; for broken marriage promises, 69, 104–5, 184–85; for domestic violence, 173–74; for murder, 172–73

race, 5, 10–11, 56, 88, 100, 130
raiding, 15–16
rape, 85–89, 102
Reaño, José, 15
residential patterns, 138–39, 188–89, 191
Rodríguez, Juana, 94, 102–3
Rodríguez Cubero, Pedro (governor), 34, 70–71
Romero, Antonio José, 129
Romero, María Manuela de la Luz, 100
Romero, Vicente, 127
Roybal, Bernardo, 44–45

Salazar, Antonio de, 88
Salazar, José Antonio, 90, 93, 95, 101
Sambrano, Antonio, 62, 125–26
Sánchez, Domingo, 127–28

Sánchez, Gertrudis, 118
Sánchez, Jacinto, 118
Sánchez, Mariano, 131
Sánchez, Úrsula Bernardina, 130
Sánchez de Oton, Gertrudis, 82
Savedra, Urgencio de Jesús, 127
Seed, Patricia, 107–8
Sena, Bernardino, 141
settlement: policies of church, 31–32; policies of state, 28–29, 31–32; policies of Vargas, 29–34
sexuality: codification, 79–80; control of, 6; defined, 79; female, 78, 89, 92–93; forms of lust, 81; male, 78, 89, 92–93; promiscuity, 83–84; "put into discourse," 80–82; sexual abuse of servants, 85–89; *vergüenza* (shame), 78; virility, 78
shame (*vergüenza*), 5, 67–68, 78, 86, 97, 99, 124
siblings, 135–37
Siete Partidas: adultery, 171; benefits of marriage, 148; betrothal (*esponsales*), 83; code of law, 39; dowry, 42; fourth *partida*, 39, 42; legitimacy, 109; marriage for stable society, 29; marriage promise, 39, 91
Silva, Felipe, 2
Silva, Francisco de, 42, 46, 118
Silva, José Manuel, 126, 128
Silveria Sanchez, María Josefa, 126, 128
Spaniards. *See* Hispanics
state: gubernatorial decree concerning family, 40; support to church, 40; views on marriage, 39–40; views on sex, 83–84
stock raising, 14, 200n30

Tafoya, Catalina Aranda, 124
Tafoya, Cristóbal, 88
Tenorio, Gregoria, 77, 90–92
Torrez, Francisca de, 156, 161–62

trade: Bourbon reforms on, 16; merchandise, 25–26; trade fairs, 15
Trujillo, Juana Teresa, 123
Trujillo, Manuel, 82
Trujillo, Tomasa, 127
Twinam, Ann, 6, 109

Ulibarrí, Antonio de, 35

Valdez, Catalina de, 145–46, 149–51, 155
Valdez, Simona, 51–52
Valencia, Juana de, 94, 122
Valencia, Juan de, 30
Varela, Diego, 30
Vargas, Diego de (governor), 4, 17, 29–32, 34, 84
Vargas, Sebastián de, 70
Vega y Coca, Miguel de la, 111
Velázquez, Antonio, 103
Vélez Cachupín, Tomás (governor), 25, 84, 86, 92, 168
Vigil, Pedro, 159
Villalpando, Catarina, 90, 134

Weeks, Jeffrey, 79
widowers, 61, 128–29
widows, 59, 61, 128–29
wives, 27, 58, 139–40, 143–44, 146–48

Yturrieta, Pedro, 1–3

www.ingramcontent.com/pod-product-compliance
Lightning Source LLC
Chambersburg PA
CBHW032223230426
43666CB00033B/821